TELL THE TRUTH UNTIL THEY BLEED

Also by Josh Alan Friedman

Books:
Any Similarity to Persons Living or Dead Is Purely Coincidental
(with Drew Friedman)
Tales of Times Square
Warts and All (with Drew Friedman)
When Sex Was Dirty
The Unspeakable Writings of Terry Southern (co-editor, with Nile Southern)
I, Goldstein: My Screwed Life (with Al Goldstein)

Albums:
Famous & Poor
The Worst!
Blacks 'n' Jews
Josh Alan Band

TELL THE TRUTH
UNTIL THEY
BLEED

Coming Clean in the Dirty World of Blues and Rock 'n' Roll

Josh Alan Friedman

Backbeat
Books

An Imprint of Hal Leonard Corporation
New York

Published in 2008 by Backbeat Books
An Imprint of Hal Leonard Corporation
19 West 21st Street, New York, NY 10010

Portions of this book appeared, in different form, in the *Dallas Observer*,
Texas Monthly, *Blab*, *Tower Records Pulse!*, Al Aronowitz's *Blacklisted Journalist*,
and WFMU's *LCD* magazine.

Printed in the United States of America

Book design by Stephen Ramirez

Lyrics acknowledgments can be found on pages 261 to 262, which constitute
an extension of this copyright page.

Library of Congress Cataloging-in-Publication Data is available upon request.

ISBN: 978-0-87930-932-9

www.backbeatbooks.com

For Chloe Mae

Contents

Introduction
Sweetheart ... Let Me Tell Ya About the Music Business ...

The old record biz was founded by tough guys and hustlers who were music fanatics with unique taste. Each carved out his own territory in jazz, folk, blues, or pop. By the 1970s, these pioneers began dying or selling off their companies. Among those who appear in this book, it is producer Joel Dorn who defines the sea change from the old music business to the new:

"The record business became a real business. It had been this magnificent cottage industry from its inception—all of a sudden, music became a part of *everybody's* business. Now there were lawyers walking around in fuckin' Nehru suits listening to the Grateful Dead, with Trans-America, Warner-Seven Arts, Gulf & Western buying up all these properties. Instead of buying a steel mill, they'd buy a record company and run it the same way."

I began these stories in the 1990s, after moving from New York to Texas. Most were done (in different form) for Robert Wilonsky at the *Dallas Observer*. The story of Leiber & Stoller is told here for the first time—anywhere.

What's so dirty about blues and rock 'n' roll? You really want the trut' about this rotten fuckin' business? Have a seat.

Josh Alan Friedman
Texas, 2007

TELL THE TRUTH UNTIL THEY BLEED

Jerry Leiber (right) and Mike Stoller (left) with the hillbilly act that
absolutely wrecked their song "Hound Dog."
(Photofest)

CHAPTER 1

Jerry Leiber
Kiss My Big Black *Tokhis*!

White Boy, Don't Tell Me How It Go!

In 1952, Lester Sill, an impeccably dressed promoter for the R&B label Modern Records in Los Angeles, took a keen interest in two Jewish boys. Sill made a date for Jerry Leiber and Mike Stoller, both nineteen, to visit bandleader Johnny Otis in his East Los Angeles garage. His twelve-piece band rehearsed there. Otis was ringmaster over a dozen R&B acts, each signed to a different label. The Johnny Otis Revue performed all across the chitlin circuit, that loose affiliation of Negro music and vaudeville clubs throughout the South. After two months of road-work he brought 'em back hot off the road to make records. Audiences assumed Otis, the embodiment of rhythm and blues, was "high yaller." But he was white, the son of Greek immigrants. Likewise, in the business of race music, folks were later taken aback to find that songwriters Leiber & Stoller were white.

At the garage, six acts awaited. Each got up on a makeshift stage to strut their best shit for the visiting white boys. Little Esther, who recorded for Savoy, begged, she screamed, and she shouted "Release Me." Three

Tons of Joy, a trio of circus-size gospel gals, waddled onto the rickety stage, nearly plummeting through the wooden planks, to offer up some old-time religion. "And each sang better than Aretha," remembers Jerry Leiber. He got a momentary flash for a song title: "1,500 Pounds of Woman Comin' Your Way." Last was Big Mama Thornton, on Don Robey's Peacock label, out of Houston. She did "Ball and Chain."

"It killed us," says Jerry.

The boys sped off to Mike Stoller's house, a fifteen-minute drive. Adrenaline pumping like a maniac—as it always did when his genius exploded—Jerry shouted dummy lyrics. He beat on the roof of the car. He had two thirds of a song finished as they pulled into the driveway. They went right to the piano. Mike didn't even sit down, just started jamming along with Jerry, filling in a rhythmic pattern and four choruses.

"I yelled, he played," remembers Leiber. "The groove came together and we finished in twelve minutes flat. I work fast. We raced right back to lay the song on Big Mama."

The six-foot, three-hundred-pound blues shouter grabbed the lyrics, which were freshly scribbled on a paper bag, out of Jerry's hand. "Her eyes bugged out at the page and she started *crooning*. As if it were 'Blue Moon.'" This was ludicrous, Jerry knew she was putting them on.

"Mama," said Jerry, "it don't go that way."

"White boy," she answered, "don't tell me how it go. I *know* how it go. It go like this." Big Mama shook, stuck out her chin, pulled apart her cheeks, and flapped her tongue like a snake, pulling some kind of grotesque Big Mammy shtick.

Johnny Otis marched over to kosher the scene. "What's going on?" She acted like a kid caught being naughty in class. "Mama, you want a hit?" said Otis. "Don't run these guys off. Be nice. These guys write hits. Maybe you already got one in your hands."

Suddenly contrite, she gave a "yassuh."

"Mama, I want you to listen at *how it go*," instructed Otis. So Mike went back to the piano and Jerry stood on the garage stage with Johnny's band and sang "Hound Dog." Halfway through, Big Mama smiled, started shaking her tail feather. Then she got up and copied what Jerry did, right to the letter.

"I threw in a few hollers to make it go," recalled Big Mama later.

Otis usually used four horns, but decided to keep only the rhythm section for "Hound Dog"—Pete Lewis's funky blues guitar figure, Albert Winston on upright bass, and Johnny Otis on drums, with the snare turned off for a hollow ring. Jerry and Mike were in the control booth. After two takes, Peacock #1612, "Hound Dog" backed with "Nightmare," was released the first week of March 1953; it froze at number one on the R&B charts for three months.

Cashbox, "Rhythm N' Blues Ramblings," March 28, 1953:

> Not in the longest time has a record hit the nation with such a startling and crashing impact as has "Hound Dog," the Willie Mae Thornton etching on Peacock label. The gal belts the rhythmic Latin tempo tune with a frenzied performance that pops your thermometer and reaction around the country simply fascinates this office as reports pour in from the R & B belt. . . .

J erry Leiber prepares lots of salami sandwiches in his Venice Beach, California, kitchen. Anybody visits, the action takes place in the kitchen. He talks like a fat man, but he's always been thin. He talks about the world's most incredible fish store in Edmonton, Canada, with hundreds of varieties of herring ("Eskimos and Jews have the same taste."). Leiber's idea of a good time: Let's go shopping for the mystical ingredients of his mother Manya's kosher chicken soup, then spend a whole Saturday cooking. Like a Yiddish mama, he needs to prepare fattening meals for guests. "You like salami? I get salamis from all over the world. This is from Genoa," he adds, with a flourish of rare mustard.

Leiber doesn't want to talk about Elvis. He's sick of it. Not even with Stoller—despite their brilliant chemistry in the studio, they drain the energy from each other when attempting to give interviews. They poison each other just standing side by side at appearances. And that is why you rarely ever see or hear them. One of the great songwriting teams of the twentieth century created their legacy while taking few bows in public—until recently.

Jerry used to be the whole floor show. But Mike, the shy, introverted one, is now rising to the occasion at society events in their honor. Without Jerry. Leiber has endured one heart attack and three bypass operations over the past twenty years. Stoller recently attended the Ghent Film Festival in Belgium to conduct a sixty-piece orchestra performing "Is That All There Is?" He received a Lifetime Achievement Award on their behalf.

"We've drifted apart in a dramatic way," says Jerry.

Fifty years to the month since Elvis released "Hound Dog" in August 1956, Jerry claims, "Elvis Presley didn't mean a fucking thing to me. The first time I heard him do 'Hound Dog,' I barely knew who he was. All I knew was that this cheap, phony hillbilly act with a greasy, boiled-up pompadour had absolutely wrecked my song, ruined it, changed the whole meaning. I wanted to sue. It was a rude awakening as a songwriter. Apparently, people thought they could change your words any way they wanted. But Mike and our publishers told me I was cutting off my nose to save my face. 'Don't be so choosy, he's selling millions of records.' 'Hard Times' by Charles Brown was the biggest R&B hit we'd had to date, a fast 120,000. I was getting astonishing reports from the Aberbachs. I remember the first call, telling us Presley was up to 900,000, right out of the gate."

Jerry thought the Elvis record had no soul or groove. But he held his peace.

The B side to "Hound Dog" was Otis Blackwell's "Don't Be Cruel." By some reports, the single sold almost eight million copies. "We learned that writing for Elvis was like having a license to print money."

Presley recorded at least twenty-four Leiber & Stoller songs, nine of them chart-toppers.

Jerry suffered when Presley serenaded a sad bloodhound on *The Steve Allen Show*. The original lyric had to do with throwing a no-good gigolo, a sponger, out of the house—sung from a hostile Negro woman's perspective:

> *You ain't nothin' but a hound dog*
> *Quit snoopin' round my do'*
> *You can wag yo' tail*
> *But I ain't gon' feed you no mo'*

Now the lyrics were changed with the fuckin' rabbit, which rendered the song meaningless:

> *You ain't nothin' but a hound dog*
> *Cryin' all the time*
> *You ain't never caught a rabbit*
> *And you ain't no friend of mine*

Leiber eventually found out where Elvis got it. Presley was headlining in Vegas early on, and walking through the hotel lounge came upon Freddie Bell & His Bell Boys, a white lounge act that covered black R&B.

"Their 'Hound Dog' moved too fast, a nervous, *okeedokee* cracker version that reminded me of Lonnie Donegan, the skiffle guy popular in England at the time," says Jerry. Freddie Bell also changed the lyrics, and issued his corrupted-version 78 of "Hound Dog" in March '55, two years after Big Mama.

"Elvis could have pulled it off like Big Mama, somewhere in that pocket—but he always covered songs the way he heard them first. He carbon-copied the Freddie Bell version. He had rotten taste. Not that it ever hurt him. If you sent him a demo with somebody farting, he'd fart on his version. He copied demos exactly, with an incredible talent for doing so. The first key he heard it in, regardless of whether it was in his range, he would thereafter sing it back in that key. Later, if I told him we could get it transposed, make it easier to sing, he'd say, 'No, thank you, sir, I like it just where it is. The way it's supposed to sound is the way it is.'"

Jerry Leiber and Mike Stoller were summoned to "knock out the sound track" for Elvis's second movie, *Jailhouse Rock*, in 1957. They entered a New York hotel room, the door blocked with a couch by their publisher, until they emerged hours later with the score. Assignment accomplished. Then back out to L.A. to record it with Elvis. And maybe back out to the beach for the endless whirl of *Girls! Girls! Girls!* (a song they'd soon write). But this was no Sandra Dee/Annette Funicello scene. The white fathers of rock 'n' roll's beach bunnies were black debutants. *Colored Girls! Colored Girls! Colored Girls!*

Songs emerge whole hog when Jerry Leiber works, in flashes of mania. Jerry and Mike also *produced* the songs for *Jailhouse Rock* (uncredited at the time), and Stoller appeared as the piano player in the movie. Jerry, a former acting student, was supposed to play the part but had a dentist appointment.

"We first met Elvis in the studio," says Jerry. "He wanted us there. And then I found how sincere he was. He had a lot of soul and groove. He was cooperative, a workhorse.

"The best interpretation of a ballad I've ever had was Elvis's record of 'Love Me.' It was unsurpassable, like melting chocolate, like Bing Crosby at his best. 'Don't' was my second favorite."

Although "Hound Dog" is synonymous with Elvis, Leiber still hates his version. "It's rare that you get an interpretation that's even close to your imagination. For every song we write, we always hope for that one definitive record, a rendition that nails it like your dreams. Most everything is a disappointment. Out of a hundred versions of 'Hound Dog,' Big Mama Thornton's remains the definitive one. I wish Elvis had heard hers first. Big Mama ain't never been topped."

But it always comes back to the salami. Leiber's cowed Fijian maid returns from a delicatessen with the wrong slice of salami. He instructs her on how to order the right cut. "See, these are too thick," he scolds, hand-feeding her a slice. Then he feeds her an exquisitely thin slice, where it melts in your mouth.

"Oh, Mr. Leiber," she says. "You know everything."

His home, designed in the style of early-twentieth-century archi-tects Greene & Greene, faces the Pacific Ocean on Venice Beach. Leiber oversaw everything. He imported rare Brazilian woods from endangered rain forests. Twelve years earlier, I accompanied him up on the beams, where he conducted a rugged crew of artisans—as if producing a record. The carpenters awaited his decision for the third-floor-window view. Jerry chose a height that framed the sky to his liking, looking out on the Pacific. There was a certain sunset he wanted to catch, a metaphor for his career.

As it does in homes in the old Jewish shtetl, a mezuzah adjoins the front door post. But here, a black Lincoln town car and a black Mercedes sedan sit in the garage, where a refrigerator is stocked full of those frosty little Coke bottles, hard to come by these days. A conjuror with barbecue, Jerry cooks up the most incredible ribs I have ever experienced. At mid-night. His skill is so precise, it's just like he's, well, producing a record. The kitchen has an exotic wood-paneled walk-in closet just for sauces.

Here are some bottles that crowd the shelves:

Famous Dave's Rich & Sassy; Gates (Kansas City's Own); Kansas City's Cowtown Night of the Living Bar B Q Sauce; Pit Boss of Kansas City; Mollie B's Incredible Smokin' Chipotle Barbecue Sauce; Arthur Bryant's Original (The President's Choice); Kansas City's Famous Zavda Original B-B-Q; Bilardo Brothers; Rockin' Roger's Soul Bar-B-Q Sauce; D. L. Jardine's Special Edition Texas Pecan; TJ's Bold & Smoky Kansas City Style; Dale and Mary's Country Club Bar-B-Que Sauce; Fiorella's; Jack Stack KC Spicy Sauce; Hayward's Pit Bar-B-Que Sauce; Uncle Levi's; Candy's Original Mexican-Indian; Stubb's Moppin' Sauce Bar-B-Q Baste; Lynchburg Tennessee Whiskey Barbecue Sauce; McHenry's Legend Heartland BBQ.

Hot sauces? That's a whole 'nother closet. Two that poke out are Ass Kickin' Original Hot Sauce and Cock Sucker Hot Sauce.

Jerry decides to work with the Gates, a Kansas City concoction.

Presented twice with a set of keys to this city, Leiber & Stoller could both probably get out of jail free. Their song "Kansas City," recorded hundreds of times since 1952, is the city's official song. A monument in honor of Jerry and Mike appears in the town square.

Flashback: Little Dick

The scene: Brill Building lobby, 1619 B'way, 1950s

The situation: Jerry Leiber's first time entering.

(Big copper elevator doors open upon two gunsels wearing dark overcoats and fedoras. They drag some poor schmuck out of the elevator into art deco lobby. Each gunsel has a leg under his arm, the shoes pointing up. Schmuck on the floor holds fedora over face, trying to keep from being recognized. Both bone-breakers are smoking and chatting casually, as if the schmuck on the floor isn't there.)

Gunsel: Carmine, who do you like in the fifth?

Carmine: I don't know. I just might be partial to Social Dancer. Who do you like?

Gunsel: Mustache Pete's been my favorite for a long time. But the fuckhead keeps running out of the money. I'll probably bet on him again anyhow.

(Suddenly the hat comes off the face on marble floor.)

Schmuck on the Floor: Little Dick. Hialeah. Fifth race.

Carmine *(turns around, snaps)*: If you were such a fuckin' rajah you wouldn't be down where you are, schmuck.

Schmuck on the Floor *(after a beat, moans)*: Little Dick in the fifth race. On my mother's grave.

Carmine *(considering)*: All right. But if it ain't, it's gonna be *your* dick on your mother's grave.

The schmuck on the floor was George Goldner.

Moishe and George

The 1950s ushered in two of the most unconscionable predators that ever stalked the music business: George Goldner and Morris Levy. "Everything about them was crooked except the perfect crease in their trousers and the impeccable part in their hair," remembers Jerry. Both gonifs opened the door for what Jerry calls "the boys in the band," and he doesn't mean musicians. "Moishe Levy was the was the most mobbed-up guy in the music biz. He was proud of every person he fucked or killed, and wore the notches on his herringbone lapel. And he'd never believe someone would actually write about him someday."

Hesh of *The Sopranos* was loosely based on Levy, though Jerry says Levy was "ten times worse." Moishe's *tokhis* shook like a money tree after the "El Watusi" Latin dance craze began on one of his labels. He then became a Jew with a horse ranch, like Hesh.

"Moishe" Levy, as he was known on the streets of the Bronx, owned Roulette Records and Birdland, the jazz mecca on Fifty-second Street. Born Morris Levy in 1927, Vito Genovese soon discovered his formidable talents for shaking down hatcheck girls, pilfering nickels and dimes from jukeboxes, and skimming coins from the men's room tip jar. Levy owned record labels and song copyrights—including, if you didn't guess, George Shearing's standard "Lullaby of Birdland." He bootlegged 78s and shipped "cutouts" from the back doors of pressing plants. He shook down songwriters, who were easy prey, forcing his name on song credits. Jerry was a street kid from the ghetto in Baltimore, so the mighty Leiber & Stoller never fell victim to song credit shakedowns. But the mob would eventually extract something worse.

Jerry thought Levy looked like Marlon Brando, only a bit taller. He was an unabashed social climber. Like Bugsy Siegel, Moishe preferred the refined snatch of aristocratic British womanhood and was always chasing after unattainable women. His own wife was once rushed to a hospital after he beat her senseless in a telephone booth. As late as 1975, Levy beat the shit out of a plainclothes cop. But the case never even went to trial. He was finally convicted of extortion in 1988 and died two years later.

Born in 1918, George Goldner began in the label business, but his labels were inside the lapels of shirts. He was originally a shmata salesman on the Lower East Side. How Garment Center moochers were able to step uptown into the music biz was amazing. But they did it, and spawned more good music than any hundred corporate lawyers today. Goldner discovered fourteen-year-old Frankie Lymon in 1956, releasing "Why Do Fools Fall in Love." (Levy forged his name onto the songwriting credit.) This record threw the music biz for a loop, spawning a hot new prototype sound. The next year Goldner released "Maybe" by the Chantels—the first of the girl groups.

For Goldner, it began with his genuine love of Latin orchestras. He loved to dance and shook his *tokhis* at the Palladium Ballroom ("Home of the Mambo") at Fifty-third and Broadway. He reminded Leiber of French romantic actor Adolphe Menjou, not a hair out of place. Goldner dressed like a used-car salesman, brandished a Tiffany cigarette case in public—and apparently wielded some mighty cock over the broads. His first wife was Gracie—George and Gracie, get it? He then married a Puerto Rican spitfire named Mona, his dancing partner and nemesis. "Goldner wasn't afraid of Al Capone, but he was terrified of Mona," remembers Jerry.

A pioneer of payola, Goldner was known to New York deejays as Mr. Pay-for-Play. He would reap spic coin with his pioneering Latin label, Tico, formed in 1948. He signed the most prominent Latin musicians in the hemisphere. Goldner supervised *timbalero* Tito Puente's landmark all-percussion album *Puente in Percussion,* on which the artist was backed by Latin/Cuban musicians whose very names were startling—Mongo Santamaria, Potato Valdes, Willie Bobo—and who were the Santanas of their generation. Tico Records was the driving force behind the mambo/cha-cha-cha craze in the early '50s.

Latin rhythm would play a big role on the records Leiber & Stoller wrote or produced. Think of "Under the Boardwalk," "Save the Last Dance for Me," "Up on the Roof," or "Spanish Harlem."

Both gonifs, Levy and Goldner, came together as one with Roulette Records in 1957. The name was a nod to George's gambling addiction. The pair had decided that rock 'n' roll, more than Latin, was where the fast buck lay—a business move that made Goldner's bookies fat and happy. They officed at 1631 Broadway. Some questionable moments in musical taste arose when their Latin, R&B, and Yiddishkeit roots clashed, resulting in 78s like "Mambo Shevitz" and Joe Loco's *cuchifrito* record of "Bei Mir Bist Du Schoen."

"If everybody in the music biz was a natural-born thief in this rotten fuckin' business, there was still honor among thieves," says Jerry. "Goldner would never fuck Morris Levy. They went to the track together, fucked women together. Goldner would fuck Joe Bananas, but not Morris Levy." Nevertheless, Goldner lost many fortunes at the racetrack. And he lost all his record labels, usually to Morris Levy.

"Goldner and Levy played mind games with Mike and me, using our heads like Ping-Pong balls," says Leiber. "We went through the meat grinder with them." And Goldner was responsible for bringing Gambino capo Sonny Franchese into the picture. "The wiseguys were as insular as Hasidic Jews: The rest of the world were goyim to them—they didn't give a fuck what anyone else thought or said. Hit records aside, we were still two green Jewish kids."

Sonny

They say the girls are somethin' else—on Broadway
But lookin' at them just gives me the blues
'Cause how ya gonna make some time
When all you got is one thin dime
And one thin dime won't even shine your shoes—on Broadway
—"On Broadway," Leiber & Stoller, Mann & Weil

One day Jerry bought two pairs of children's suspenders from a street vendor while strolling down Broadway. As he approached the Brill Building, a hulking black fellow suddenly draped an arm over his shoulder.

"You're Jerry Leiber, right?" he asked. "I've been wanting to meet you for years. I love your music."

The come-on was suspect. Anyone on the street who loved Leiber & Stoller records, say a musician or hipster, would usually say, *I dig your shit*, or, *Love your stuff, man*. Not so formal. Grinning, the big man continued. "I've got some friends who really wanna meet you."

Jerry said he'd love to but had another appointment. But the man insisted, motioning toward some joint on the side of the Brill Building.

"Don't worry. They're right in there."

Asking if they might meet later instead, Jerry said his office was right upstairs.

"We know," said the man.

"You do?"

"Yeah, everybody knows where you are," he said.

"Tell you what, I'll give you my number, give me a call, I'll tell you when I'm free, around one o'clock."

"We don't make appointments."

"Well, I've got to make this meeting," said Jerry.

"I really don't think you *gotta*," the stranger said, friendly as pie. "I think *our* meeting is very important and you oughta cancel. So why don't you call your secretary, tell her to call that appointment off, and tell them you'll meet *them* later. If you could meet us at one o'clock, then meet *them* at one o'clock."

Checkmate. Not wanting to look scared out of his wits, Jerry reconsidered. There was a telephone booth on the corner of Forty-ninth and Broadway, infested by every broken-down pimp and bookie within ten blocks of Times Square. Jerry sized the guy up, in case he'd have to pick him out of a lineup later. He was about 6' 2", although he seemed seven feet tall. Jerry called his secretary, Faith.

"This big black guy grabbed me in front of the Brill Building and said he loves my work and he loves me and he wants me to come meet his friends because they love my work and are dying to meet me. He's taking me to some deli downstairs."

Faith just said, "Go."

Leiber exited the phone booth and said, "Take me to your leader, Jack."

Jerry's escort turned out to be Notorious Nate McCollough, an outside hitter connected to the Genovese mob. Word had it he was a highly decorated former Marine officer, once a member of the black honor guard for the president of the United States. Upon his release he became Morris Levy's right-hand enforcer. Nate would meet his end three years later in Florida, a bullet through the eye, the same fate as Bugsy Siegel. At the moment, however, he remained lethal.

Leiber had worked at the Brill Building for years and knew something about New York delicatessens. Yet somehow, he'd never noticed this little deli nudged against the Brill Building, smack-dab next door to Jack Dempsey's on the ground floor. The entrance was five feet deep, with a meat-case diorama showcasing pastrami, corned beef, hot dogs. An old guy, about eighty, stood watch over the store while his younger counterman carved the sandwiches. The old man regarded Nate with suspicion, squinting at him as if he might hold up the joint. "Whaddaya want, whaddaya want?"

Polite as always, Nate said, "We wanna join our friends for lunch."

The old Jew broke into a smile. "Of course," he said. "Follow me."

When they reached to the back of the deli, Jerry's heart stopped. Eleven of the ugliest guys he'd ever seen sat twiddling their thumbs. Each one looked like a gargoyle skewed on top of a church steeple in Paris. All had their backs to the wall—except one. And he sat facing the others, his back to Leiber. Nate introduced him to Sonny, a bull-necked *balagula* with a limp-dick handshake. "Siddown," he said. "Have somp'n' to eat. A steak. A beer. Anything ya want."

It was 11 A.M.—a steak, a beer? Jerry was ready to throw up just looking at him. But he sat down and ordered.

"Hey, I've heard a lot about you. You write good music."

"Thanks," Jerry said, "but I write the words."

"Oh. Well, words are good too." All the gargoyles nodded in agreement. Jerry put the paper bag with the suspenders in it on the table.

"You wrote for Elvis . . . whatizname?"

"Yeah."

"'Blue Suede Shoes,' right?

"No, I didn't write 'Blue Suede Shoes.'"

"You didn't? Which one did you write?"

"'Hound Dog.' I wrote 'Hound Dog.'"

"Oh, 'Hound Dog.' That's pretty good, too. Made a lot of money, huh?"

"Yeah."

"How long's it take to write a song like that?"

"Ten minutes."

"Whad you make off it?"

"About a quarter-million."

He did some calculating on his fingers. "Twenty-five grand a minute? Not bad . . . How's the business? I hear you and your partner are doin' real well."

By now, Leiber figured this was a shakedown. Sonny had both gnarly hands open flat on the table, massaging the top. One of his fingers slid against the paper bag. The tip of one of Jerry's son's suspenders poked out.

"What are these? You mind?"

He held up the little red suspenders in front of the jury of gargoyles. "Hey, lookit these. Suspenders. Kids' suspenders. I love kids. This guy loves kids!" He eyed Jerry sincerely. "Jerry, I got kids. I love 'em too."

Leiber would soon learn that this guy who loved kids was Genovese capo Sonny Franchese. Growing up on the streets of Baltimore, Jerry had met some tough longshoremen. But Sonny Franchese chilled him to the bone. The mobster eventually served a full twenty-five-year stretch in federal prison. Sonny's fingers came to a halt on the table and he took dead aim, eye to eye.

"You wanna hear a riddle?" He turned to a greasy blond-haired Quasimodo with bulbous blue eyes. "Not a riddle. I mean an antidote."

"It ain't antidote," came Blue Eyes. "It's *anecdote.*"

"You know what the fuck I mean. Lemme ask Jerry a few questions. Jerry—where does a Cat'lic boy go when he gets into trouble?"

"I don't know, where does a Catholic boy go?"

"He goes to see his priest," Sonny said, satisfied. "You're a Jewboy, right?"

"Yeah."

"Where does a Jewboy—I mean Jewish boy—go when he gets into trouble?"

Jerry thought he'd be cute and answered, "To his lawyer."

Sonny laughed, which was not endearing, and pointed to his henchmen, who started tittering. "Isn't he funny?"

Then Sonny fixed his stare upon Jerry Leiber; the laughter dried up, and his face shriveled into a prune. "You're funny. But you're wrong. You're a Jew. A Jewboy goes to his rabbi. And guess what? I'm your rabbi. And you got trouble. . . ."

Whatever happened next is deeply buried in the shadows of music business lore. The mob reclaimed Times Square in the 1960s, a turf they lost after Prohibition ended. I've heard tall tales, like one about Jerry being hung outside the Brill Building penthouse by his ankles. Jerry and Mike made a pact never to discuss it, and remain paranoid forty-five years later.

But the upshot of the lunch with Sonny was devastating: Leiber & Stoller sold their empire, Red Bird Music, to George Goldner for one dollar.

Gargoyles with cauliflower ears became unnerving visitors to the Brill Building, intimidating songwriters and effectively destroying the careers of Jerry and Mike's girl groups. Leiber & Stoller's stable included the Ad Libs ("The Boy from New York City"), the Exciters ("Do Wah Diddy Diddy") the Dixie Cups ("Chapel of Love"), and the tough-white-chick Shangri-Las ("Leader of the Pack"). Jerry and Mike fled, and avoided making records for three years. In their place, artistic decisions were influenced by guys with names like Punchy and Sluggo and Sally Meatballs—plunging the era of the Brill Building into its demise.

Diamond Don

Leiber & Stoller didn't get a dime for "Hound Dog" until twelve years after it was written. The rights were commandeered by Diamond Don Robey, the most powerful Negro gangster in the South. A figure in the Houston Mafia, he hated whites and ran Fifth Ward gambling on the dark side of the tracks. When Las Vegas opened up, the white gangsters left him behind and bitter in Houston. In his book *A History of the Blues*, Francis Davis brands Robey "100 percent sleazeball," and adds, ". . . as if claiming co-composer credit for most of his performers' songs wasn't bad enough, he also threatened them with bodily harm or death when they objected."

Nobody would have written this when Robey was alive.

R&B wild man Andre Williams recalled Robey firing a gun past Little Richard's head in the studio, after a sassy remark. "And also, Richard was downtown, sellin' fish!" said Williams. "And Don Robey drove up and seen him down *sellin' fish*, and took a fish out the fish cart and slapped him over the head and told him his artists *don't sell no fish!*"*

As mountains of contracts in the Leiber-Stoller archives attest, the money trail of a profitable song is labyrinthine.

"We missed out on the big money with 'Hound Dog,'" Jerry explains. "We had to go to court to get Johnny Otis and Robey's copyright off of it. Otis did all the paperwork and registered the song in his, Big Mama's, and Robey's name—and left ours off. We were nineteen, too young to sign a legal contract. Don Robey got all the publishing money around the world from the Presley record, nine times more than us. Therefore, he was responsible for paying us. Twelve years later, we finally got their names removed as songwriters and collected ASCAP performance money, paid to us as writers directly. Robey couldn't get that."

Leiber never knew that Robey was born half-Jewish. "But it now makes sense," he figures. "No black man could be that dishonest and

*Andre Williams, from interview by John Nova Lomax in the *Houston Post*, February 24, 2005.

devious. He was tall, light-skinned, resembled James Earl Jones, a froglike face."

Born in Houston in 1903, Robey dropped out of school to become a professional gambler. In the late '30s, he ran a taxicab company and opened the Harlem Grill on Los Angeles's "Brown Broadway" strip. Returning to Houston, he opened the famed Bronze Peacock Dinner Club in 1945, along with a record store, and then slithered into music management. He launched twenty-three-year-old jump-blues artist Clarence Gatemouth Brown. Like Morris Levy in New York, who parlayed nightclubs into records, Robey spun the Peacock Club into Peacock Records in 1949.

Leiber met Diamond Don at Johnny Otis's house in L.A. Jerry always sized men up by their threads, as in his song "Shopping for Clothes."

"He wore a suit and tie with a yellow diamond on his finger as big as my nose. I told Otis the diamond stickpin on Diamond Don's tie was yellowish. Otis said, 'You don't know what the fuck you're talking about. It's supposed to be yellow. High yaller.'"

Leiber & Stoller were stationed at the top of the music biz by 1960, in the top floors of the Brill Building. Robey phoned from Houston one day. Leiber was easy to reach—nobody paid to keep their phone number out of the directory yet.

"This is Don Robey. Is this Jerome Leiber? How are you, man?"

"Fine."

"I'm gonna do you a big favor," said Robey. "This is going to be one of those lucky days in your life. I'm going to give you the privilege and opportunity of buying your song back."

"You're kiddin' me?"

"No. I'm gonna sell you 'Hound Dog.'"

"What're you gonna charge me?

"A hundred grand," said Robey.

"A hundred grand!"

"That's all, boy," said Robey. Leiber still didn't understand the economics of songs. A hundred grand sounded like the cost of the Empire State Building then.

"Are you out of your fuckin' mind?" came Leiber. "You've been stealing from us for years. Go fuck yourself."

Robey was quiet. Jerry said, "Can you hear me, Jack?"

Robey waited a beat, then said, "Boy, all I can tell you is count your blessings you're not down here in Texas."

Jerry now states, "I made a big mistake, because a hundred grand for 'Hound Dog' at that time was one twentieth of what it was worth. Irving Berlin would have known, I can tell you that."

Jerry has never been to Texas in his life, and Don Robey is probably the reason why. "I found out later there were graveyards in Texas filled with people who so much as looked at him wrong. He had a network; he could find you in a hole in the wall in Siberia."

Most ironic, Diamond Don also kept an iron fist over "The Gospel Highway"—the catchphrase that symbolized the thousands of miles and performers who crisscrossed the heartland, spreading salvation through music. They played churches, barns, and cotton fields. Like the Shuberts owned Broadway, Robey owned a piece of every venue his gospel singers appeared in, even had a lock on their church appearances.

"Don't be fooled by old publicity pictures of Robey in a suit and tie with black-rimmed glasses, like a legit businessman," says Jerry. "Just like those jive-ass evangelist preachers, he didn't pay anybody. He owned every gospel singer from Mahalia Jackson on down. He was the Joe Bananas of Texas music. I'm sure he was cozy with the Italians in New York. Anybody promoting a Joe Louis fight, even in the South, hadda been involved with [Madison Square Garden fight fixer] Frankie Carbo, give those boys a slice of his action."

Robey had dead ears for music but knew enough to listen to advisors. His recording legacy, if such could be said, came from a great gospel roster, including the Dixie Hummingbirds, the Mighty Clouds of Joy, the Five Blind Boys of Mississippi, and the Sensational Nightingales. Robey had a little dinky pressing plant with four pressing tables. Like his New York counterpart, Moishe Levy, when not releasing his own distorted-output records, he would bootleg others. He demanded that his gospel groups and drummers follow a metronome with a red light in the studio—as if anybody could align their soul to a metronome dial going back and forth. It was supposed to be the same meter as the beat of a human heart.

"Hound Dog" spawned a hundred covers and, more irritating, dozens of answer songs in the dog-fuck-dog music racket. Jerry had contempt for answer songs, a common rejoinder in the race records market since the 1920s. "It's an opportunistic way to shamelessly hitch your record to a recent hit."

Jump-blues singer Roy Brown did "Mr. Hound Dog's in Town":

> *Hey everybody, Mr. Hound Dog's in town*
> *I'm here to stop the lie*
> *That gal has spread around*

Even country bumpkins Homer & Jethro chimed in with "Houn' Dawg," and Yiddish comedian Mickey Katz with "You're a Doity Dog." But Rufus Thomas, who deejayed the Sepia Swing Club on WDIA in Memphis (supposedly the only major station that didn't accept payola*), had the biggest hit, "Bear Cat," scrawled out by Sam Phillips:

> *You know what you said about me, woman?*
> *Well . . . you ain't nothin' but a bearcat*
> *Scratchin' at my door. . . .*
> *You can purr, pretty kitty*
> *But I ain't gonna rub you no more. . . .*

Diamond Don sued Sam Phillips and won 2 percent of Sun Records' profits from "Bear Cat," plus court costs. Robey sold Duke/ Peacock to ABC in 1973, two years before he died.

*From interview with WDIA program director David J. Mattis, by George A. Moonoogian and Roger Meeden, in *Whiskey, Women, and . . .* Number 14, June 1984.

The Kind of Shit We're Looking For

In 1966, the young Randy Newman came to Jerry's office to audition his songs. "He said he'd always wanted to meet me," Jerry recalls, "and sat down at the piano. He played one song after another. When he finished, he slunk down in self-defeat."

"I thought my songs were good," Newman said, "but they all sound like shit. Nothing but shit."

"Let me tell you a story," Jerry told him.

"When Mike and I were young, around 1950, you needed a letter of intro to publishers. We'd had a few records, but this was before 'Hound Dog.'"

Through Lester Sill, they got an appointment with Harry Goodman, Benny Goodman's brother, at Arc Music Publishing. Harry once played upright bass in the Benny Goodman Orchestra. Arc Music handled Chess Records, which had Jerry's favorite roster—the down-in-the-ditch blues of Wolf, Muddy, Memphis Slim.

"We went to his office. He looked like a hippo behind his desk. Mike sat down at the upright piano. We played him our first number. I always sang holding a piece of paper with the lyrics. Harry the Hippo grabbed the lyric sheet, studied it, crumpled it up and tossed it right in the garbage. 'This is shit,' he said.

"Mike and I looked at each other.

"'Don't worry, not everything can be great,' came Goodman. 'Do another.' So Mike and I played the next song. He asked to see lyric sheet, crumpled it up, tossed it in the garbage. 'This is shit.'

"We played our third song; he did the same thing. We hadn't yet smoked marijuana, but the cigarette in his hand smelled sickeningly sweet. I leaned over to Mike and whispered, 'I think he's high. Let's get the fuck outta here.' So I said, 'Excuse us, my partner has to take a leak.' But Mike came back, so we tried one more. This time I crumpled the paper, tossed it in the garbage.

"'What are you doing?' asked Goodman.

"'I saved you the trouble.'

"'Wait a minute,' said Goodman. 'Get that paper.' I went to the garbage pail and retrieved it. He smoothed out the paper, looked at it hard and said, 'This is shit. But it's exactly the kind of shit we're looking for.'"

Randy Newman ended up as the arranger for Leiber & Stoller on "Is That All There Is?"

Excuse Me, I Didn't Know You Were White

"We walked in on Wynonie 'Mr. Blues' Harris ['Mr. Blues is Back in Town!,' 'Good Rockin' Tonight,' 'Grandma Plays the Numbers']. He stayed in this little hotel on Central Avenue, the pulse of L.A.'s black nightlife. Wynonie had these monumental 'Battles of the Blues,' pitting himself against T-Bone Walker at Club Harlem in Watts and Club Alabam on Central. Women would line up and throw hard-earned cash at their favorite. We told the concierge at the front desk that we were Leiber & Stoller. He looked at us blankly. Who?

"'We're here to see Wynonie Harris.'

"'May I ask your business?'

"'We're songwriters,' I said, 'and we've written some new material for Wynonie Harris, which he commissioned.' Which was not true. We were just bringing some songs that Lester Sill told us to take. We rang the bell, he comes to the door, looks at us, and his eyes get big as saucers.

"'Hello. Leiber & Stoller, I presume?' He spoke in the tone of some Gilbert & Sullivan operetta. 'You caught me a little by surprise. I just got out of the shower.' He wore a white terry-cloth robe with fresh conk grease running down the side of his face. 'If you don't mind boys, I must admit, I didn't know you were white.' We'd run into this a number of times. James Brown thought we were black, too.

"I was about to say, 'We didn't know you were black,' but I didn't.

"'Lester Sill sent ya, right? Great guy, great guy.'

"He had an upright piano in the room. An unmade king-size bed had a big hump under the covers.

"'Well, whaddya got for me?'

"'Three hits,' I said.

"'Only three?'

"'Yeah, we got three hits.'

"'Is it okay if I be the judge of that?'

"'No problem, you be the judge.' I had gall back then, told him you're gonna love 'em. Mike went to the piano almost paralyzed with fear. I always wondered if his fingers would work because he was so frightened playing in front of anybody. We did the first of three songs.

Sittin' in the Blue Light Diner
Knowin' life could be much finer
Nothin' here but the smell of beer and men
But I'm so down I can't be choosey
And here come old Side-Order Susie
Shake 'em up and let 'em roll, let 'em roll again

"He liked two of the three songs a lot. 'Well, fellas, when you gonna get me lead sheets?'

"Mike said, 'Tomorrow.'

"'Gotta get 'em to me soon, rehearsal's in two days.' He was playing L.A. deejay Gene Norman's Blues Jubilee at the Shrine Auditorium.

"'Come on over, let's have a little drink on it, man,' he said. We sat on the edge of the bed and he pulled out a bottle of scotch, which I hated and still do. I was a bourbon man. He took a swig and handed it to Mike, who said, 'No, thanks.' I could see that Wynonie's eyebrows dropped a hair. I looked at Mike as if to say, 'You idiot, he thinks you're turning it down because he *nigger-lipped* it.' Wynonie took another swig, smiled weakly and said, 'How 'bout you?' I said, 'Are you kiddin'?' I grabbed the fuckin' bottle and drank a quarter of it just to show him my appreciation. I got so whacked I could hardly stand up. He smiled, slapped me on the back, and felt good again. He corked the bottle and threw it on the bedsheet. We're bullshittin' and ready to go. Then, out of the corner of my eye, I see an enormous black feminine hand, with ruby red nails a mile fuckin' long. It feels around like a blind crab and hits on the whiskey bottle and starts to pull it in under the covers. Wynonie turns, sees the hand, and whacks it hard like a mosquito.

"'Bitch! I told you this was a business meeting!'"

Lust & Greed

The Leiber & Stoller "playlets" were personified by songs they wrote like "Jailhouse Rock," "Young Blood," "Poison Ivy," "Charlie Brown," "Along Came Jones," "Love Potion #9," "Shopping for Clothes," "Yakety Yak," "Little Egypt," "Riot in Cell Block #9," "Smokey Joe's Cafe," "Nosey Joe," etc. Their stated mission: Make Black Folks Laugh.

Jerry always worked on the studio floor, not in the control room. He set the tempo and groove, conducted the rhythm section while Mike was off arranging the horns or strings. Jerry did "head" arrangements, didn't use charts. He stuttered sax solos into King Curtis's ear on the studio floor, the most legendary being that of "Yakety Yak." Record by record, they incrementally assembled an ensemble of percussive instruments that came to be known at the rental agency—and in the industry—as the "Leiber-Stoller kit." The kit arranged ten different percussion instruments: congas, standing tom-toms, timpani, triangles, marimbas, and big, bowl-shaped African hairy drums with skin heads that still had animal hair growing out.

Leiber first saw these ethnic instruments in L.A. around 1955 in a small club on the strip. They were played by a Mexican quartet led by Joe Karioka. The group played Jerry's favorite sound track piece, "Anna," a Brazilian *baion* (samba) from the 1951 Italian movie of the same name starring Sylvana Mangano.

"The theme absolutely drove me crazy. It had the only beat I ever discovered that could keep a slow ballad moving and cooking, to remain interesting. It was also very clarified, translucent, precise—you could hear and see through all the percussion, even with five guitars going. We added one instrument at a time, record by record. It was like brain surgery. You could hear the strings, the violas, the violins and brass through it.

"I eventually taught everybody how to use the Leiber-Stoller kit. Burt Bacharach had a tendency to write ballads, with arrangements that would sound turgid and boring—we laid this on him and he used this rhythm on every hit for thirty-five years."

Thousands of pop records utilized the same rhythm, and still do to this day without their creators knowing it. Atlantic engineer Tom Dowd also helped refine the Leiber-Stoller kit. They first used it on the Drifters' "There Goes My Baby" in 1959, the first rock 'n' roll record of its kind to also introduce a large string section. Though the strings sounded bizarre and convoluted behind Ben E. King's vocal, the record set off a pop music trend for the next few years. Leiber & Stoller produced about thirty big hits, including "Spanish Harlem," "On Broadway," "Stand By Me," and "Save the Last Dance for Me," with that Latin beat. It provided a way to give a beat to ballads, make all sorts of songs swing that wouldn't have otherwise.

The first independent production deal ever made in the record business happened through Leiber & Stoller's first contract with Jerry Wexler and Ahmet Ertegun at Atlantic. Leiber & Stoller produced and arranged their own records but were not yet credited or paid for that. Just as songwriters. They also never took advances for songwriting, under Atlantic's publishing arm, Progressive Music.

"All songwriters contracted under publishers took salary or advances, but we never did. We were too proud. Someone once asked Sammy Cahn, 'What comes first, the music or the lyric?' He said, 'The check.' I was cocky in those days. I don't know why; maybe 'cause we'd had some hits. But we decided we wanted credit for arranging and *producing* [called "supervision" back then].

Jerry Wexler, who'd recently helped coin the term *rock 'n' roll* for the market, barked, "You're already getting paid as writers; what else do you want?" He offered another half cent per record. Leiber said they wanted more. Wex said, "You and your buddy, Lust & Greed, want *more?*"

"Who am I?" asked Jerry. "Lust or Greed? Another credit meant more notoriety, attention . . . more money. I sensed Wex was programmed to argue for argument's sake, but had no solid reasoning behind him. He was just arm-wrestling us.

"I told him, 'You're not taking any chances other than studio costs. You're not paying publishing money up front. So we want another credit.'"

It was an arm-wrestle between a Yiddish slum kid from Baltimore and an older Washington Heights *shtarker* that would set the precedent for the next fifty years.

"So what do you want to be called? The captain, the pilot, the *commandant*? The director? Are you Cecil B. DeMille or something?"

"How about . . . producer?"

Thus was christened what became the most dubious title in all the music biz: "record producer." Henceforth, Leiber & Stoller's producer/arranger credit appeared as a separate creative entity in the making of records. Their first record for Atlantic in this new capacity as an independent production team was "Searchin'," with the Coasters, in January 1957. Backed by "Young Blood," it sold 1.2 million 45s, at $1.28 a pop, Atlantic's first million-seller before Bobby Darin.

The Coasters

Leiber & Stoller reached their early zenith with the Coasters. They charted twenty-four times with their pet project, which personified the playlets—two-and-a-half-minute musical radio plays.

The Coasters were a group of vaudevillians, tummlers, comedians to boot, and comedians receive sustenance in delicatessens. "They ate white food, pastrami sandwiches, never ribs and cornbread," says Jerry. "In fact, ordering pastrami was the secret of their success."

Fifty years later, the following songs are still on the tip of everyone's tongue: "Charlie Brown," "Yakety Yak," "Little Egypt," "Poison Ivy," "Along Came Jones," "Searchin'," and "Young Blood."

Even though the brilliant "Down Home Girl" and "D. W. Washburn" were covered by the Stones and the Monkees, respectively, it's these lesser-known tracks that are most fascinating today: "Shopping for Clothes," "The Slime," "Idol with the Golden Head," "Run Red Run," "The Shadow Knows," "Three Cool Cats," "Bad Blood," "Wake Me, Shake Me," "Down in Mexico," "Turtle Dovin'," and "Soul Pad."

"When we prepared dates for the Coasters, we'd write four or five songs, always an extra song or two in case one broke off," says Jerry. "We worked the Coasters until they dropped. We'd rehearse the guys three to five days, a cappella—or 'acapulco,' as the Coasters used to say—before going in the studio. And we'd finish right before three hours. That's why Jerry Wexler loved us—our records came in under budget, cost almost nothing to make, then made millions."

All memories confirm there were big laughs in the studio, everybody falling down.

Cornell Gunther of the Coasters was prancing gay, Jerry recalls, but also the toughest of the bunch. He once took out four guys in a parking lot, who made kissing sounds as the Coasters exited a building.

"Get in the car honey, lock the doors," he said to Billy Guy, Carl Gardner, and William "Dub" Jones, the great bass voice you hear on "Charlie Brown." Then Gunther turned around, called the gang "faggots," and beat up all four. The moral: Never mess with a tough fag.

Though the Drifters and the Coasters were produced by Leiber & Stoller, each group sounded like they came from a different planet. The Drifters were pure, adult-sounding singers, not comedians, and their records never pandered to teens. Yet they were a manager-owned entity with revolving members on a weekly salary; they didn't get royalties.

By the mid-'60s it was over for both groups. Thereafter, they became a loose assemblage of package-deal oldies acts. You might see a group called the "Drifters" booked the same night in Pittsburgh, Las Vegas, and Honolulu, with audiences none the wiser. In the age of *Shaft*, the only material that would have made sense for the Coasters was too incendiary and stayed in Leiber's trunk, like the unreleased "Colored Folks," or this nifty nugget of race bait called "Whitey!":

Who dropped the bomb and started the war?
An' when you're over there fightin', who you fightin' for?
When you come back and you can't get a job

And the only way to make it is to hustle and rob—
Hey, who you gonna hustle?
And who you gonna rob?

The Clovers

Jerry always wanted to write for the Clovers, a great early '50s Atlantic
R&B outfit. "One Mint Julep," with Harry Van Walls' tinkly piano, and
"Your Cash Ain't Nothin' but Trash" both sound like they could have
been written by Leiber & Stoller.

Atlantic dropped them by the late '50s.

"Their manager, Lou Krefetz, was from Baltimore, like me," says
Jerry. "The only person who knew how miserable our neighborhood
was, and one of the few who came out alive. Lou took 'em to United
Artists, did one or two sessions, couldn't get it on. So he came to us.
'Hey, Jerry, you gotta do me a big favor. I fuckin' need a hit. Not only
are the boys gonna starve, but I'm gonna starve. I can't book 'em, nothin's happening. Just look in the trunk—maybe you got a Coasters reject
you can make fit.'

"We had this song, 'Love Potion #9.' I told Mike, Lou really needs
it, he's on the balls of his ass. Mike said, 'How can we take it away from
the Coasters? They're our group, our boys, our kids?' I said, 'We wrote
fifty songs for them already, twenty hits. One song won't kill 'em. The
Clovers need a hit.' Mike said, 'How do you know it's a hit?' I said,
'How do I know anything, I just think it's a hit. It's our A-side for the
Coasters' next session.' So we did it for Clovers, and it sold a million
and a half. They were back in biz for life."

The Searchers also had a smash with "Love Potion" in 1965. "The
British rock 'n' roll versions of our R&B songs were great."

Back on the charts in 1959, the Clovers were thrilled to be booked
in some expensive, swank nightclub, wearing tuxedos. The bass vocalist
had the richest speaking voice, so the club asked him to announce the
group onstage. Ahmet was in the dressing room, where he called Jerry
and held up the phone.

"Ladies and gentlemen, we'd like to perform a Billy Eckstine number for you called 'You've Changed.'"

You've changed
That sparkle in your eye
Have *gone. . . .*

To Know Him Is to Loathe Him

"I want you to do me a favor and take in this kid Phil Spector," said Lester Sill, calling from California in 1960. "I think he's talented, a little crazy—but you understand that, right, Jer? Haw haw."

"That's fattening frogs for snakes," said Jerry. "He's gonna steal our licks and tricks and go out and compete. Why should we take him in?"

"Because you owe me," said Lester. And that was good enough for Jerry.

"One more favor," said Lester. "I want you to pay his airline ticket."

Like Jerry, Spector lost his father tragically when young, and moved with his mother from the East Coast (the Bronx) to Los Angeles in 1953. From out of the blue, teenage Spector scored a number-one smash in 1958, "To Know Him Is to Love Him," with his group, the Teddy Bears. Even so, they broke up the next year.

During his apprenticeship with Leiber & Stoller, Spector revealed this story. While on tour, The Teddy Bears played a gig at some Texas roadhouse. And this was back when Texas was mean. After their set, Phil entered the men's room and was followed by a biker gang. They tapped his shoulder at the urinal, Phil turned around, and they all whipped out their peckers and pissed on him.

"Phil got in on the British invasion right from the git-go," says Jerry. "But even before that, he was wearing these George Washington ruffled shirts and high-heeled boots in the early '60s. So he might have been pissed on more than once. As he started making money, he got paranoid, talked about hiring bodyguards, as if the whole world was gonna tap his shoulder and piss on him."

Once the bodyguards, who looked like Green Berets, were in place, Phil began to concoct these hero-saves-the-day psychodramas. He'd come to the rescue of girls being harassed by one of his bodyguards. Pulling a gun, he'd scare the guy off, and the girl would be rescued.

"But Spector was one of greatest cowards I ever met," says Jerry. "He couldn't chase away a pigeon."

Jerry sensed his killer instinct immediately. He looked upon Phil as a nasty teenager who laughed at other people's hardships. "I had a house in East Hampton since '58 and let Phil stay there around the summer of '61. He had no money. He had separation anxiety—'Where you going, when you coming back,' every time I left house. I think, through drugs and mental illness, this progressed years later to where he held people hostage at gunpoint so they wouldn't leave his house after parties."

Leiber & Stoller provided Spector with his first commission as producer on Ray Peterson's 1961 hit with "Corrina, Corrina." Phil pestered Jerry to play on sessions. Like a ward boss granting patronage, Jerry slipped him into the lineup. Phil shares guitar credits on the Coasters' vaudevillian treasure "Shopping for Clothes," and on one of Paul McCartney's faves, "Thumbin' a Ride." Phil's strumming is virtually imperceptible. But notably, he did the guitar solo in the Drifters' "On Broadway."

"He was a pretty good guitar player and helped Jack Nitzsche, who did the arrangements."

After Jerry provided Phil the keys to his office, Phil pilfered his own contract from the files, went back to L.A., and started his own record company, Phillies, under Lester Sill. "Still, we kept his business jumpin'," says Jerry. "Mike and I sent him seventeen smash hits from the songwriters in our publishing stable."

It is indisputable that the great Brill Building teams wrote most prolifically under Jerry and Mike's watch: Pomus & Shuman, Goffin & King, Mann & Weil, Barry & Greenwich.

"Phil was a thick-skinned pig and would shake down the songwriters and take a lot of the rewards. I wasn't there, so I don't know exactly what Phil contributed to each song—I suspect it was always good, but minor." Jerry won't bring himself to say that Spector committed outright forgery. He puts it like this: "I can vouch that song X was written by Ellie Greenwich and Jeff Barry and we sent it to Phil, who recorded it, and when it came out it had all three names on it as writers."

Spector might shoehorn in some bridge or relief. Like the three-chord break before the last chorus of Barry Mann & Cynthia Weil's "You've Lost That Lovin' Feelin'," or other songs that came pretty much fully conceived. Nevertheless, Phil's golden production alone could mean the difference between a song moldering unfinished in a trunk or becoming a hit for the ages.

"I always had nothing but contempt for cannibals who forced their names on songwriting credits," Leiber says. "I didn't have a lot of scruples in this rotten fuckin' business, because you can't survive with too many. But guys who added their names to songwriting credits because they owned the company, or ran the band, like Benny Goodman—any of those cocksuckers. It shows a brutal greediness, grasping and rapacious. If the pattern and idea is set up, *any* asshole can inject a line into a song. It's all there. But even though they come up with a line that rhymes in correct meter, it's the worst line in the song. It's always forced. Because they're not songwriters. They're not living in the idea and having fun with it. They're merely bullying their name onto it."

Otis Blackwell's songs included "All Shook Up," "Return to Sender," "Fever," "Great Balls of Fire," "Breathless," and "Handy Man."

"Such a sweetheart, and one bitch of a writer," says Jerry. "He wrote songs by himself. But he'd have to share credit on all those songs with someone who had a big connection he didn't have. They chewed him up in pieces."

Typical for Blackwell, he once sold away a six-song package of demos, which included "Don't Be Cruel," for $150.

Jerry and Phil wrote "Spanish Harlem" at Jerry's brownstone on Seventy-second Street. "In those days we had dinner with the kids around five. The writing session was for six. Mike was invited, but called in at seven, he had to take his son Peter to dinner. Could he come in now? I told him don't bother, we finished. So months later at the session, Mike contributed the opening bars to 'Spanish Harlem,' which he wrote on the spot. But *he* didn't share song credit."

(Lenny Bruce bought the single, played it onstage and said, "Listen to these lyrics. This is like a Puerto Rican *Porgy and Bess*.")*

Leiber & Stoller's stock only seems to rise, as Spector's reputation plummets by the year. Jerry was glad to bump into poor old Phil at sax player Nino Tempo's local gig in 2007. He came up behind Phil and whispered, "I know you didn't do it." Aside from murder charges, Spector has weathered the indignity of being mixed out of history on McCartney's *Naked* release of the *Let It Be* album, sans Spector's post-production. And before George Harrison left this earth, he wrote in his opening liner notes for the thirtieth-anniversary CD of *All Things Must Pass*, which Phil coproduced:

> It was difficult to resist re-mixing every track. All these years later I would like to liberate some of the songs from the big production that seemed appropriate at the time, but now seem a bit over the top with the reverb in the wall of sound.

After decades of gun-swaggering bravado, the Tycoon of Teen's gun finally went off in some poor girl's head, and he faces the prospect of dying in prison.

"My son Jed once dated the chick who Spector shot," says Jerry. "She was a great girl. Spector would drink Manischewitz while doing coke—a horrible concoction."

Jerry Wexler and Doc Pomus had a much higher regard for Spector as maestro, but Jerry doesn't cut him much slack. The mythic celebration of Spector's "Wall of Sound" must have worn on Jerry's nerves. Was it really *that* big an advance over the Leiber & Stoller template?

"Spector never acknowledged us," says Jerry. "He never said thank you."

*From the CD liner notes for Lenny Bruce, *Let the Buyer Beware*, © 2004 Shout Factory D6K 37109.

Manya from Yuppitz

Jerry's mother, Manya, was from a shtetl that she called Yuppitz. She always said it ironically. There was no such place. But everyone from her village always answered, "Yuppitz," when asked where they were from. It meant nowhere. Both his parents were orphaned children. "They had all the psychological quirks that orphaned children have," says Jerry. "And they passed all this crap on in the most generous way to me and my sister. We grew up scared and crazy." Yet Manya wasn't scared, and she wasn't crazy.

In Poland she was a bartender and barmaid on the overnight shift. She described the inn as a rough joint, but was prone to understatement. Russian Cossacks didn't just enter; they rode horses right up to the bar counter. The ceilings inside were high, but the Cossacks would have to bend in half to get through the entrance. A wide berth separated the bar from the tables. Horses would shit on the floor and peasants would not dare complain. Six Cossacks at once would burst in and demand their customary vodkas. Things could turn nasty when they got drunk. If they didn't like the way the vodka was tipped off, they wouldn't ask for more—they'd smack the bartender in the face with their riding crops. The server knew right away she'd fucked up with the drink. After they had their fill, they'd gallop off.

One night, the owner of the inn asked Manya to fill in for the deliveryman. It was fifty miles to Warsaw, quite a haul by horse and wagon. He traveled by two-horse cart to Warsaw every week to refill six-foot barrels of beer. The guy refused to do it one week. He'd been robbed and beaten during the last trip. Bandits lay in wait for travelers along one particularly treacherous stretch. The owner couldn't get anyone, so he asked his barmaid, Jerry's mother. She bargained for four times the kopecks he offered and got it. He said he would pay up front. She told him to hold the money. If she returned unmolested, with the barrels nearly full, he should give her twice as much, because a portion of the beer was always hijacked. Obviously, if she didn't return, he could keep the money, she said.

So she set sail. She was only eighteen, a good-looking woman. Tramps and gypsies ran to the edge of the road and flagged her down at a crossroad lit by a bonfire. This was where the delivery guy would start galloping. But Manya waved back and stopped the wagon. She confronted the leader, told him she was going to Warsaw to fill the barrels. Feigning innocence, she said she'd heard it was treacherous, that there were bandits in hiding. (Guys who might have gone into the record business if they'd been born here.) If they agreed to protect her, she would throw a party when she got back with the beer, and pay them. In a spirit of comradeship, with an opportunity to do a good deed for this fine young woman, they agreed.

She rode on to Warsaw and returned with enough beer to drown the Russian army. The bandits got loaded, danced, hugged and kissed her. When she left, they blew kisses and waved good-bye. She arrived back safe in Yuppitz and collected her reward.

Haulin' Coal

Jerry Leiber's parents arrived by ship in Baltimore in 1925. Though his father had been a teacher in Poland, they opened a general store. Jerry was born in his parents' house in 1933, where only Yiddish was spoken. His father died when Jerry was five, a terrible calamity in which he had contracted tuberculosis *and* lung cancer, succumbing to bronchial pneumonia after a year in Baltimore's Mt. Sinai Hospital.

"I slipped and almost fell into his grave during the funeral," says Jerry. "Maybe I should have gone in with him. My mother had no money, and we moved to the worst place in the world. The worst slum in Baltimore. My cousins and uncles were all grocery people. They shopped around to find this basement vestibule for my mother to open a store. The place stank. She opened the windows, did Lysol, but couldn't get rid of the smell. Cousin Ely and Betty were in tears, telling her not to buy it, we'd get robbed, assaulted.

"The first day, these Polish and Irish-Catholic kids walked by bouncing a ball as I sat out on the tenement steps. One spit and said: *"Jew ain't nothing but a nigga turned inside out.'"*

The blacks, however, didn't know about ethnic divisions. They only knew white. Baltimore is on the Mason-Dixon Line. Jerry remembers colored-only water fountains, segregated movies and restaurants. "It was more pronounced than the deep Southern states. Baltimore was Calvinist, and more racist than Mississippi."

Manya opened her tiny basement store, with twisted Coca-Cola and Dr. Pepper signs outside. The store had no name, but everyone called it Mary's. She sold canned goods, Campbell's, Del Monte, Heinz, had a fully stocked meat case, cold cuts. Kids thought Jerry was lucky because his mother's store sold rock candy. "But I never ate candy, just sour pickles," says Jerry. "The store even carried rubber orthopedic stockings for old ladies with varicose veins. As stuff came in she moved it around, somehow made it fit. She got up 5:30 every morning, went to bed at midnight. She was a one-man band."

Waving a fork in the auditorium, a teacher asked first-grade kids what it was. Jerry's hand shot up. He said, "It's a *gopl*!" The teacher said, "What?!" The whole auditorium broke into wild laughter. When the next little girl said fork, the whole auditorium applauded. "I knew a *gopl* is a fork, a *shlisl* is a key, and a *leffl* is a spoon. Even the other Jewish kids didn't know what these were."

Manya read Polish, Russian, and Hebrew but had trouble with English. Calling Jerry "incorrigible," the principal sent home a note demanding a meeting with his mother.

"Jerome," said Manya, proudly, "I knew you were such a good boy! I know what incorrigible means. With a little encouragement, you'll go a long way."

Yiddish curses rang out in the Leiber household: I'll put you in hell. . . . It should be as dark in your eyes as it is in mine. . . . Jerome, don't worry about nothin', cause nothin's gonna be all right.

"When I was five, playing in the kitchen on the floor, my mother would wring her hands, then point to me and tell her four-hundred-pound friend, in Yiddish, 'Bela, Bela, he lays in my stomach and grows like a stone. He's like a cancer.'"

"Here is the big thing that made me what I am," reveals Jerry. "Had it not happened, I would have remained Yiddish. My mother, against friends' and families' advice, decided to extend credit to black families. No other grocery store in Baltimore would do this. She didn't like the idea of giving a Polish Catholic woman credit—whom she knew in her heart would send my mother, her children, and every Jew she ever met to Auschwitz—but deny some black laundress down the street. Suddenly everybody in the black neighborhood came to her store. But she had something else that nobody ever offered any black family. Free delivery. It raised self-esteem. And guess what? I was the delivery boy. It sounds like Abe fuckin' Lincoln, but I delivered groceries, five-gallon cans of kerosene, and five-pound bags of soft coal for fireplaces from my mother's store."

One household Jerry delivered to was that of Dunbar, a black kid five years his senior who became a surrogate big brother. Dunbar fought at the YMCA and taught Jerry to box. Jerry was often invited in for supper. He found that he loved pig's knuckles, cabbage, and chitlins.

Epiphany #1: Receiving solace from the Negro side of life.

"I could sleep in the gutter and nobody would lay a finger on me. I got this sense of belonging to the black race. I loved them and they loved me. I felt enormous pride and power, the way kids would talk about their big brothers or fathers—which I didn't have. But every nigger in the world was my friend."

Some Negro homes had no electricity, only kerosene lamps and coal fires. And so, as Jerry hauled sacks of coal into dimly lit rooms, he heard strange music coming out of radios. As mammies fussed over their little white coal boy, he played with other kids, while collards and pork steamed over the oven. Jerry's third-grade teacher warned him that listening to Negro radio would end him up in the electric chair.

As Jerry returned from yeshiva once when he was eight, a crowd gathered in front of his mother's store. He kept his Hebrew books concealed in a brown paper bag. Four kids from his neighborhood gang, who would intermittently turn on him, waited in ambush. One tripped him and the books came sliding out. A feeding frenzy started—"Hey, what's this Hymie heebie-jeebie shit!?" Two Baltimore cops stood grinning outside their police Buicks. The books lay sacrilegiously on the ground. As Jerry bent over to pick one up, he was shoved from behind and the books scattered again. The crowd played soccer with his Hebrew books. Then Rodney Smedly, his archenemy, came up the middle. The crowd started to chant, "Kill the Jew! Kill the Jew!"

"Even the cops made bets, so I realized nobody's gonna save me. I took stock of the situation as Smedly came at me and made this firm decision: *I'm gonna kill that motherfucker*."

The training with Dunbar paid off as he beat Smedly to a pulp. The cops had to pull Jerry off as he banged Smedly's head into the pavement. He then sacked his Hebrew books like groceries and made his way through the hushed crowd. He was bleeding around one eye, but felt great as he entered Manya's store. It might not have ended this way in Yuppitz, only in America.

"You're late. What happened?"

"I told her I got in a fight," says Jerry. "Then she banged me in the head harder than all of Smedly's punches put together. I thought my brains were coming out of my ears. 'Didn't I tell you not to fight? You'll end up in jail, in the *electric chair*, Jerome! You're giving me such a *meesa masheena*. The electric chair, Jerome!'"

Move to L.A.

Jerry was twelve in 1945, when he and Manya boarded a Greyhound bus for Los Angeles. "Every few hours I'd have to hold up a blanket while she struggled out of a girdle or corset, the whole bus looking on while I stood mortified."

They stopped at Sante Fe. An Indian wearing a coon-tail hat sold tchotchkes at a stand. Jerry told him they were moving to L.A.

"Be careful in L.A.," he said.

"Why?"

"People who go to L.A. fall asleep."

"I never forgot this sage wisdom," says Jerry. "Only someone from an ancient culture could make such a cosmic observation."

The Greyhound depot in Los Angeles was right across from the Brown Derby on Vine. They were greeted by jubilation and a brass marching band parade, soldiers dancing.

"Jerome, find out what the noise is," asked Manya. So Jerry asked the bus driver.

"It's V-J Day, man. The war is over!"

He went back to his mother and said, "The war is over!"

She turned to scratch a piece of lint off her lapel. "Oh."

Los Angeles, with ocean, palms, and orange trees, was paradise compared to the Baltimore slums. Jerry was soon working as a busboy and dishwasher at Clifton's Cafeteria. A Filipino short-order cook stood watch, his elbows resting upon the lower part of a Dutch door. "I had to pass him with dirty dishes, down two flights of slippery stairs to the dishwasher. 'Caw-ful, caw-ful,' he warned, every time I passed. A Mexican dishwasher made fun of his accent, and he charged out with a butcher knife. The owner chewed out the Filipino, and as the owner left, the cook spit on the ground and shouted, 'Puck you!'"

The cook, who Jerry later realized was constantly stoned, had a tiny radio. He listened to Hunter Hancock's programs, like *Harlem Holiday* and *Harlematinee*. "One night I heard the most incredible voice."

Epiphany #2: Hearing Jimmy Witherspoon sing "Ain't Nobody's Business."

"It *killed* me," says Jerry. "But I thought, 'I can do that.'"

Considering rock's cultural dominance over the last fifty years, it's hard to imagine just how rare it was to find a white kid digging ditch blues, alley music, race records, whatever you want to call it—in the 1940s. Even more astonishing that a white kid would write himself some black blues. Doc Pomus, Mose Allison, and Johnny Otis come to mind. That's it. (This might be as astonishing today as well . . . an inner-city homeboy writing Yiddish cantorial music.) The ascendancy of rhythm & blues into rock 'n' roll was propelled by a handful of creators, of which

Leiber & Stoller were the prime force. Jerry would soon have his first record, "Real Ugly Woman," with Jimmy Witherspoon, in 1950. He and Mike were seventeen.

Love Me, Love My Awards

Many, many awards line Leiber's exquisite hallways, reminding all who pass, but mainly himself, of his early greatness. Leiber has to play catch-up in the *classiness* department, as befitting someone from a Depression-era working-poor *Yiddishe* household. Love me, love my awards. Five honorary doctorates. I've tried to convey that I admire a man's work, not his awards. But Jerry says, rightfully so, that most people admire awards more. Besides, the awards are really acknowledgements for making lots of money. A random sample, all engraved with his name:

Two Grammys on the living room mantle; NAS Lifetime Achievement Award, bearing the Washington Monument; 2002 Foreign Composition Award for "Stand By Me" from JASRAC (Japanese Society for Rights of Authors, Composers and Publishers); some country music award for writing "Jackson" (*"We got married in a fever"*); President's Award to Leiber & Stoller, July 15, 1986, from National Music Publishers' Association; two awards for "Kansas City," each with its own set of keys to the city; Distinguished Artists Award, Club 100 of the Music Center, November 3, 1997; fitted in glass: LACC Leiber & Stoller Pioneering Rock and Roll Songwriters Distinguished Alumni Award, 2005; World Soundtrack Award 2005, presented by the Flanders International Film Festival; a shofar horn reads, PRESENTED TO JERRY LEIBER, WHOSE SONGS HAVE MADE OUR CULTURE MORE MELODIC, ENTERTAINING, HAPPY AND GROOVY—the Creative Arts Temple, November 14, 2004; a modest trophy from the Cleveland Clinic Heart Center for being a model patient.

"Most awards are boring, you get terrible food, old ladies sitting next to you with expensive perfume floating over the rot," says Jerry. But at the Ivor Novello Awards in London, Elton John came onstage before thousands of people. He wore a tux, his bow tie hanging down off the collar, patting his forehead with a handkerchief. "Ladies and gentlemen, you wouldn't believe what just happened," said Elton. "I was coming down the elevator, and at the second floor on walks perhaps the most beautiful man I've ever seen. My heart went pitter-pat. And this young man looked at me with melting doe eyes. It was love at first sight. I didn't want to come to the stage but had to. For Leiber & Stoller. I'm so flustered. I had a few words to say but lost the paper. Without L&S, I wouldn't be up on the stage here, sweating."

"Then came George Martin, master of ceremonies," remembers Jerry. "Elegant, articulate, laudatory in all right areas, made a speech about us—if I wrote it myself, I couldn't be more satisfied. Then he said I'd like to introduce a friend—Paul McCartney. Paul said he saw the same guy as Elton on the elevator. He made a speech even more lauda-tory. 'Without Leiber & Stoller, I wouldn't be up here tonight. They were the models from which I and a couple other buddies in the band modeled ourselves. We've never really publicly given them credit. They are number one.'"

Seven Leiber & Stoller songs were (officially released) on Beatles albums. After "Kansas City," six appear on posthumous releases *Live at the BBC* and *Anthology*—three of them Coasters songs.

As recently as July 2007, Leiber & Stoller and their entourage were flown to Paris by the French jeweler Cartier and put up at the Bristol Hotel. Enfeebled by various ailments, Jerry took two epidural shots for the New York–to-Paris flight, stretched out in a sleeper pod, and woke up refreshed in Paris. French luminaries gave speeches, thanking them for inventing rock 'n' roll, while Little Richard, at seventy-four, brought down the house on piano.

"I once stood next to Little Richard for a group picture where we all had our arms around each other. I used to be a wrestler, could size up somebody quickly, and his shoulders felt powerful—he was much taller than I expected, strong as an ox. I figured he'd have been slight, effete. But he wasn't. 'Can I ask you something personal?' I said. 'How'd you get to be so fuckin' strong?'

"'King Cotton, baby, King Cotton,' he said."

41

The rule unwrit has always been that Jerry and I are friends on an equal basis—but underneath should always be my sense of awe, and when I violate respect for his awards, he loses it. I have to intermittently present a certain level of reverence, so he can swat it away with self-deprecation—"I'm not Irving Berlin." "Oh, yes, you are."

And, in fact, I do believe he is Irving Berlin.

Blue Skies

Leiber's family settled in a small apartment on Larchmont Boulevard in L.A. RKO and Paramount Studios were two blocks down at Melrose. Jerry hung out at the gate and schmoozed with guards. He'd bring them packs of cigarettes and Cokes. Sometimes they'd let him inside the studios. One day a little man walked out of nowhere, impeccably attired in a navy blue double-breasted suit with fine gray pinstripes and pointy black shoes. It was a loading dock; a place you only saw workers. The man stood at the edge of a big puddle of rainwater, looking up at the sky and moving his lips.

"Who's the nut?" Jerry asked.

"Nut?" the guard said. "You should only be such a nut. That's Irving fucking Berlin."

"The songwriter? Wow." Jerry didn't know he was still alive. "Can I meet him?"

"You must be kiddin'. No."

"Can I just say hello?"

"No, you can't do that neither."

"Why is he moving his lips like that? He looks crazy."

"You should be so crazy," came the guard. "He's writing a song."

Then the guard took pity. "Look, kid, when he stops moving his lips like that, he's not writing the song anymore. Then you can go in. Here's what you do. Are you listening? You go up and say, 'Mr. Berlin, can I shake your hand? I think you're great.' Or maybe you say, 'Mr. Berlin, I think you're great. May I shake your hand?' If he looks at you and smiles, then you shake his hand and say thanks, turn around, and come back out. Don't ask for his autograph or nothin'. Got it?"

After a minute or two Berlin stopped moving his lips. The guard gave the signal. Jerry walked to the guardrail and asked Mr. Berlin if he could shake his hand. Berlin smiled, offered his hand, and said, "Put it there, pal." Jerry walked through the puddle feeling cold water sluicing through his shoes. But he'd shaken Berlin's hand and was in heaven.

I'm Gonna Be a Songwriter

By 1948, when he was fifteen, Jerry was working at Norty's Record Shop on Fairfax, across from Cantor's Deli. He stocked records and worked behind the counter after school. The store carried no race records or jazz, no Billie Holiday or Lester Young. Norty's had two kinds of clientele: those who bought big band records—the Andrews Sisters, Patti Page, Georgia Gibbs— or those who bought albums of cantorial music, like Rabbi Ysidor Bularski and folksingers who did "Belz Mayn Shtetele, Belz," one of the standard Yiddish songs of yearning for one's old shtetl, or Jewish ghetto. The clientele of Norty's included Russian, Polish, and Ukrainian immigrants. These records sold in every small Yiddish enclave in any city around the world.

Yiddish is the centuries-old, guttural street language shared by Eastern European Jews, be they from Poland, Russia, Hungary, Romania, France, or Germany. It might be a stretch to call Yiddish a metaphorical sister tongue to the language of blues. No Jew was a stranger to another when traveling over the continent, if he knew the secret language.

A hundred or so Yiddish words have been assimilated into English. For example: *chutzpah, klutz, mishmosh, meshugga, boo-boo* (brought into common usage by Jerry Lewis), *schmuck, shlong, shlemiel, schlock, schmaltz, shlep, shmeer, shmooze, shnook, spritz, shtick . . . tokhis.*

By the late '40s and '50s, nothing could be less hip than Yiddish. It reeked of old-country impoverishment, pogroms, *mockeys* with pushcarts, the lived-in, centuries-old kitchen aroma of mama's boiled flanken. Everything an upwardly mobile street sharpie even remotely like Budd Schulberg's Sammy Glick was running from. Yiddish culture was in free fall. Its scholars, playwrights, and intellectuals had been incinerated during the war. Israel turned its back on Yiddish in favor of adopting the proper Biblical tongue of Hebrew for its new state in 1948.

"Take it from me," says Jerry. "Hebrew is not funny, it's not pithy, it's not juicy, it's not colorful. I never heard any joy in it. It's all business. Philosophy, science, politics."*

One afternoon, the best-dressed man Jerry ever saw walked into Norty's Record Store with a briefcase. Jerry never forgets a man's wardrobe, and describes it like food: he wore a tan, double-breasted suit with an almost imperceptibly thin sky-blue pinstripe going through it. While local Hollywood elites like Cary Grant dressed in Saville Row, the top bookies, pimps, and gamblers went to Sy Devore on Vine Street. And so ran Lester Sill's impeccable taste—to the nines.

Lester was a song entrepreneur. He opened his tan leather briefcase and presented five new 78s. He asked if he could play them for Jerry behind the counter.

"You wanna see what *I* think? What for?"

"Well, you're the salesman here. I want to know if you think they'll sell here."

The first he played was John Lee Hooker's "Boogie Chillen." Jerry told him it was dynamite.

"You like that, huh?"

"I like it a whole lot."

"Do you think it would sell?"

"It would sell to me. But not anyone else here. Lemme play *you* something." Jerry pulled out a cantorial album by Rabbi Ysidor Bularski, put it on the Victrola, and Lester held his face like he'd gotten shot in the head. Jerry also played a Tony Bennett ballad, Johnny Ray's

---

*Seemingly down for the final count, Yiddish is making an ironic comeback in cyberspace, as one of the hot new languages of the twenty-first century.

"Cry," Frankie Lane's "Mule Train," and then Mickey Katz's Yiddish version of "Mule Train." That's what sold there.

"So whaddya want to be when you grow up?"

"I am grown up."

"Well, of course, you are," Lester apologized. "But what are you gonna be?"

"I'm gonna be a songwriter."

"You're kidding?"

"No."

"You wanna sing me a song?"

Norty, the owner, was taking inventory, and Jerry told Lester he could get fired. But Lester said don't worry, he'd take care of Norty, he'd known him forever.

"Well, I've got no written music, but they're all the same anyway. They're blues."

Jerry sang one. Lester liked it and said he *was* going to be a songwriter. He asked Jerry to sing another, told him that was a good song, too, so Jerry sang a third. Norty finally walked over, asked, "What the hell's going on, what're you doing with my boy?" Lester explained that he was doing an audition. Then he handed Leiber his card: LESTER SILL, MODERN RECORDS, HEAD OF SALES AND PROMOTION.

"Call me one of these days. You got these lyrics down in a book, right? You've gotta get lead sheets, ever heard of that? Lead sheets are the sheets of music where every note is under every syllable of every word and the chords are on top. You need that in order to demonstrate a song to a singer, with a piano player. Do you know somebody who can do that for you?"

Jerry said he'd look around.

Meeting Mike

A European journalist interviewing Leiber & Stoller once said, "I finally get it. You're the motor, Mike's the brakes. Together you're a car."

"For fifty years Mike kept me from jumping off of cliffs or going to jail," says Jerry. "Mike was also the businessman. He's mathematical, literal. He signed all the checks and I've never questioned one of them. Mike has thirty thousand records, inventoried, cataloged—he can locate any one in five seconds. I don't even have any Elvis or Coasters records in my home."

One day a ragged group came in to audition, wearing work shirts. Two of them wore filthy turbans. Jerry and Mike asked what their name was.

"The Farrows," they said.

"You mean Pharaohs?" asked Mike. "Like Egypt, the pyramids?"

"Yeah, the pyramids."

"Well," goes Mike, "Indians and Arabs wear turbans. Not Pharaohs. How do you spell it?"

"F-a-r-r-o-w-s."

"Oh," says Stoller. "A farrow is a litter of pigs."

They looked like they were going to lynch him.

Leiber & Stoller were both born in 1933. Leiber came up tough, Stoller didn't. Stoller was from Sunnyside, Queens, New York, the last place anyone would go to catch some sun. He attended an interracial summer camp in 1940, where he watched older Negro children play upright piano in a barn. When they left, he'd try to make his hands do what theirs did, but couldn't. Then, at age ten, he received piano lessons from James P. Johnson, who taught Fats Waller. Mike admired Joe Turner's piano man, ("Roll 'Em") Pete Johnson, as well as Albert Ammons and Meade Lux Lewis—preferring boogie-woogie men to stride players. As a teenager, he hung out at the Famous Door on Fifty-second Street, where Dizzy Gillespie and Charlie Parker played for themselves. The Stoller family moved to Los Angeles in 1949.

"The first few years we collaborated, he was contemptuous of what we were doing," says Jerry. "He didn't love the blues. If it wasn't Thelonious Monk, it was junk."

Leiber was writing songs with a working drummer named Jerry Horowitz at Fairfax High. When Horowitz's father died, he had to quit music and get a full-time job. But the young drummer recommended the piano player in his band. The guy wasn't bad, he studied with some composer—maybe Jerry could call him to write songs with.

"I took Stoller's number," says Jerry. "Somebody picked up the phone. 'Hello, is this Mike Stoller?' 'Yeah.' 'You play piano?' 'Yes.' 'Same Mike Stoller who played gigs with Jerry Horowitz in Boyle Heights?' He said, 'Yep.' 'You read music?' 'Yep.' 'You can write notes down, lead sheets?' 'Yep.' 'How would you like to write songs?' 'You mean that moon-June-spoon shit? I don't dig that shit. Not interested.' I said, 'I don't write no moon-June-spoon shit. I write blues.' He said, 'I don't do blues.' 'What do you like?' 'I like Gershwin, Cole Porter, Jerome Kern.' I said, 'That's all right, my mom digs that shit. I think Irving Berlin's the greatest. I got a notebook with lyrics I can show you.' He said, 'I really hate songs. I like Diz and Thelonious, Miles, Charlie Parker. You ever hear of those guys?' I said no. But I talked Mike into me coming over."

The boys wrote blues songs together through the summer of 1950. They dated black debs, got drunk, and spun around in Mike's '37 Plymouth. They went to ghetto dances and hung out with spade hipsters at Club Alabam on Central Avenue—leaving the white world behind.

Mike's father accused Jerry's mentor, Lester Sill, of being a thief. But Lester took Jerry and Mike, who wrote songs that summer, to Modern Records and introduced them to Sol and Joe Bahari. They immediately cut a few songs with the Robins. Then Lester took the boys across the street to Aladdin, where Charles Brown, Amos Milburn, and, to Stoller's delight, Lester Young recorded. They cut "Hard Times" with Charles Brown, which went to number one on the race records chart.

"That's where we learned to produce records. From Maxwell Davis. He arranged all the sessions at Aladdin, a triple threat, did every tenor sax solo. He could write or play anything, the coolest guy, never got excited or upset, just took out his ruler went to work. His stuff always swang. He got swang, we used to say."

Mike and Jerry formed an independent label, Spark Records, in 1953. They wrote for Amos Milburn, and Ray Charles when he was still imitating Nat King Cole, before he became black again. They did "Riot in Cell Block #9" for the Robins (with the perennial refrain, *There's a riot goin' on*). Like a radio drama, it used an arresting staccato tommy gun and police sirens, narrating a prison riot under a Muddy Waters Delta blues riff. This playlet became the signature style Leiber & Stoller mastered as they turned the Robins into history's favorite doo-wop group—the Coasters.

One very dark episode: Flush with cash, Jerry bought himself a Jaguar. One night at an Italian restaurant James Dean challenged Jerry to a drag race.

"What kind of car you got?"

"Jag."

"That's an old lady's car," said Dean, who drove a Porsche. Both young hipsters psyched each other out and quit before gunning the engines. Before Dean fatally crashed his Porsche, Jerry was demonstrating his automotive bravado to two black girls. But these weren't debutantes, they were hookers. They were all over him in the front seat, egging him on to go faster. "Hurry up, gotta make another trick!" one yelled, stomping her big foot over his on the gas pedal. The car crashed, killing one of the girls. Leiber was charged with vehicular manslaughter. He doesn't discuss it, of course, but her ghost has haunted him the rest of his life.

Nesuhi Ertegun

The beloved Nesuhi Ertegun, Ahmet's older brother, opened up the floodgates for Leiber & Stoller. High-society sons of Turkish ambassador Munir Ertegun, the Ertegun brothers were raised in Washington, D.C. They had Dixieland bands come up to the Turkish embassy for parties. Nesuhi would found Atlantic's jazz division, producing the era's gold-standard albums with Coltrane, Mingus, and the Modern Jazz Quartet. But in the early '50s, Nesuhi lived a modest life with his wife, running a specialty store in L.A. called the Jazzman Record Shop.

The first release of "Kansas City" with Little Willie Littlefield came out in 1952. "It was a hit in San Francisco and one town in Texas, but did nothing in L.A," says Jerry. Likewise with the Robins' "Riot in

Cell Block #9" and other now-classic records, including "Framed" and "Smokey Joe's Café."

"None of our records made the Top 10 in *Cashbox* or anywhere," says Jerry.

In 1955, Nesuhi picked up Leiber & Stoller's "Ruby Baby" for the Drifters (later a hit for Dion and Steely Dan), on his brother's label, Atlantic. He asked Jerry why their records didn't sell nationally. Jerry told him what Ertegun already knew—Spark Records didn't really have national distribution.

"You guys make great records," said Nesuhi, "but you don't know anything about manufacturing, distribution, or promotion. You're wasting your time. You ought to be making these records for my brother at Atlantic. I can assure you you'll sell records."

"I played Nesuhi a coupla demos," says Jerry, "and he asked, 'Who's singing?' I said, 'It's me.' He said, 'Come on, you're pulling my leg. You don't sound Jewish.' I said, 'It's me, Nesuhi, it's me, I make all the demos. I can imitate a twenty-two-year-old drunk or an eleven-year-old girl.' He said, 'I wanna sign you. You're the best white blues singer I've heard in a long time.' I figured he didn't know much about this business if he wanted to sign me, because I wouldn't sign me and I got pretty good ears. But I sounded like Memphis Slim and was better than a lot of black blues singers around L.A. at that time. But I felt it was unacceptable for a white guy to sing blues."

Jerry finally humored Neshui. "I cut a record around '54, with Shorty Rogers, Shelly Mann, and all those guys. I was Elmo Glick, a combination of Elmore James and Sammy Glick, the antihero of Budd Schulberg's *What Makes Sammy Run?* It was a terrible record."*

Stoller and his wife, Meryl, spent their 1956 honeymoon in Italy. They returned on the ill-fated Italian ocean liner, the *Andrea Doria*. Both were among the survivors the night it sank in the North Atlantic. Jerry, who'd

*Two better tracks: Leiber sings lead on the Coasters' "Shake 'Em Up and Let 'Em Roll," and the bridge (*That ain't no freight train coming down the track*) on "Baby, That Is Rock & Roll."

spent a day frantic over whether his partner was alive, met them at the dock in New York with a new silk suit for Mike.

He informed Mike that a song of theirs, "Hound Dog," was on its way to number one. Stoller wasn't yet sure who Elvis was.

Leiber & Stoller moved to New York in 1957 to direct A&R at RCA, a short-lived gig. They dissolved Spark Records in order to begin their groundbreaking production deal with Atlantic Records, which their RCA contract allowed. Coming from the West Coast with two of the Robins, lead singer Carl Gardner and bass Bobby Nunn, they added tenor Leon Hughes and comedy singer Billy Guy (Jerry's vocal alter ego)—and the Coasters were born.

Leiber & Stoller became the pulse of teenage America, and their output over the next decade fills up music encyclopedias.

Atlantic

Two dentists played a significant role in the formation of Atlantic Records. With so many tooth doctors around, you'd think a free dental plan came written into each artist contract, but that wasn't the case. The first dentist, Herb Abramson, cofounded Atlantic with Ahmet in 1947.

"*He* was the man, the real soul and brains of the operation," says Leiber. "Ahmet was a figurehead, a great social creature; he could sit down with the hippest motherfucker on earth and out-mother him. Herb was the *music* man, matchless in his sensibility and production. The innovative guy, but not the toughest. He dressed like Laurence Olivier. And a dentist by profession. He made the best records, like 'High-Heel Sneakers.' Herbie did the Ravens, and you didn't get no hipper than the Ravens when I was a kid. Jimmy Ricks was the greatest bass vocalist in the business. They were funkier than the Ames Brothers and Mills Brothers. The Mills Brothers sang behind Bing, but the Ravens were too black for Bing."

Herb's wife, Miriam, was the backbone of Atlantic, according to Leiber. She was head of production—she ran the manufacturing. Herb came back from the Korean War after a few years to find the group had bonded. Ahmet, Jerry Wexler, and Miriam Abramson, "who had more balls than the men." She then divorced Herbie, left Atlantic, and married Freddie Bienstock.

Leiber believes Ahmet, Miriam, and Dr. Vahdi Sabit (the Ertegun family dentist, who originally bankrolled Atlantic) drummed Herbie out. They divested Herb's piece of Atlantic in 1958.

Leiber, who at times considered producer Jerry Wexler his second-closest friend, says Wex became the tough guy. "Wex was burrowed to the roots of *Billboard* and *Cashbox*. He had an illustrious rep and great gift for gab in order to pay off people to get on the charts. He was the *schmeichler*."

In addition to being the *schmeichler*, Wexler was, according to Al Bell, the black chairman of Stax/Volt Records, also "the mother and father of what became known as R&B and then soul music. He heard it, he loved it, he respected it, and he taught America and then the world to love and respect it."

Also a man of exquisite taste, the great "Omelet" Ertegun (as doo-wop groups mispronounced it) had difficulty in matters of intimacy. In his later years, he had the aristocratic stamp and kidney of a world-weary squire who'd been quite handsome in his youth, but actually never was.

Chanteuse Phoebe Legere, a hot blonde at the time, was one of many young ladies who had the distinction of being stalked by Ahmet's limo. Ertegun's limo was known to troll down side streets behind model types who'd piqued his interest in a bar or nightclub earlier. Legere recalled a strange encounter. Knowing who he was, she agreed to have him up to her East Village apartment, a five-floor walk-up. Midway up the stairs, Ertegun following, he suddenly lunged under her skirt and in one fell swoop was able to slide under her panties and penetrate his middle finger *deep into her rectum*. Maybe some ancient Turkish sleight of hand. He quickly unplugged himself and bolted down the steps, having mined his gold, as she froze in astonishment. One can then imagine the urbane connoisseur in the back seat of his limo, finger glistening victoriously under his nose. *Laissez les bon temps rouler*! Baby, let the good times roll!

As Leiber and Stoller both said, "We didn't write songs, we wrote records." And few people, when the stakes were high, have ever known *exactly what to do* with such precision as Leiber & Stoller. General Patton, perhaps, when drawing up battle plans. "If I said, 'March,' when we were in the studio, then I expected them to *march*," says Jerry. Mike and Jerry inspired, supervised, and edited songwriters, assigning them to singers and groups. They employed up to ten songwriting teams in their publishing office, working nine to five (but really around the clock). The smaller the cubicle, the bigger the hit—and they wrote hundreds: Goffin & King, Mann & Weil, Pomus & Shuman, Greenwich & Barry, Gamble & Huff, Shadow Morton, Burt Bacharach (before Hal David), and Van McCoy (before disco). Jerry even signed Neil Diamond.

Red Bird

"Mike and I made most of our hits with complete unknowns, starting from scratch. Like the naive kids we were, we signed all of the acts we discovered over to Atlantic," says Leiber. "So we didn't own our own acts, we didn't *own* the Coasters—Atlantic did. We had no autonomy; it was not like we could take them with us."

An accounting dispute led to a falling-out. "We were suddenly discharged from Atlantic and all of our artists we'd been producing for ten years. They gave us the Drifters; they were a graveyard at that point. But we felt we had nowhere to go. Mike and I had little kids and were not by any means rich yet."

Though beset by momentary insecurity, it's hard to imagine the "Wizards of Wax," as *Life* mag dubbed them, not being the most sought-after musical entity in pre-Beatles America. Jerry and Mike rolled up their sleeves and crossed the street to United Artists, where they were greeted warmly.

"The first group we signed was Jay & the Americans, who walked in off the street. The first record, right off the bat, was 'She Cried,' which sold 1.8 million and went to number five on the charts in '62. U.A.

had been starving—this was their first million-seller. Then we produced "The Boy from New York City" with the Ad Libs. Bing, bing, bing, like magic. Four or five hits. Then we said, 'Fuck this, let's go into the record business.' So we started Red Bird Records in 1964."

Leiber & Stoller produced a run of hits with Jay & the Americans, who would also put "This Magic Moment" back up on the charts. Reminiscent of the Drifters, they were a clean-cut, pseudo-doo-wop "boy group" of Jewish collegians. Their records utilized Leiber & Stoller's Latin groove, which in this case sounded hokey. "They were okay, not great," shrugs Jerry. "You didn't have to like the lead singer's voice."

"Only in America" was first recorded by the Drifters—where it would have implied a Coaster-esque put-on:

> *Only in Am-er-i-ca*
> *Could a kid without a cent*
> *Get a break and maybe grow up to be president*

Jerry Wexler nixed the Drifters version. The irony was too dicey and provocative for a black group. Jay & the Americans' vocals were added to the original tracks, and it became a milquetoast hit, losing Leiber & Stoller's original intent.

The Stage

Some of greatest songwriters were also the most unpleasant, if not ugly-looking, people.

"Jule Styne was nasty to everyone else but nice to me," says Jerry, of the great *Gypsy* composer. "The guys who wrote the most beautiful melodies were usually nasty motherfuckers, pricks, lady-killers. And nice guys like me wrote mean, shitty sentiments. Opposites play in everything."

It is also axiomatic that the most repulsive-looking restaurateurs serve the most delicious food. As if the quality of the menu is in inverse proportion to the repulsiveness of the proprietor. Especially delicatessen men.

Max Asnis, who owned the Stage Delicatessen at West Fifty-fifth Street and Seventh Avenue, with his partner, Hymie Weiss, for decades, was a Yiddish Quasimodo. His Hirschfeld caricature adorned the menu and walls.

"I used to come into the Stage and the only ones present were Shecky Green, Milton Berle, and two hookers—and it seemed crowded. Asnis tried to keep the Stage for local theater professionals, not tourists. Max usually never talked to me when I had lunch at the Stage, which was every day for nineteen years. I used to meet [legendary Broadway director] Harold Clurman at 10:30 for breakfast.

"One morning, I sat across from Clurman, having my chopped herring, bagel, and coffee, reading *Variety*. A group of women entered wearing pale pastel suits and Kresky's jewelry, with HELLO labels attached to their lapels. Midwestern Sunday schoolmarms from a knitting convention at the Americana Hotel. Max viewed them with typical *schutzim* goy contempt. So he walks up to my table and loudly asks, 'Jerry, vy dey call a pussy a cunt?' I heard silverware drop on the ladies' plates.

"'Max, you're gonna chase the ladies outta here.'

"'Don't tell me how to run my store. You wanna be my friend, you gonna do dis act with me or not?' He made a face like he'd poison me if I didn't join in.

"'Now ask me back dis question, and don't visper,' he said. 'Are you ready? Vy dey call a pussy a cunt?'

"'Why, Max? Why do they call a pussy a cunt?'

"'Because it looks like one.'"

Maybe this heady mixture of pastrami and cunt jokes is what kept knitting club ladies coming back. Asnis finally succumbed to the blue-haired ladies.

"One morning in the '70s I walked into the Stage to meet Clurman and we saw it was all over. Overnight. There were fifty-year-old pot-bellied barmaids in black lace stockings and shorty dresses. They opened a new bar and served drinks at 10 A.M. In came the stampede of blue-haired ladies from the Americana Hotel across the street."

Rock 'n' Roll

The blues is a century-old tradition, like baseball, with an abundant history. Blues history wasn't deconstructed and tied together into a continuum until more recent times. Charlie Patton may be traditional now, but then he was absolutely radical. Now, the way baseball players compete in the present against past achievements, so do bluesmen.

But Jerry has a major problem with rock 'n' roll:

"The term was invented by people like Alan Freed. And Jerry Wexler, who might find it embarrassing to admit now, but he promoted the name into usage, around the time of Joe Turner's 'Shake, Rattle and Roll.'

"It's a misnomer that tries to cover stuff that's too diverse. Some was just plain country, some was jazz-oriented blues, some was pop. But everything was suddenly called rock 'n' roll. The identity is stretched so far, it's not definable. It's been over-populated genetically, it's got so many strains going at once.

"Rock 'n' roll is like a culture that no longer has a universal character. If we call it rock, or rock 'n' roll, we destroy the knowledge of what its origin is. Rock is a generalization that flattens out and neutralizes meaning. We're getting away from the specificity of meaning. I'm not passionate about too many things, but I am about the use of words, and the dilution of meaning. Words like *outage* bother me. It means a power outage. Twenty-five years ago, you wouldn't know what the fuck that meant. Someone traded in the phrase *power failure* for the quicker word *outage*, which is an inferior description. All to make time for more commercials, to trim seconds off a newscast so an extra toilet paper commercial can fit. A kid says a candy bar is *awesome*. It's a distortion and exaggeration of a simple thing. So is rock 'n' roll."

Songwriters

At the height of Leiber & Stoller's run, Mike Stoller considered their rock 'n' roll records transient, ephemeral, for the market of the minute. All the standards of American music had already been written. No Broadway, jazz or modern composer would give them a moment's recognition. Aside from the pop charts, the only pats on the back came from a small circle of peers in the insular music biz.

"We eventually bought into this self-disgust for years," says Jerry. "I know Mike's proud of our achievements. But he's also embarrassed, thinks it's lowbrow, backward, stupid. He thinks jazz is a higher art. Some of this rubbed off on me. It's heartbreaking. It took me years to rediscover for myself what I'd done, who I was."

Eventually tidal waves of cultural redemption and appreciation would come. Still, Jerry Leiber rarely looks sideways to admire musical contemporaries, perhaps because he gave so many their start. But he still looks up to the standard-bearers of an older generation. He was friends with the likes of Sammy Cahn, Jule Styne, Frank Loesser, Ira Gershwin—all of whom loathed rock 'n' roll.

Harold Arlen (né Hyman Arluck) was the son of a cantor. Like *The Jazz Singer*, he dropped out of school, to his parents' dismay, to play red-light districts in Buffalo.

"He did hipper stuff than Gershwin or Cole Porter," says Jerry. "I don't mean 'Somewhere Over the Rainbow.' I mean stuff he did at the Cotton Club, big band things that really cook."

Among his standards: "Stormy Weather," "Ac-Cent-Tchu-Ate the Positive," "I've Got the World on a String," "Between the Devil and the Deep Blue Sea," "Blues in the Night," "That Old Black Magic," "One for My Baby (and One More for the Road)" "Come Rain or Come Shine."

"His stuff does not sound like a *take*," says Jerry. "Gershwin, whom I love regardless, sounds like he's doing a take on pickaninnies. Arlen sounds like he's one of the boys."

Leiber is of the school that believes that one man stands above all other songwriters:

"I used to make lunch money by asking, 'Who wrote "God Bless America"?' They'd answer, 'Nobody. It's a street song, the government commissioned some poet or took John Philip Sousa's music and stuck a lyric.' I'd make a bet. 'Okay. Irving Berlin wrote it.' 'He didn't write it, "God Bless America" is the anthem.' '"God Bless America" isn't the anthem, "The Star-Spangled Banner" is the anthem.' 'Hey, you're right.'"

Like Leiber, Russian-born Irving Berlin's first language was Yiddish and he also lost his father as a young boy. Berlin worked the streets to survive and slept in nickel flophouses with old bums when he was six years old. At a Berlin tribute, Jerry heard Harold Arlen say: "I've been in love with his work ever since I could hear. His songs were not actually written, they were born."

"I'm not crazy about all the people who sang them," says Jerry. "But I love Berlin's songs the most."

The dichotomy veers south from Berlin: "After him, my favorite stuff was Muddy, Wolf, Memphis Slim, Little Walter, Sticks McGee, Furry Lewis, John Lee Hooker . . . and 'Bad Bad Whiskey' by Amos Milburn. But I still consider Berlin the greatest craftsman of all time. The marriage of music and words was unparalleled. His stuff is so collectively perfect, not just technically, but aesthetically, poetically. I sat down for months, like doing crossword puzzles, with a lead sheet and tried to improve on Berlin's lyrics with a one-word connective—an *and* or *up* or an *under* or *over*. I couldn't do it. Not once. His craft is so natural and effortless, you can't see the stitching or the bolts in any of the work.

"Berlin's stuff is the universal writing of the world—'Easter Parade,' 'White Christmas,' 'Alexander's Ragtime Band'—his standards are as important as the fucking 'Star-Spangled Banner.' Sammy Cahn, Frank Loesser, Richard Rodgers, Sondheim—any of them would say Irving Berlin without hesitating."

The writer of *Guys & Dolls* talked like a bookie but was as well educated as they come. Frank Loesser ran his own publishing company, Frank Music, and knew more about copyright law than his copyright lawyers. "We used to go out for drinks. He smoked Chesterfields, I smoked Camels. When I drank bourbon at his house and ran out of Camels, it wasn't so bad, 'cause he had Chesterfields. That was our bond together. Stoller smoked Parliaments, which was like toilet paper to me."

Jerry's tough on Stephen Sondheim. During Jerry's long marriage to stage director Gabby Rodgers, he held sway as a Broadway raconteur, if not an impresario. Excepting the hit jukebox musical, *Smokey Joe's Café*, Leiber & Stoller have been stymied in all attempts to launch an original Broadway musical—partly because Jerry's genius only extends to three minutes, but mainly due to Leiber's dark side, when he turns into what he calls "Grandma Hyde," as in Dr. Jekyll and. He has a notorious rep for turning tyrant and welching on collaborators. (And trying to shoehorn inappropriate old songs into new projects.) Nevertheless, Leiber & Stoller became de facto publishers of eighty gold-standard Broadway musical scores, including those of Sondheim, after buying out the stock of companies like Times Square Music.

"Sondheim never had a hit *record*. Standards, yes, great songs recorded over and over, but never a hit record. Jule Styne and Sammy Cahn wrote hit records for Broadway shows."

Well, if nothing from *West Side Story* or *Gypsy* murdered the pop charts, how about "Send in the Clowns?"

"Sentimental, self-pitying, self-serving, really clunky. But the seams in between the phrases have been well soldered. The melody is derivative in the broad sense; it has all the earmarks of a categorically predictable show tune ballad."

He's equally ruthless about "I'm Still Here": "It's great for old actresses, but one of those rah-rah-for-me songs."

Favorite Sondheim number: "I Never Do Anything Twice."

Gypsy, *Guys & Dolls* and *Follies* are among the four scores most often proclaimed Greatest Broadway Score. The fourth, Lerner & Lowe's *My Fair Lady*, gets Jerry's vote hands down.

"It's as perfect, per bar of music, per line, per song, in refinement, as anything ever done. A seamless web between book and songs, which is usually impossible. Alan Jay Lerner was a gentleman junkie who wore white gloves. Lerner actually improved G. B. Shaw's language in the lyrics. Only Gilbert & Sullivan were better."

When Jerry Leiber X-rays a song or score, you're liable to suddenly admire or lose respect for it.

"Even *Fiddler on the Roof* was watered down compared to the Yiddish theater my mother took me to in Baltimore," he says. "Zero's performance was a Catskills version of Yiddish—compared to Menasha Skulnik ("the Yiddish Charlie Chaplin," himself half Jewish), Leo Fuchs ("the Yiddish Fred Astaire"), or Molly Picon. When he shrugged his shoulders and held up his hand in the pose of the Yiddish tailor, saying, '*Nascusha*'—'not great'—in answer to 'How ya doin'?'—it seemed more Borscht Belt than authentic. And I own the publishing to *Fiddler*."

A perfect song: "September Song" (Kurt Weill, Maxwell Anderson): "It thoroughly captures the emotional moment of getting older and dying, in such an elegant and touching manner. It's discreet, never gets sloshy or sentimental."

Favorite rendition: Walter Huston in *Knickerbocker Holiday*.

Other songs Jerry considers bulletproof: "Where or When" (Rodgers & Hart), "I'll Be Seeing You" (Sammy Fain, Irving Kahal), "As Time Goes By" (Herman Hupfeld), "All Alone by the Telephone" (Berlin).

Leiber has instigated fights over his opinion that Bob Dylan is "a fraud, a covert liar, inauthentic." Obviously, he was deeply shaken by how Dylan changed songwriting. Dylan could have never worked nine to five at the Brill Building.

"He took too many lyrics from old folk records. It's not natural for a middle-class Jew from Minnesota, not in his genes. Such a sloppy white motherfucker with no rhythm. He came to visit us in the studio in the early '60s, when we were recording John Hammond, where he met the Band for the first time. Wearing a hat, white makeup, and lipstick, he was a clown from the neck up. He was playing a role—I never believed he was real. Had a lot of chicks? So did Mickey Rooney. The fact that he was so hip, inscrutable, and quiet—this motherfucker is self-aggrandizing and full of shit."

Jerry is relieved to hear that great American novelist Nelson Algren agreed, and said as much in his last book, *The Devil's Stocking*.

What bothers Jerry the most about Dylan:

"His father was a pharmacist."

I don't know, Jerry. What the fuck does that mean?

"What does it mean? Doesn't that just say it all?"

Blacks and Jews

"I always felt that most other white songwriters were imitating the blues, things they'd heard about, variations on the theme. I never trust writing that's self-conscious, mannered, worked-over, revised and shined. But blues became my language, my métier, my life. Impulsive phrases came out of my mouth extemporaneously. I didn't imitate language or attitude. It was second nature."

Being Jewish is not what Leiber & Stoller are about whatsoever, in song or person. All the greats were assimilated: Berlin, Gershwin, Arlen, Rodgers & Hammerstein, Leonard Bernstein, Sondheim, Paul Simon, on and on. Only Boch & Harnick and, oddly, Dylan (momentarily), embraced themes of Jewish heritage.

Nevertheless, Leiber is a missing link, the Cro-Magnon Jew in the alchemy that propelled R&B into rock 'n' roll. The subject is not one he cares to examine, an affront to his work as a professional or a hipster. However:

"The combination of Yiddish and Negro strains of humor is the wildest synthesis I ever came across. Hooking up from different tributaries happens subliminally and by chance. A lot of what I've written is informed by Yiddish timing, rhythm, and sensibility; and by black timing, rhythm, and humor. Both worlds are not the same by any stretch. But there are similarities in the irony, futility, and sense of the lower depths. A cheerful attitude about bad luck. The Jewish guy who shrugs with his hands open to the sun, after a car accident."

Shake 'em up and let it roll. There were sly moments when Jerry snuck in irresistible rejoinders, like Dub Jones' bass background kicker, "ooga booga, shuga booga," on "Bad Detective." Or the mention of bagels and lox in "Soul Pad."

After the Martin Luther King assassination, when Newark and Detroit were burning in 1968, the black political Left suddenly turned nasty on the music business. At the National Association of TV and Radio Announcers convention in Miami, record men received death threats and pistol-whippings at their hotels. A Black Power revolt overtook the stage, as irate demands rang out for black takeover of radio and record companies. Jerry Wexler was supposedly hanged in effigy. King Curtis and a gun-strapped Titus Turner hurried Wexler out of the auditorium when they got word he was targeted for a hit.

Jerry Leiber took this harder than anyone. He felt he should be exempt from any backlash.

"We felt the sting of betrayal from black musicians; we felt stabbed in the back. LeRoi Jones put a tourniquet on a part of me when he came out with anti-Semitic accusations, accusing Leiber & Stoller of stealing from the black man. It seemed we could bestow a lifetime of musical fame, if not fortune, on virtually anyone we wanted to produce, cherry-pick them from nowhere.

"Before this, there were nothing but common bonds, at least in music. Dizzy Gillespie spoke Yiddish to his manager—a sign of cooperation and respect. Ray Charles—and he didn't have to kiss nobody's ass—spoke generously of the Jews, said if there was anybody could sing the blues besides the black man, it would be a Jew."

No matter that R&B and '50s rock 'n' roll were a bridge between the races—heavily segregated by culture and by law—that helped change everything. It wouldn't have happened without the music. Not that altruism was the guiding force behind the indie record companies, predominantly run by Jews. The most despicable was Herman Lubinsky of Savoy Records, whose methods damaged everyone he came in contact with. Vee-Jay, a black-owned label, was also tough on black asses, and then there was Don Robey. But many Jews operated valiantly, if such can be said of the record biz, like the Chess Brothers in Chicago, Milt Gabler of Commodore, Art Rupe of Specialty, Art Sheridan of Chance. They loved the music. Even the slobbering Neanderthal Syd Nathan of King Records in Cincinnati hired black executives and launched James Brown, Wynonie Harris, Bull Moose Jackson, and the Dominoes with Clyde McPhatter.

Atlantic Records was always in a class by itself, the gold standard in rhythm and blues—a category coined by Jerry Wexler when he worked for *Billboard* in 1949. It replaced the hoary term *race records* on the charts. Rhythm and blues was bound to the far right end of the AM radio dial, the ghostly low frequencies consigned to nigra music. Through statesmanship, fifty-dollar handshakes, and arm-twisting, perhaps nobody toiled harder than Wexler to push this music to the center of the radio dial.

Sweetheart . . . Let Me Tell Ya About the Music Business. . . .

Leiber & Stoller have wielded ownership over some 100,000 song copyrights (exclusive rights), which their company manages on Sunset Strip. The 250 golden-age songs that they penned themselves are in perpetual play at every moment around the world. They are sampled by rappers and heard on radio, TV, Broadway, and commercials; in elevators, carnival rides, dentists' offices, and Hollywood movies (most indies can't afford them).

I crack open a totally random page in one of Jerry's many thick leather-bound publishing folders on his office shelf. There's "The Good Ship Lollipop"—and all other songs associated with Shirley Temple. Jerry was unaware he even owned it.

Like the most fertile plantation in the antebellum South, these songs keep giving and giving. The tunes are out there working, slaving, earning lots and lots of dollars. Bringing exotic slices of Balik salmon (reserved for the Tsars) and Gaspe Nova to the Leiber breakfast table. But there's one thing no amount of money could buy:

"Nobody knows how to make bagels anymore in Los Angeles—it's all over. Cantor's still has pretty good corn rye, but forget the bagels and bialys. The last place was New York Bagels, but they were bought out by some *goyishe* outfit and the bagels look and feel like doughnuts."

By the late '60s, after losing Red Bird Music to *the boys in the band*, Leiber & Stoller were left nearly broke—relative to their standing as city and country squires. Then something happened that changed this forever. As Jerry perused *The New York Times* one morning at the Stage, chopped herring thumbprints aligning the margins, he turned to the financial section. He never even read or understood the financial section. But buried deep there was a bland story on Commonwealth United, a "leisure" company that sold boat basins, mobile homes, pinball and slot machines. Among the labyrinthine assets they were spinning off were some huge publishing catalogs of popular songs. All sorts of goodies, like the Lovin' Spoonful, Bobby Darin, Tim Hardin's "If I Were a Carpenter." Nobody else spotted it.

"I thought to myself, 'Man this is a deal made in heaven.'" Moving like a jackrabbit, Jerry lined up Stoller and their publishing partner, Freddy Bienstock, to do the number crunching.

"Freddy said with maybe a half mil, we might be able to make a dent in the Commonwealth holdings, they're going for 40 to 50 percent of worth. So there was no way."

Leiber's grand East Hampton neighbor Gene Coleman astonished him with a loan for four hundred grand.

"I walked into Freddy's office, Mike was there, and I said, 'I got it, guys. The money to buy Commonwealth United.' They said, 'C'mon, Leiber, it's too fuckin' early in the morning for this bullshit.' I put the check on Freddy's desk. 'How do you know this is any good?' 'He's a friend of mine.' Freddy called the bank. They called back twenty minutes later, and the check was good. We bought Commonwealth."

Using leverage from the Commonwealth stock, the three kept the ball rolling. Lin Broadcasting's stock took a dive, and they wanted to dump their music assets. "The best R&B shit ever," says Jerry. Thousands of song copyrights, including Bull Moose Jackson, Earl Bostick, Wynonie Harris, Clyde McPhatter; thousands of country songs, including early Hank Williams, Flatt & Scruggs, Homer & Jethro; labels like King, Queen, Deluxe, and Federal, with James Brown's catalog.

And to top it off, they bought a third division of music subsidiaries, languishing in the late 1960s under the clueless ownership of a newspaper company—*The New York Times*. The catalogs of Times Square Music and Herald Square Music contained some eighty Broadway scores, each containing about twenty songs—*Fiddler on Roof, West Side Story, Gypsy, Zorba, The Apple Tree, Cabaret.* . . .

"You couldn't accumulate this kind of catalog unless you're Max Dreyfus. All these companies bought publishing catalogs, then fired the music pros that managed them. Their accountants told them to dump overhead. Run by schmucks who had no music contacts, of course it went to pieces, lost tons of money, so they decided to spin them off for a tax loss."

Leiber, Stoller, and Freddy Bienstock had music contacts. They knew about managing songs. By the turn of the twenty-first century, the publishing catalogs they acquired for a mere $400,000 had increased more than two hundred–fold in value.

Music publishing is the ownership, promotion, and administration of songs. It's where the big money hides, deeply entrenched behind the scenes. The concept of the "publisher" dates back to the nineteenth century, when songs were literally sold through sheet music. The songwriter's craft was a separate entity from that of the performer who sang it. Tunesmiths were moon-June-spoon dreamers, without the patience to discern the matrix of publishing. Like johns waiting for hookers, they'd sign anything; they couldn't sit still and study contracts. Royalty channels dictated an equal split between songwriter and publisher.

Freddy Bienstock was a younger cousin of the Aberbachs, who owned Hill & Range, one of the biggest publishing companies in the world. Jerry always assumed he was the Aberbachs' nephew. "I hired him after his uncles fired him," says Jerry. "His uncles were in partnership with Colonel Parker and RCA. They owned all the music rights to everything Presley did. Freddy sifted through and selected all the songs for Presley sessions. So everyone in the world was sending him cars, money, and girls. He was the conduit to Elvis recordings, worth millions."

Bienstock began as an office boy and song plugger for the Aberbachs. It's relevant here to consider the song plugger's creed:

He is who, by all the arts of persuasion, intrigue, bribery, mayhem, malfeasance, cajolery, entreaty, threat, insinuation, persistence and whatever else he has, sees to it that his employer's music shall be heard.
—Isaac Goldberg, *Tin Pan Alley*, 1930

In a shadow world behind labyrinthine lairs of deception and thievery, men like Bienstock and the Aberbachs ruled. Freddy ran a smooth game as point man for Elvis. And he didn't even like rock 'n' roll.

"For instance, Aaron Schroeder was a writer who couldn't get arrested," says Jerry. "Aaron made more money than we did with Elvis, and we had nine hits. Aaron never had a hit. So how did he make more money? Freddy got him every B-side of every potential Elvis hit. He only wrote shitty songs. They used to call him Backside Schroeder. Aaron took a free ride on the back of Otis Blackwell's songs. I think he was kicking back 15 or 20 percent to Freddy. As long as Freddy was confident he had a hit on the A-side, he was free to put anybody on the backside. Aaron was off to the races."

With *Clambake*-caliber songs like "Stuck on You," "I Got Stung," and "A Big Hunk o' Love," it's no wonder Colonel Parker must have loved him. Schroeder became a publisher with January Music and Aaron Schroeder International.

"Then some British writer he fucked for all those years sued him, won, and put his lights out, destroyed him financially," says Jerry. "A major lawsuit, an international embarrassment, that caused Schroeder to leave the music biz and go into the toy clock business or some other *mishegoss*."

"The Aberbachs are one family I wish I could have driven to the gates of Auschwitz," says Jerry. But the pyramid went even higher. The Aberbachs began under the auspices of Max Dreyfus. Dreyfus was the Babe Ruth of song publishing through the first half of the twentieth century. His mere name elicits awe in the eyes of Jerry Leiber. He was the dean of Tin Pan Alley—named as such for the cacophony of out-of-tune pianos clashing at once on West Twenty-eighth Street. This is where the business of songwriting—Jerry's business—developed. There was no waiting around for inspiration—you wrote songs to order.

Max Dreyfus's stable included young Irving Berlin, Victor Herbert, Jerome Kern, Irving Caesar, Harold Arlen, Vincent Youmans, George and Ira Gershwin, Cole Porter, Rodgers & Hammerstein, Johnny Mercer, Lou Donaldson . . . you get the idea. All were nurtured by Dreyfus when they were young. Most lasted out their careers with him, and, like Leiber & Stoller, his songwriters respected him.

"God answered to Max," says Jerry. "If God was a song plugger, Max owned the company."

Jean Aberbach started as an office boy and song plugger for Dreyfus. His brother Julian, meanwhile, started Hill & Range in 1943, cornering 75 percent of Nashville's burgeoning country music publishing, including Hank Williams's on RCA. He recommended Colonel Parker to the Presley family, when Parker was managing Eddy Arnold.

"I believe Hill & Range was bankrolled by Max Dreyfus," says Jerry. "It was the first major company signed by BMI to compete with ASCAP. Jules overcame some obstacles, had to talk to Negroes. He had a thick Prussian-Austrian accent. He worked his way up, a very clever, ambitious opportunist."

So Hill & Range, with the Aberbachs and Bienstock, was literally stationed on top of the Brill Building in the penthouse. Even though Freddy "couldn't carry Frank Military's (Sinatra's song screener) briefcase," Jerry and Mike became fond of him.

"Bienstock's lawyer, Jules Kerse, looked like a Neanderthal gorilla with a low protruding forehead. He came over one day and said, 'Those pricks Jean and Julian Aberbach really fucked him over good.' 'Freddy's Viennese uncles who ran Hill & Range fired him? What for?' 'I don't know, those fuckin' Nazis.' The Aberbachs were Viennese Jews, but their manners were Germanic, and people referred to them as 'those Nazis.'

"The lawyer said, 'He's out of a job with two kids, he's staying on the Lido in Venice and can't pay his hotel bill. Can you help him out?'

'Yeah, sure. We'll give him an office and a phone—we'll cover till he scores.' Freddy flew in a week later.

"When we bought *The New York Times* catalog, there were stacks of contracts ten inches high, the whole length of a conference table. Resignatures on songwriters contracts, renewals, foreign rights, and transfers, a monumental scale, for scores of eighty shows. It took us a day and a half to sign all the necessary transfers for this sale. Freddy inherited the main lawyer after his uncles got rid of him. So he was "our" in-house lawyer. He told us the papers were okay to sign. Mike and I signed without looking—there was too much to read. We later found out that all of the foreign copyrights—Europe, Far East, United Kingdom—millions of dollars in rights, were signed away to Bienstock. We always signed things with trust among friends. I wanted all the contracts declared null and void, but we lost in court."

It was then that Jerry found out that Bienstock had been fired by his uncles for something similar. "He'd slip every other song into his own shell company at his uncles' expense. One for me, one for you, fifty-fifty. That's a no-no. If Joe Bananas was involved, say good-bye. So we're in business for seven years before I found out."

Years later, in his seventies, Freddy Bienstock received a Friars Club tribute at the Walter Kerr Theatre on Broadway. Bienstock's daughter, Caroline, who now runs the company, had little trouble convincing Jerry and Mike to show up. She's a gorgeous broad. So they did a testimonial.

In 2006, Leiber & Stoller sold the publishing catalogs they'd acquired with Bienstock to the Japanese.

"Freddy called," says Jerry, "and thanked me for half the company I left him."

That half amounted to $62.5 million.

Parker's Last Stand

One New York afternoon in the late '60s, Leiber fainted on the street. He caught a walking pneumonia. A Good Samaritan Greek cabdriver picked him up out of the gutter and drove him to four different hospitals.

Leiber didn't have his wallet. None would admit him without I.D., money, or insurance. This guardian angel cabdriver finally got him admitted at the Italian hospital in Harlem, where he was put in intensive care. He stayed for two weeks. The cabdriver hadn't even triggered his meter, did the whole thing off duty, then left the hospital without Jerry ever knowing who he was.

When Jerry returned to his apartment, where he lived alone at the time, there were thirty Western Union telegrams in his mailbox. Affixed to the door were two manila envelopes. Each one was from Colonel Parker or the Aberbachs.

They said, "Elvis is waiting for you. He will not go into the studio without you. Please contact the Colonel immediately and come to L.A." The first telegram was signed "the Aberbachs," the second, "Colonel Parker." Then they started being signed "the Aberbachs and Colonel Parker" together, each ensuing message more friendly and urgent. The last said, "Please come to L.A. immediately," and was signed "Tom."

"So I called Colonel Parker," says Jerry.

The Colonel answered, "Where ya been?"

"I've been in the hospital."

"*Haw, haw,* hospital's for sick people," rasped the Colonel, like a good ol' boy. "Whad'ya have?"

"Walking pneumonia."

"Well, if it's *walkin'*, it couldn't be that bad. You must be walkin'. We need you out here immediately. Leave this moment."

"I can't come tonight, I just got out of the hospital."

"Well, if they released you from the hospital, they wouldn't release you unless you were ready to come out. We don't have time for any of this sissy business, here. We got work to do right now. This has *gotta* be done immediately."

The Colonel said to check the contracts, sign them, and send them right back. Jerry told him to hold, he had another call.

"Call me back, I don't hold for anyone," said the Colonel.

Jerry found a manila envelope with MGM–Colonel Tom Parker stationery, requiring his signature at the bottom.

"But somehow, the contracts were missing," says Jerry. "Only the signing page was there. So I decided not to sign, and to involve Mike in this—so he couldn't later say, 'You idiot, why did you sign, you lost us a million,' or even, 'Why *didn't* you sign, you lost us a million?'

"I called Mike and, as always, he never takes a stand, letting me make decisions. Mike's intensely private, they never know when he walks out of the office whether he's going home, to a poker game, or the men's room. He doesn't tell anyone."

"What do you think?" asked Mike.

"No, tell me what *you* think this time," said Jerry. "I've had enough with Elvis, even with all the money. I'm ready to give it up, can't take it any more."

"Tell him to go fuck himself," said Mike.

"That's my boy," said Jerry, proud of his partner.

Jerry called the Colonel back.

"There's a problem. There are no contracts under the first page."

"Just sign it," said the Colonel. "We'll fill it in later." As if Leiber & Stoller, Presley's primary hit makers, whom he called his "good-luck charms," were suddenly street-corner chumps.

"I talked to my partner, Mike," said Jerry.

"How's Mike?"

"Fine."

"What'd he say?" asked the Colonel.

"Mike says to go *fuck* yourself." Jerry hung up before the Colonel even had time to threaten him.

Leiber & Stoller never graced Elvis with another hit, or heard from the Colonel again. As Presley continued his descent into *Clambake*, he was reduced to recording a dozen Leiber & Stoller chestnuts as covers—not first releases. And they sounded like schlock, just the way the Colonel liked it.

Is That All There Is?

Peggy Lee's 1975 album, *Mirrors*, might represent the last great work Leiber & Stoller produced. "Is That All There Is," the single, became an improbable smash in 1969. It featured a remarkable arrangement by Randy Newman, which Jerry considered "a beautiful gift." Lee went on the road for five years before finishing other songs intended for the album. By 1975, *Mirrors* could no longer capitalize on the single's momentum, and fell through the cracks. Furthermore, the album was mixed so poorly, the lyrics and intent were lost.

Only recently were the tracks revived for a 2005 CD package, *Peggy Lee Sings Leiber & Stoller*. The songs emerge in a sparkling remix done by Peter Stoller at Jed Leiber's studio. Acts of redemption by the sons, showcasing the Brechtian scope of their fathers' work beyond rock 'n' roll.

"Is That All There Is?" was sent to Barbra Streisand first. "But the demo remained on her manager's desk," recalls Jerry. "One night Streisand heard Peggy Lee do the song live in Las Vegas. She asked, 'How come I don't get songs like that sent to me?' I said, 'As a matter of fact, it was sent to you first." She asked her manager, who said it was still on his desk. So she fired him."

"Is That All There Is?" was written with Lotte Lenya in mind.

"I was obliquely influenced by the atmosphere and attitude of a Thomas Mann story, 'Disillusionment.' But it really came from a song Marlene Dietrich did in an early movie. I used it as a dummy melody for the line 'Is that all there is, is that all there is?' I'd been singing that phrase for fifteen years before writing the song. When I finished, I couldn't separate the line from the Dietrich melody. Do you think it's a nick?"

Well, Leiber took the song to Marlene Dietrich. He'd signed Burt Bacharach to his first publishing deal, when young Bacharach was musical director for Marlene Dietrich.

"I asked Burt a favor, because there was no other way to get to her. So he set it up. Mike, who's always suffered from stage fright, didn't think he could play in front of Dietrich. So Bacharach learned the piano part before we plugged it to her. Marlene had just gotten back from Hyannisport and raved on about the Kennedys for over an hour. Then Burt played it, I sung it."

Dietrich asked Jerry if he'd ever seen her perform live.

"I almost said yes. But the truth was, I hadn't. I figured she'd spot a lie. So I said, 'I never had the opportunity to see you.'"

"I'm glad you're honest," said Dietrich. "That song is *who* I am. But *not* what I am onstage."

Another song, "I Ain't Here," had the rejoinder "kiss my ass," which Peggy Lee refused to sing. "So we changed it to 'kiss my foot,' which she delivered so convincingly, it was as good as if she'd sung, 'kiss my *black* ass.'"

"Ready to Begin Again (Manya's Song)" was named after Jerry's mother.

> *When my teeth are at rest*
> *In the glass by my bed*
> *And my hair lies somewhere in a drawer. . . .*

It was around this time that Manya went up to Israeli Foreign Minister Abba Eban, as he descended the podium after a speech, in broad view of the entire audience. She grabbed his hand in a sturdy grip. "Mr. Ambassador, I'd like you to meet my son, Jerome. Have you ever hoid 'Hound Dog'?"

"Some Cats Know" cooks with Ray Brown's devastating bass lines. The song was conceived for another of Jerry's unrealized musicals, an adaptation of *One Hundred Dollar Misunderstanding.* Written with Billie Holiday's voice in mind, it almost hurts to hear Peggy Lee sing it, imagining what Holiday could have done. A record with Billie Holiday, who died in 1959, was one of two "big trophies" that Jerry never bagged.

It was only after "Is That All There Is?" that Leiber & Stoller were inducted into the Songwriters Hall of Fame. Johnny Mercer asked, "I bet you're wondering why you're here?"

"Yeah?" said Jerry.

"Because you finally wrote a good song."

Showdown at Elaine's Corral

From the 1960s through the '80s, "Midnight" Jerry Leiber spent his nights at Elaine's, table four. Table four was home base to Bruce Jay Friedman, Jack Richardson, Terry Southern, Norman Mailer, William Styron, Arthur Kopit, Tom Wolfe, James Jones, Kurt Vonnegut, Irwin Shaw, Gay Talese, George Plimpton, David Newman, Bob Brown and the great alto sax man, Paul Desmond.

"I was one of the original cowboys," says Jerry. However, his drinking cronies, being chiefly novelists, were never particularly impressed by "Jailhouse Rock" or "Charlie Brown," much less Leiber's immense influence over pop music. Their generation was rooted to Sinatra.

Many a deal got started at this table. And here is where an unfortunate side of J. L. comes into play, that can't be ignored. Leiber cannot write prose and requires collaborators. When not consumed by flights of grandiosity, he can be self-deprecating. "I know I'm a low-class Jew who can't punctuate a sentence." An initiator of book, stage, and movie endeavors, Leiber gained a hard-earned reputation as *the* time waster nonpareil. He has abused the time of Ben Hecht, Mordecai Richler, Bruce Jay Friedman, Christopher Durang, Albert Goldman, William Friedkin, Martin Scorsese, Taylor Hackford, Ishmael Reed, Leonard Bernstein, Jerome Robbins, Wilfred Sheed, Bob Spitz—all seduced by Jerry's initial largesse and immensely enjoyable company. All were forced to flee when Leiber's medications faltered, and he turned radioactive, diving off the deep end. The writer Michael Roloff wrote an unpublished book about Leiber's dysfunctions, and the price Roloff suffered from years of abandoned projects. Only the mighty Stoller has endured—which probably explains the wintry distance of his gaze.

Jerry's inability to complete projects began sometime after Leiber & Stoller's last hurrah in the '70s. They produced an all-star album for T-Bone Walker, which along with the Peggy Lee album set the bar for 1970s studio rhythm sections. The wistful "Pearl's a Singer" for Elkie Brooks in England. Two Procol Harum and two Stealers Wheel albums, producing the hit single, "Stuck in the Middle with You." After which Leiber forever remained stuck in the middle himself. Spending ten years on lithium and four decades in psychoanalysis, Leiber likely sent his analysts into analysis. "Lithium kills 90 percent of your sex drive," he says, "while the personalities of most women kill the other 10 percent."

Leiber & Stoller could never launch an original Broadway show, before or after *Smokey Joe's Café*. The best of their musicals-that-might-have-been is *Oscar*. Had it been produced before, say, *La Cage Aux Folles*, it might have been the toast of the town. By now, its fancy-pants-and-poof take on Oscar Wilde might fall upon audiences beset by fag fatigue. Though *Oscar* is easily the caliber of a Kander & Ebb musical, Jerry feels less qualified than Alan Jay Lerner to mess with the Queen's English. In the same way he didn't feel qualified to sing blues. And if it ain't *My Fair Lady*, Jerry asks, why bother?

And so, he spent more time at Elaine's.

One night, Buzz Farber, Norman Mailer, and former light-heavy-weight champ José Torres come in slightly drunk. Torres just lost a fight. "Apparently, he ain't no Sugar Ray Robinson," Jerry cracks to his friends. Jerry looks up at Buzz, a tight crony of writers and fighters, and says, "How you doin'?"

Buzz heard the Sugar Ray remark and is irritated. Jerry had hooked Buzz up with a job at CBS, which sent him to Spain for some bullfighting documentary. But Buzz fucked it up, returned only with photos of himself in the bullfighting ring. Now Buzz mumbles he'll throw Jerry through the window.

Jerry starts flipping through his mental Rolodex, names of Moishe Levy hitters, fight-fixer Tommy Eboli, Genovese gargoyles, all the underworld connections he's had to deal with. Buzz is a weightlifter and forty pounds heavier. But Jerry takes the bait.

"If you throw me through the window, you better come out and stomp me to death. Because I will have you killed. I have the money and connections to do it, and you know it."

"Fuck you and your money," goes Buzz. "Let's go outside."

"I will not," says Jerry.

So Buzz challenges him to an arm-wrestle. Besides having been a bantam-weight wrestler in high school, Jerry was a gymnast. He could still perform an "iron cross" on the hand rings.

"Okay," says Jerry. "A thousand bucks."

"Whaddaya mean a thousand. You know I don't have a thousand."

"Then go fuck yourself," says Jerry.

Buzz demands to arm wrestle anyway. So Jerry agrees. But Elaine overhears the argument by now and comes over. "What the fuck's goin" on?" She's the Big Mama, mother hen to all the writers. Buzz instantly deflates, kisses her.

"Oh, just a friendly arm-wrestle for drinks," says Buzz.

"All right," comes Elaine. "I'll be the judge."

They walk to the bar, where Elaine was calculating the bar tabs. One, two, three. Jerry pins him in a second. Buzz is furious. He yells, "You cheated, you jumped the gun, took me by surprise. Let's do it again."

"Take it like a man," says Jerry. "You lost, that's all you get." Buzz swallows with the perennial schoolyard threat, "I'll get you later."

So Jerry returns to his table, with Terry and Carol Southern and publisher Dick Seaver with his wife. Jerry leans back on the chair, his feet up. Suddenly an arm encases his neck in a stranglehold. At first he thinks it's an affectionate squeeze, but it's violent. The attacker pulls him off the chair.

Jerry grips the table and kicks them both back into the wall. Plaster flies all over, cuts Jerry's face, and covers the face of attacker. Jerry gets a good punch into the attacker's neck and the plaster clears. It's Norman Mailer.

Mailer digs his fingers into Jerry's eyes. Ellio, the headwaiter, comes over, puts his two hard thumbs into Mailer's eyes and says, "Let go." Mailer screams. Elaine comes over, taps Ellio, and says, "Let go of him." Ellio lets go of Mailer, Mailer lets go of Jerry.

Blinded, Mailer staggers toward the jukebox up front. Jerry is so angry he wants to kill him. He sets up his punch, ready to cold-cock Mailer. But the whole restaurant yells, "Jerry, don't! He's crazy, he's sick, leave him alone!"

Then the final word: "Jerry, if you do it," warns Elaine, "I'll make you regret it the rest of your life." She watches over her writers first. Jerry lets his arm drop.

The implication was clear. Norman's big ol' inebriated skull was more valuable than Jerry's. Mailer was a roaring lion of the literary world. Jerry was just a ditch-blues, rock 'n' roll songwriter.

The Big Trophy—Sinatra

Leiber never caught *any* of his groups live—including the Coasters, the Drifters, or Elvis. He only went to small dives or saloons. But he did see Sinatra once in concert at Carnegie Hall in 1987. He claims it would have meant more, aesthetically, to have *one* record with Sinatra than thirty with Elvis.

"We'd gotten just about everybody we've ever wanted, except for Sinatra and Billie Holiday. I began to like Sinatra as I got older and learned about superior songwriting. Nobody else announced songwriters and arrangers onstage. [Film director] Billy Friedkin called me up. 'How'd you like to go see Sinatra?' I'd heard him in saloons, but never a concert. What are we gonna do, sit there in a suit and tie next to some old lady who smells like Midnight in Paris? I hate crowds, I'm claustrophobic. Billy said they had a bar at Carnegie Hall, so I said okay."

Sinatra did a half dozen numbers, the orchestra dispersed, and he stood by his pianist with no arrangement. He said, "These two kids, Jerry Leiber and Mike Stoller, wrote this. They used to write rock 'n' roll, Elvis hits, I don't know what kinda crap. But they grew up, finally wrote a beautiful song."

The song was "The Girls I Never Kissed."

"His timing was off," Jerry remembers. "But I was *thrilled*. We wrote it for him, not anyone else."

"The Girls I Never Kissed" was never released in Sinatra's lifetime.

"We were sitting at the Friars Club on Fifty-fifth Street with Hy Weiss, the only Jew in New York who would tell Joe Bananas to go fuck himself.

Very big balls. Ran Old Town Records, had a great baritone singer, Arthur Prysock, and killer group that did 'So Fine.' We're talking about the business in general, and that getting laid ain't no fun any more."

Also at the table with Jerry and Mike was Frank Military, Sinatra's point man, like Bienstock was to Elvis. "The very best music man in the business," by Jerry's estimate. On a whole 'nother plane than mere song pluggers, he screened songs for *Sinatra*—who himself chose the most flaw-less songs in history. Military dressed elegant, a fresh flower in his lapel, and came into the city by chauffeur-driven Bentley from Connecticut.

Frank Military suddenly said, "Jer, I'm really getting sick of the business."

"What do you mean?"

"I mean, people only talk about 'product.' We used to sit down at Luchow's with Jerome Kern, all the charter members of ASCAP, and make world-shaking decisions. But we also talked about songs. I want to murder the next motherfucker that looks, dresses, and says *product*. Nobody goes, 'Hey, did you hear that lyric?' Nobody's excited about the content, just sales. They're murdering everything I love about this business. Boy, would I like somebody to walk up and say, 'Frank, I got a bitch of a song.'"

Jerry said, "Frank, I got a bitch of a song."

"Go fuck yourself," said Military.

"Frank, I got a bitch of a song and I wanna show it to you."

"All right, wiseguy, what's it called?"

"The Girls I Never Kissed."

"You ain't kiddin'? Where is it?"

"I'll have it on your desk Monday morning."

"That's what everybody says. I wanna hear it *now*. Where is it?"

"You're in luck," said Jerry, who lived a few blocks up from the Friars, at the Galleria on Fifty-seventh Street.

As they strolled along, Military said, "I can't tell you how light I feel. This is something I haven't done in years. It's like getting laid for the first time."

Jerry poured drinks and Mike sat down at the piano. They plugged the song.

"It's a fuckin' smash!" was Military's reaction. "Frank'll kiss my dick on Forty-second Street! Gimme the lead sheet."

He kissed Jerry and Mike, then left. Ten days later Jerry received notice that Sinatra was cutting it. After the session, Military called. "I don't know what to tell you, Jerry, it was pathetic. He couldn't sing it. I know you've been waiting all your life for this."

It was a heartbreaker. But then Military said, "Take it easy, there might be another shot. He's surprising, he comes back from the dead. Sinatra heard the playbacks and he's talking about another session."

A week later, another call from Military. "Jer, Frank just called Billy May. He's booking another session for 'The Girls I Never Kissed.' Just the one song."

Three days later: "Jer, I don't know what to tell ya, this is really heartbreaking, but he was worse this time. You know what Sinatra said at the end of the session? I'll get it next time."

There was no next time, and Jerry never heard from Military again.

It's long after midnight in Venice Beach. The ribs are a fond, greasy memory, and ditch blues float through Jerry's living room speakers. The older Jer gets, the more he comes home to the blues. The broken-down kind, rife with mispronunciations, sung by sharecroppers who make Pigmeat Markham seem like Henry Higgins. He slaps his knee and sings along to his own songs, like the original Alvin Robinson version of "Down Home Girl." All of the slick CD packages sent to him remain forever unopened on the shelf.

I pick one up. *Sinatra Live from Las Vegas*, an official 2005 posthumous release. There it is, on track ten: "The Girls I Never Kissed."

"Here," I say, unwrapping the CD. "Doesn't that count? You've got your big trophy."

"Oh," says Leiber, with nary a shrug. The same way Manya reacted to the end of World War II.

—2007

Doc Pomus: So much wisdom disguised in simple street language.

(Sharyn Felder-Bratton)

CHAPTER 2

Doc Pomus
Tell the Truth Until They Bleed

D oc Pomus's loss to New York City was, to me, like losing the
Statue of Liberty. His Buddha-like presence, holding court in
music saloons, would now fade into Big Apple legend, where
the past seemed greater with each passing year. "At least now they can't
say I died young," he cracked at his sixtieth birthday. He was sixty-five
when he passed away in 1991.

Doc Pomus was no Damon Runyon character; he was a leading
man, a stabilizing figure of integrity in a music industry that had come
to resemble a corporate cesspool.

I met him after he emerged from a sorrowful decade of retirement
to collaborate with Dr. John in 1977. He retained his lyrical brilliance—
so much wisdom disguised in simple street language—decades after his
peers let theirs dissolve.

Shortly after Elvis died, I wrote the first of four articles on Doc,
commemorating his comeback in a *Soho News* piece. In the curious way
Americans honor their heroes after death, Elvis royalties intensified
like a rejuvenated oil well. But Doc Pomus, who wrote twenty-five songs
for Elvis, never met his foremost interpreter. They'd only conferred a

few minutes by phone, Elvis calling for late-night instructions during an early '60s recording session; Doc didn't even know who he was talking to.

Doc came within inches of meeting Presley at a 1974 Hilton Hotel press conference. But the hard-assed Colonel Parker, whom Doc knew well in the old days, wouldn't let Pomus through. Doc introduced himself to Vernon, who said his son would love to meet him, but Elvis had just left the hotel. Doc was heartbroken. Three years later, Doc and Elvis made solid arrangements to meet. But Presley died a week before the meeting, leaving Doc totally spooked.

Nevertheless, when I met Doc in 1977, he'd just coproduced the debut album for Roomful of Blues, the first white boys to revive Kansas City swing. He'd also produced the very first (henceforth unreleased) Fabulous Thunderbirds album, plucking the band out of Austin when they were woolly local upstarts. (The T-Birds single-handedly ended the era of white blues bands looking and playing like hippies.)

He'd written the title song for some Elvis revival show on Broadway. But his track record—Doc had written maybe two thousand songs, sixty of them charting—intimidated potential collaborators. Even friends were often dumbstruck ("You wrote *that?*"). Other than Cher, to her credit, nobody recorded any of his recent material. He was hungry to write, and that was the thrust of my article.

I've done all sorts of magazine interviews, but Doc Pomus was the only one who ever gave me a warm postpublication call. I fell into the inner sanctum of his West Seventy-second Street apartment, the all-night rock 'n' roll whirl. Doc presided bolt upright in his king-size invalid's bed. He was surrounded by piles of blues records shipped in from Chicago, promotional cassettes, music biz correspondence. A cable-TV channel switcher and phone operated over a swing table. He would put me at ease with his stories, fielding phone calls with childlike disbelief at the outside world. Some cracker-trash country singer called at 3 A.M. wondering if Doc knew how to lure his cat down from the roof. "Can you believe this shit?" Doc would mutter, hanging up. There were more fakers and poseurs in the music biz than anywhere, and Doc was blessed with knowing all the assholes. "Everybody's a *genius,*" he would say, mocking the instant accolades accorded some schlock producer who that week scored a hit.

Johnny, the current driver of Doc's bus, was Fats Domino's former road manager, who cut his teeth collecting Domino's nightly box office receipts. When Johnny went home, Doc would buzz in guests through the electronic lock on his eleventh-floor door. Here I met such after-midnight visitors as Otis Blackwell, the Brooklyn pants presser who *invented* the rockabilly pop record ("All Shook Up" and "Don't Be Cruel"). Doc once sang in all the blues joints of Brooklyn with Otis for eight dollars a night. When in town, Big Joe Turner would drop in, feeble with a cane, yet still able to shout blues all night long, and every song in the key of C. So integral was Big Joe's fifty-year role in R&B evolution, Doc believed, that rock 'n' roll would never have happened had not Turner existed. Doc was often on the phone to the committably insane Phil Spector, who gave no other man but Doc full respect.

A happenstance visit by Ronnie Spector to Doc's apartment resulted in a breakneck romance that sucked every minute of my life for four months. Ronnie was Godzilla disguised as Gidget. Doc helped me regain my sanity in the year it took to recover.

Dr. John—aka Mac Rebennack—became Doc's new collaborator. A small grubby keyboard was always present in the living room. Their first songs were lyrical beauties that triggered a renaissance in Doc's career: "Dance the Night Away with You," "He's A Hero," and the title track for *City Lights*, a 1978 Dr. John album.

> *Too many city lights*
> *Too many midnights on the wrong side of life*
> *Too many honky-tonk-never-happen women*
> *Gave me no time to find*
> *A good wife of my own*

Pomus could turn the spin on a clichéd phrase and deliver it as a knockout punch, such as the gospel gem "One More Time," recorded by B. B. King and Joe Cocker. The two doctors (Doc and Dr. John) wrote concept albums for B. B. King ("There Must Be a Better World Somewhere"), Jimmy Witherspoon ("Midnight Lady Called the Blues"), and Jose Feliciano, Ray Charles, Irma Thomas, and Johnny Adams.

During songwriting sessions, Mac would retire to the bathroom for a half hour. Each time, Doc sweated out whether he'd emerge alive or have to be carted out by ambulance. Mac later credited Doc for inspiring him to give up an old habit.

According to Mac, one of the five purest traditional blues motifs was created by Doc in the song "Lonely Avenue," recorded by Ray Charles in 1956. "Mac always said that was the 'junker blues'—*junker* being the old term for *junkie*," explained Doc. "It's a certain kind of monotonous, sad, melodic and lyrical line that, because of the continuity involved, for some reason has always attracted junkies. Da-dum, da-dum, da-dum—I imagine they're shuffling along to it or something. All the junkies, Mac told me, thought I was a junkie. They said somebody who wasn't could never have written 'Lonely Avenue.' Mac couldn't believe how straight I was."

Broadly imitated (hear Iron Butterfly's "Butterfly Bleu"), the riff became a prototype blues. During a serendipitous night going through Doc's buried closet, I found the original reel-to-reel—a spontaneous outburst while Doc's car was stalled in traffic in 1956. I also found crumbling tapes of Doc live at the Musicale in Manhattan, with Mickey Baker and King Curtis, circa 1954. These I transferred on my Teac to fresh tape.

In a master songwriting class he gave from his apartment, I sat as an observer. A lot of Doc's philosophy was black-and-white: "I look at music one way. It's either soulful . . . or not. If it's internal, it's great; if it's external, it's not great. I can tell where a songwriter has sat with a line for two weeks. To me, any artist who sits there analyzing the lines should be a mathematician instead."

Twenty songwriters would have their weekly assignment—a love song or a novelty song—critiqued by the class. Then Doc would point out the weaknesses and strong points. Guests like Dr. John, Otis Blackwell, Tom Waits, and Marshall Crenshaw added their two cents. Doc explained to the class why they shouldn't think in a shallow hit-song mentality. How he derived more satisfaction from a soulful rendition of an original song on a Jimmy Witherspoon record that sold ten thousand copies than a hit he wrote for, say, Andy Williams (who refused to sing Doc's "Can't Get Used to Losing You" on his TV show until it reached number one). How they should immerse themselves in a regional genre of music, say, that of New Orleans, before attempting to write honestly in that form—not just do a cynical quick study. How to listen to a singer's entire output before tailoring a song specifically for him, learning what he *can* sing.

In the '50s, the managers of a questionable singer named Fabian approached Doc and his partner, Mort Shuman. "They gave us an assignment to write songs for someone who couldn't carry a tune. That's very difficult to do."

Fabian was a heartthrob among teenyboppers even before he cut a successful record. Fabian's first two hits, "Turn Me Loose" and "I'm a Man," originally written for Elvis, were watered down melodically and lyrically for his limited chops. "I was proud of the fact that I was able to get a guy like that off the ground," Doc said.

The career of Jerome Felder—aka Doc Pomus—might be divided into three periods. The first was as a blues singer. In 1944, at age nineteen, his debut 78 record was released on the Apollo label. A middle-class Jewish kid from Brooklyn, he changed his name to "Doc" so his dad, a ghetto lawyer, and his mom, a proper Englishwoman, wouldn't know he was headlining at Negro joints. He handpicked rookie musicians King Curtis and Mickey Baker for his live backup band. Curtis became the seminal rock 'n' roll sax player of all time, and Baker the most prolific studio guitarist of the 1950s. On record, Doc was backed by sidemen from the Basie, Ellington, and Louis Armstrong bands. He recorded some thirty sides for Apollo, Chess, and Savoy. As a sideline, he wrote killer material for all the early Atlantic Records artists—LaVern Baker, Gatemouth Moore, and his idol, Big Joe Turner.

In this era, Doc Pomus may have been the *only* white big-city blues singer in America. He always had a record out, and in those days a blues single that sold twenty thousand copies was a huge hit. But unlike his dark-skinned contemporaries, he couldn't work the South, where a white man was forbidden on the chitlin circuit. In what he once referred to as "Crow Jim-ism," he was restricted to the colored joints of the Northeast, mainly a dozen establishments in Brooklyn, Harlem, and New Jersey. Until he was thirty-two he never earned more than two grand a year, lived in fleabag hotels, and feared he'd wind up on the streets.

Somewhere around the time of his last and strongest single, "Heartlessly," he had an affair with actress Veronica Lake. Alan Freed broke the song into heavy rotation on New York airwaves in 1955. This was a strong indicator it was destined to chart. As was common practice when a small-label release made this impact, a major label—in this case RCA—bought the master. And then, for reasons forever unknown, RCA killed the record, never released it. (Perhaps because they found out Doc was on crutches, unmarketable as a teen idol.) The experience so soured him he quit singing forever. Surely had Elvis released the rockin' ballad "Heartlessly" identical to Doc's single, it would be a standard today. (*Send for the Doctor*, a collection of sixteen Doc Pomus singles, was released on the "Whiskey, Women, and . . ." label from Sweden in 1984.)

Doc's songs helped form the dawn of rock 'n' roll, a movement he never figured would last more than a year or two. "Man, I been in a room with so many hits. If you wrote half a song and needed an ending, anybody who was around would come in and help, and you would do the same for them. Whenever a record was produced, we'd all be there in the rehearsals. And now it's all big-secret business. When I talk with contemporary artists, they're more involved with the mechanics of business than they are with the craft."

During a forty-minute car ride from Manhattan to Great Neck, Jerry Wexler gave Jerry Leiber the title of an unfinished song Doc was stumped by. Showing off his chops, Leiber turned the title into a finished lyric by the time they arrived. The title came with Doc's blessing, for which Leiber & Stoller gave him a third interest. Returning from his honeymoon in early 1957, Doc and his wife stopped at a diner, a few dollars left to their name. Doc noticed a new song, "Young Blood" by the Coasters, on the jukebox and threw in his nickel. It was the same idea he'd given Leiber & Stoller, entirely reworked. Delighted, Doc phoned Ahmet Ertegun at Atlantic Records, who wired him a $1,500 advance on the single, congratulating him on his first national hit.

In the mid-'50s, Doc mentored a teenage pianist from Brooklyn with great chops. Mort Shuman became his partner. Like Jerry Leiber, Mort grew up in a Yiddish-speaking household. From a penthouse cubbyhole in the Brill Building, Doc and Mort set out to *reap teen coin*, crafting hundreds of bluesy pop songs. They wrote twenty-five for Elvis ("Little Sister," "His Latest Flame," "Whole Mess of Blues," "Suspicion"), hits for the Drifters ("Save the Last Dance For Me," "This Magic Moment."), Dion & the Belmonts ("A Teenager in Love"), Bobby Darin ("Plain Jane"). Twelve songs a week they wrote, overpowering the odds of reaching the charts by sheer abundance. Doc estimates he did 80 percent of the lyrics, 20 percent of the melody.

"In the '50s, the kind of songs I wrote were associated with sleaze and juvenile delinquency," he said. "I was married to an actress [Willi Burke] at the time, and she was embarrassed by it all 'cause all her friends were theater people."

With Shuman as partner, Doc's yearly income shot up to fifty grand: "I had a house, a swimming pool, all that shit, and we had nothing but these Broadway characters hanging around. None of them paid any attention to me, and if they asked what kind of songs I wrote, I felt embarrassed. If I had written a fifth-rate Broadway song, my God, they would have been proud."

Now, consider the context in which "Last Dance" was written. Here's Doc, married to this gorgeous blond Broadway actress, and all her Broadway cronies are contemptuous of rock 'n' roll. A childhood victim of polio, Doc was on crutches, never able to walk. One night he was at a dance with his wife, waiting for her to finish dancing with a bevy of partners, patient and cool on the sidelines. Though he never said so, it likely provided the inspiration for these lines: "Don't forget who's taking you home / And in whose arms you're gonna be / So, darling, save the last dance for me." This much-covered Drifters hit, with the Cubano-Ricano rhythms of the early '60s, has passed the lips of several generations—none hip to the hidden meaning.

After 1965, one of pop's great songwriting teams disbanded when Mort jumped ship. By sheer coincidence, Doc's wife walked out the same week. In crutches since polio took the use of his legs during early childhood, Doc fell down a flight of stairs and wound up in a wheelchair, where he would thereafter remain.

Throughout the Beatles and Woodstock years, Doc Pomus stopped writing songs. He became a gambler, part of a sad Broadway underworld where high-stakes card games sometimes ended in robberies or kidnappings. He had no respect for his past work; his songs meant nothing to him. There were no rock critics back then, no awards or artistic recognition beyond his immediate comrades. Only once, during a 1960 trip to Europe where "A Teenager In Love" held three positions in the British Top 10, were he and Morty baffled to find newspaper reporters and cognoscenti interested in their songs.

And so by 1975, when he gave up gambling, Doc resurfaced to find a different world opinion. His songs had lasted, were in fact frequently rerecorded. The pop music he once saw as a passing trend for fifteen-year-olds had contained so many simple truths that it prevailed. "And what could be more valid than the truth," he realized. "Thank God I learned to appreciate what I had written."

I worked at Regent Sound Studios, a job I landed fresh out of high school, where former Atlantic Records producer Joel Dorn kept his offices. There on the wall was a huge custom-size poster of a proud Dorn, arm around this imposing, bearded figure in a wheelchair, with Stetson hat and fat turquoise rings. At the time of the photo, Doc had discovered and coached a young Bette Midler. He introduced her to Dorn, who produced her first album. Dorn encouraged Doc to resume writing. Thus began the third stage of Doc's career, in partnership with Dr. John.

At the time, Doc would arrange unique gigs for the Lone Star Cafe in New York, corralling the likes of Van "Piano Man" Walls, the premier Atlantic Records session pianist of the 1950s. Walls never appeared without his trademark Sherlock Holmes cape, deerstalker cap, and Calabash pipe. In the old days, he often had Big Maybelle on his arm. After Walls played on Doc's "Boogie Woogie Country Girl," a Big Joe Turner record, he left the country. Decades later, Doc found him in Montreal and summoned him to the Lone Star Cafe. The Lone Star merely provided Doc a reserved table as thanks—for all the legends only he could summon to their stage. But never a free bar tab.

When out on the town, Doc wore snazzy alligator shoes, which he purchased in the '50s at Leighton's on Broadway, where all the blues singers, gamblers, and pimps then shopped. The shoes lasted thirty years simply because he never walked in them. Doc's bus, known as the Docmobile, had a custom pneumatic elevator lift for his wheelchair. Like a musical Ironside, he conducted business on the road from a locked-in desk by his wheelchair, and escaped to music clubs several nights each week. The bands Doc brought to the Lone Star often divided up their cash in the bus at 4 A.M.

But Doc was plagued by a chronic succession of chauffeurs who would disappear under bizarre circumstances. "I could write a book about drivers," he constantly complained, having to interview replacements while stuck for weeks in his apartment. The sheer logistics of getting around Manhattan, deciding which invitations to honor, lest they leave him stranded without wheelchair access, was overwhelming. These lifelong dilemmas he never once weighed upon his friends.

Doc's driver was a full-time on-call employee, required to transport him to his stomping grounds—clubs whose entrances could accommodate a wheelchair. Drivers were to check back periodically but inevitably left him trapped amid torturous rock bands at Kenny's Castaways. The moment the driver arrived, the wheelchair vanished backward like a ghost. This image, which I witnessed a hundred times, was a metaphor for bad music.

Most drivers, after a few weeks of good service, felt they were entitled to a songwriting partnership, or to be sponsored in some crazed business venture. Once Doc hooked up with an impeccable, well-mannered gentleman in his forties, who drove perfectly and kept his mouth shut. Sure enough, after several sterling months, the cops came by. Turned out he was a wanted pederast, a ranking member of NAMBLA, who suddenly ran off to Belgium to resume a relationship with a thirteen-year-old boy. Inevitably, this type of news hit Doc when the bus was double parked, the driver making a run for it and stranding him in a crowded club with a loud, poodle-faced, cucumber-pants band.

Perhaps the worst night of musical torture for both of us was the night we caught Bruce Springsteen at his Palladium debut. Passes were arranged by Karen McAvoy, a femme fatale I introduced to Doc who became one of his "downhill women." Karen periodically conned Doc out of a few bucks, stood him up, or hoisted her skirt over her head in public. He swore her off a dozen times. But we were both hope-lessly enamored, and she warmed her way back into his life by cooking remarkable dinners.

The former girlfriend of Springsteen/Conan drummer Max Weinberg, she arranged passage for us to witness the Springsteen phenom. Karen was an hour late with the tickets. When we arrived at the Palladium there was great confusion, Doc having to be wheeled through a maze of roped-off passageways. The night grew worse as the driver abandoned us for three hours of the most tedious mediocrity I'd ever heard. Springsteen's lyrics were *so* hackneyed and the tunes *so* derivative, it seemed baffling that such an act could even get a record deal, much less be lionized in the media.

"Man, this stinks," Doc said. I never saw him so pained to leave a show, as Springsteen, a great crowd pleaser, kept pouring it on. Bruce dedicated a song to Doc, but only Weinberg emerged afterward to shake his hand.

Doc was the only guy I enjoyed club hopping with, and some of our better evenings were spent as a foursome, with Ronnie Spector and Karen, in 1978. From rock 'n' roll revivals, where I'd have to defend Ronnie's questionable honor amongst horny, balding, doo-wop singers, on to the Bottom Line and the Lone Star. We'd fuel up on hot dogs from Nathan's, or stop the Docmobile at Barking Fish, a remarkable, though short-lived, Cajun take-out restaurant insanely located at the corner of Forty-second and Eighth. Doc believed they served "the most authentic cornbread" in New York.

By sunrise, we'd pass out back at his apartment. I'd seen plenty of hot girls strewn across his bed in the wee hours, in various states of consciousness. But what Doc could do at this stage remained a mystery.

The yearly Doc Pomus birthday parties were attended by a few hundred guests, spilling out into the hallway of his one-bedroom apartment. There were vats of Popeye's fried chicken and dirty rice. John Belushi often provided a crate of champagne on ice in the bathtub. Otis Blackwell came alive by 2 A.M., reenacting his original demos for Elvis as he loosened the white handkerchief around his sweaty neck. Blackwell was one of a handful of people in rock history on whom Doc bestowed the title of genius.

Big Joe Turner, a huge squat frog in a chair beside Doc all night, abruptly woke up at 4 A.M., cried out, "How come the dog don't bark every time *he* come to our door?" then collapsed back asleep. Nobody paid poor Tiny Grimes any mind, as he quietly played four-string tenor guitar in the corner all night. (An Atlantic Records star of the late '40s, Grimes was a founder of the Art Tatum Trio, and recorded with Charlie Parker on Savoy.)

"Tell the truth until they bleed!" cackled Jerry Leiber, in call-and-response, as Doc lashed out at the memory of some thieving record company president they once knew. People always came clean around Doc—he had no tolerance for hype or grandiosity. The older blues legends had a mystical connection with Doc Pomus, and spoke guardedly to the white rock critics. Doc would tap his coffee cup, flattered as celebs paid their respects or whispered in his ear.

I sat at Doc's table when Mort Shuman returned after a twenty-year split to collaborate again. Shuman conceived and starred in the 1968 off-Broadway musical hit *Jacques Brel Is Alive and Well and Living in Paris*. Then he moved to France and became a pop star there. Dolly Parton had just recharted their song "Save the Last Dance for Me" and offered some prospective assignments, along with Julio Iglesias.

Shuman turned out to be a large, barrel-chested neo-Frenchman, who seemed to eat the furniture around him. Doc was well over three hundred pounds in his Stetson hat, so together Pomus and Shuman appeared larger than life. Their combined charisma electrified the Lone Star, where Charlie Thomas and the Drifters kept an onstage patter going toward them. Mort heckled like a banshee, belting out strange new harmonies to "Hushabye," "I Count the Tears," and other Drifters songs he'd cowritten. Doc rolled his eyes, ever the straight man, but seemed humbled by this lusty animal, Mort Shuman, who had been his partner in glory. The reunion was brief, however, Doc strangely hurt once again, while Shuman returned to France. (Doc and Mort's life always crossed in mystical ways. Mere months after Doc died, the much younger Shuman came down with a liver disease and died in France.)

Doc taught me how blues was tongue-in-cheek, often self-mocking, all that self-pity not meant in earnest. There were happy blues and sad blues. But the two classic distinctions were between urban and Delta blues. The urban had more to do with jazz, swing, and big bands. City and ghetto life. Whereas the Delta blues was folksy, using bottleneck guitars, cigar-box instruments. "Guys mumbling," as Doc saw it. "Ya never knew what the hell they were talkin' about. The Chicago people were crossover guys, like Muddy Waters, who I eventually liked," he said.

"You know what's amazing?" he continued. "When I made my 78 records, we used to laugh at all the singers like Muddy Waters. When the rock stars started using them as opening acts, all of a sudden these guys became well known. My group of people—Joe Turner, King Curtis, Mickey Baker—used to laugh at all the country-blues singers who were backwards musically. John Lee Hooker and Lightnin' Hopkins sang out of meter—we couldn't respect them."

Naturally, the off-meter and slurred-word syndrome became copied and immortalized in the annals of rock. "Most of the black guys that sing with a rasp have a voice that's been misused from early life, from drinking and smoking since they were nine. My contention is that it comes from misusing the voice, not knowing anything about proper vocal techniques. So you get a white guy who has no reason for this— his speaking voice is clear—and he suddenly affects a rasp," he said, referring to certain hippie blues bands of the '60s and '70s. "They must practice all day in college. There are black guys with very nice speaking voices, like B. B. King, who don't sing with a rasp. Joe Turner's singing the blues for fifty years; he don't have a raspy voice. He could have been an opera singer."

When Big Joe Turner died in 1985, his widow, Pat, bestowed upon Doc a shopping bag. It contained Big Joe's personal effects. The bag was spooky and Doc was unsure what the hell to do with it. He summoned me over to go through the contents, which resembled the last worldly belongings of a blues Mahatma Gandhi.

I felt like I was invading a dead man's privacy. Without hesitation, Doc dumped across his bed the items of his childhood idol, the hero of Chuck Berry, Bill Haley, and Ray Charles. There were assorted voodoo charms and a mojo stick. A campy gold cigarette lighter, tacky rings, a watch, a gold phone directory with no numbers. (Turner was illiterate. He memorized in quick study the songs Doc wrote for him, and never forgot a lyric). A pair of shoes, and Big Joe's *wallet*, for Christ's sake.

"*Just* what you'd expect a great blues singer to leave," said Doc. Within the wallet were five business cards that read:

BIG JOE TURNER
"BOSS OF THE BLUES"
AVAILABLE FOR:
CLUBS · CONCERTS · PARTIES · TELEVISION · RADIO
JOE & PAT TURNER
(213) 751-6500

I took one.

When things went bad for Turner, he'd abandon a wife, house, Cadillac, with no forwarding address, saying, "I left all those troubles behind." Doc wrote the first new song Turner recorded in twenty years, "Blues Train." He brought Turner to New York from L.A. to do one last album, backed by Roomful of Blues, and booked Joe a long engagement at Tramps. Turner left copyrights under previous wives' names. Doc discovered that ten years' worth of Turner's royalty checks had disappeared. Two of Turner's songs, including "Flip, Flop and Fly," were on the two-million-selling *Blues Brothers* album. Untangling the mess, Doc stopped a $26,000 check sent out that week to an ex-wife, Lou Willie Turner, who'd been quietly collecting the checks in Florida. The check was rerouted to a startled Joe Turner, who'd never even heard of *The Blues Brothers*. Thus began Doc's philanthropic work with the Rhythm & Blues Foundation in Washington, aiding impoverished R&B pioneers.

Doc and I seemed to share a mutual recognition of the thievery, self-deception, and pomposity manifested by certain people in charge. Prominent music industry no-talents, poseurs. Lies and misinformation printed in *Rolling Stone.* "High priests of nothing," to use a phrase from one of Doc's songs. They were all part of Doc's nighttime gallery.

He collaborated with Willie DeVille, who affected a cotton-picker's doo-rag look. Privately, he was dumbstruck that DeVille could sit for hours strumming a guitar aimlessly without an idea in his head. (Their collaboration did yield several acclaimed albums.)

Neil Sedaka, whom Doc fixed up with his first publisher in the '50s, met with Doc in the '80s for a potential collaboration. Sedaka went off into a greatest-hits medley, so lost in his piano lullabies that Doc's driver removed him, backwards, without Sedaka knowing. Dylan showed up once, wanting to collaborate. Then never called again. The bullshit seemed to get to him more as time marched on.

I'd already moved to Texas when Doc Pomus passed away in 1991, and couldn't make the funeral. His last days of lung cancer were painless, his daughter, Sharyn, said. Big Joe Turner records played quietly in the hospital room. Doc's standing-room-only farewell at Riverside Chapel was said to be the most astonishing music funeral New York ever saw. A new record deal was scored on the spot by forgotten singer Little Jimmy Scott—who brought the audience to tears. Doc's own songs rang out, gospel-style, as the audience stood and joined in. This was exactly the kind of irony Doc strove to prevent for so many of his friends. He knew their funerals would be sold out—it was while they were alive that he worked to fill the seats, get them some cash—if only enough for a new set of dentures for some old sax player, or stage threads for a singer who couldn't make the rent. But mostly, to allow them the hard-earned dignity to keep playing their songs.

—1991

Personal Management
Phil Spector

THE RONETTES

Exclusive Recording
Artist
Philles Records Inc.

Ronnie Spector (center): "Baby, my love's goin' down da toilet with you.
Tellin' you to your teeth."
(James J. Kriegsmann)

CHAPTER 3

Mr. Nobody

I am what some in the business refer to as a "ponce." That is, I'm the emasculated man behind a famous female, from whom I derive my sense of self-worth, and from whose stardom I live through. Sound the trumpets: I am Ronnie Spector's Boyfriend. Someday, I hope to be Mr. Ronnie Spector.

We are currently on tour, exiting the lobby of the Hilton, two blocks from the Hempstead Dinner Theatre. It's right before show-time. Ronnie and I rendezvous with her backup singers in the lobby. I personally pass out the girls' costumes from the one-hour French cleaners—a standard poncely duty.

This is Ronnie's umpteenth backup duo, since her original early '60s girl group. These generic Ronettes are gorgeous Puerto Rican chicks, both nineteen, accompanied by their Italian boyfriends. Both guys have blow-dried coifs and three-piece vested suits, just like John Travolta in *Saturday Night Fever*, the top film out now. They, too, are disco princes, each with his own Corvette.

It's raining outside. Boyfriend #1 pulls up to the entrance in his Corvette. His girl squeals, jumps in. Then Boyfriend #2 screeches his wheels to a halt, popping open the passenger door for his chick, who proudly hops in. And I'm standing there with Ronnie, who's in sequins, heels, and stage makeup. I'm carrying this tiny travel umbrella, barely big enough for one, which I pop open as I lead her out the door. It's the longest two-block walk of my life:

"You mean to say I'm the fuckin' star, and I have to watch my backup singers get into expensive cars—which *their* boyfriends are considerate enough to provide—while I have to walk in the fuckin' rain to my own fuckin' concert, in front of my singers, in front of my fans, in front of the whole tour bus! Do you know how embarrassed I am, what this makes me look like? Couldn't you have at least rented a car?"

"It's only two blocks. I should rent a car to travel two blocks?"

"If you knew how to treat me like a lady—which you don't have a clue—you'd have rented a limo. I'm only the fuckin' star."

"I spent my last twenty bucks just to get here from the city. I am totally broke."

"You ain't broke. You cheap! Where the fuck you get that umbrella?"

"It's a travel umbrella."

"You cheap, baby, that's all there is to it, too cheap to get a regular size. Tellin' you to your teeth."

I don't exactly manage Ronnie, which is the province of suitcase pimps and agents. Or usually some former garage mechanic who shacks up with a beauty queen, declares himself "manager," then fancies himself a showbiz impresario—until his big plans glean nothing. No, I'm a guit-tar player. At least I'm not a drummer, something Ronnie doesn't even consider to be a musician. Ronnie's never heard my band, and frankly, I think I'd freeze up.

Friends and employers have stopped calling; they know I'm pretty heavy into this relationship. She always insists I make more time for Us. Tonight's the first family Thanksgiving I ever missed. Ronnie accused me of being a child for wanting to go home to the folks. Thanksgiving was just another work night on her Roy Rayden Vaudeville Tour itinerary.

We enter the theater wet. Sure enough, some of the performers in the show see us walk in. Ronnie, radiating smiles, chats a moment with Joe Frazier, former heavyweight champ. His nightly spot is to walk onstage amidst applause and lift Eddie Fisher up over his head as he sings—reminiscent of the film scene in which Mighty Joe Young rises from beneath the bandstand, Atlas-style, holding aloft the pianist.

"Joe Frazier thinks you a fuckin' mo-ron," Ronnie tells me.

"Whaddya mean? We never met."

"You wanna go argue with Joe Frazier? That's what he said when he walked by. Is *that* your boyfriend? He called you a *that* and gave me a look, like, 'What're you doin' with such a loser?'"

"What? He stands onstage every night like a circus ape."

"I'm embarrassed to face him again."

"You'll manage."

"I have to tour with these people. Throw that fuckin' umbrella away!"

So now I pace the Hempstead Dinner Theatre dressing room as Ronnie Spector and the Ronettes take the stage. A ponce in shining armor. I dread walking her back to the hotel, while the two disco boyfriends anticipate whisking their doo-wop dates to Long Island dance clubs. Spoiled Mafia grandsons. Though they're polite—I'm with the star who employs their girlfriends—they don't chat much to me. I've yet to spot Rayden: I keep an eye out for anyone resembling a disco Jack Ruby. The three of us sit chain-smoking, as we have numerous times, in locker rooms at high school gymnasiums, armories, or wherever rock 'n' roll oldies shows are held. As a backstage entity, you might call us the Ronettes' Boyfriends.

Ronnie shares the bill with seven other nostalgia acts. Only Eddie Fisher, the '50s crooner who dumped his wife Debbie Reynolds to marry Liz Taylor, gets his own dressing room. For all this hard travel, she only does two songs each night. Always the same two, at every rock 'n' roll revival or disease telethon. The same two songs, which were hits fifteen years ago. But damned if she doesn't belt 'em out each time, pulls out all the vocal trills she's famous for. She always gets her ovation.

But last week, during her adorable curtsy, Ronnie continued sinking and collapsed. She had to be carted offstage by the Drifters, on deck.

Ronnie insisted on her own limo for the three-week tour. "Only Eddie Fisher gets a limo," Roy Rayden decreed.

"So I have to ride the bus—with the musicians," she complains with disgust. "Some of them told me that they had extra jobs—like being a plumber. Ugh!"

Yesterday I received this paranoid call: "Honey, you better get up there," warns one of Ronnie's only two friends, a gay set designer. "Protect your woman, if you love her."

"Of course I love her. From what?"

"Roy Rayden."

Rayden has the nostalgia circuit practically sewn up. He can't crack the movies, or break a new act into disco radio. He weaves in and out of his tours in a limousine, while his "cavalcade of stars" ride coach.

"Roy will forcibly compromise her virtue."

"Say what?"

"That's what Roy Rayden does. He books fading teen queens on these shitty Vaudeville bus tours. When they're exhausted, depressed and disoriented by the third week, he offers his limo, slips 'em champagne spiked with elephant tranquilizer or something. And baby, that's when they get *discoed*. They're never sure what happened. He's raped a few aging *Beach Blanket Bingo* bimbos and a Mouseketeer or two. He's a nostalgia rapist."

"A nostalgia rapist? I'll kill the bastard."

Although Ronnie is only thirty, she claims—a far cry from prehistoric, but ten years older than me—she is now labeled an oldies act. Her heyday of hits peaked when she was seventeen. That "oldies" tag riles her, so please don't say that word; she'll pitch a fit, and I'll be the one who has to sweep up the broken dishes. Being thirty is apparently so grotesque, it's turning her gray.

I grilled her this afternoon, as she made up for the show. "Have you been in Rayden's limo?"

"Once."

"Did he do anything unusual?"

"Had me autograph an album."

"Which one?"

"The Santa cover."

"Anything else?"

 "He winked."

I shudder over the connotation of a wink from a nostalgia rapist. "Baby, I don't think you should get in there again. He's a bad-news motherfucker."

"At least he has class," snips Ronnie, chugging a cheap bottle of sherry upside down over her bee-stung lips as she struts around like a venomous Harlem street hooker. "The tour bus is da pits, babe, and Roy, well, he invited me to Philly tomorrow—in that nice, warm limo."

"We'll ride the bus."

"What! Baby, my love's goin' down da toilet with you. Tellin' you to your teeth."

Ronnie was all Borscht Belt charm during our first few months. After the Rock 'n' Roll Is Here to Stay concert at Madison Square Garden, she felt like the greatest toy in the world. A hoarse-voiced, ninety-eight-pound kewpie doll. My own little historical showpiece, spinning 'round like a giddy ballerina. On the bill that night were the aging Righteous Brothers, our "blue-eyed soul brothers," who weren't even real brothers. Their behavior was less than righteous, as they rubbed up against each of her legs like dogs. When Ronnie introduced me, they looked the other way when shaking hands with her lowly escort, a cock blocker, some young ponce, Mr. Nobody, in charge of fetching luggage and costumes. But it was my responsibility to take care of this toy, to hand-feed it milk and cookies before bed, put it in its nightie and tuck it in.

She spent a whole night teaching me how to wink. "It's da sexiest thing a guy can do—if done right." Her own wink was devastating. Then, with utter seriousness, she presented her nurse's diploma and took my blood pressure.

One night, Ronnie sat upon my lap and poleaxed me with Beatle yarns until dawn. How the Ronettes were invited up to their hotel suite in the Plaza. How Lennon tried to feel her up on the night of their first Ed Sullivan Show, seen by 73 million, the defining moment of rock music history.

"You denied John Lennon one measly feel of your tit?

"He was a fuckin' musician."

Somehow, the Ronettes were aloof to musicians, frustrating the mightiest of rock stars. They swaggered like wet dreams onstage, but Ronnie, the leader and the youngest, was only seventeen at the height of their fame. Mama protected the girls' virtue, Mama shooed away the Harlem musicians—whom she considered as a whole class to be shit.

The Ronettes granted the British groups platonic dates for publicity. Which was more than they ever did for any Motown group. "We never went out with black guys," Ronnie said. The Ronettes spurned the most clean-cut, churchgoing gospel singers—who came abuzzin' 'round their beehives.

"Baby, we were a sensation downtown at the Peppermint Lounge. Got our eight-by-ten publicity shots from the Kriegsmann studio, where all da Broadway stars went." She handed me the famous photo. "That was da pose by which all girl groups were measured."

Ronnie's older sister and cousin flanked her, palms up in a come-hither gesture. Dueling beehives of voluptuous, teased black hair. They wore tight white bridesmaid skirts, slit above the knee, and Kleenex-stuffed bras. Three light-skinned, racially ambiguous, tough-lookin' Harlem chicks. "Fans thought we were Puerto Rican Polynesians. That was our gimmick, with Oriental eyeliner." Street fights between black and Hispanic gangs broke out, each claiming the Ronettes as their own ethnic group.

"My father, wherever the hell he is, was white and Irish. My mother, if you must know, was partly black—but mostly Comanche Indian."

In bed, Ronnie blurts out she loves me more than her ex-husband. But the distant Tycoon of Teen sometimes calls in the wee hours. By the time Ronnie hangs up, she's catatonic. This trance is something Nadia the psychologist is working to break. He can sabotage any record deal she has going, making sure she remains a Golden Oldie.

I'd threaten to go after him, but for the fact he pays her $750 a week alimony, and is raising their eight-year-old adopted son. She chokes up whenever the kid is mentioned. Ronnie's child was awarded paternal custody to a notoriously eccentric, reclusive nut. So she felt the court was saying, in its own ironclad, heartbreaking little way, that she was a Bad Mommy.

Phil Spector put his golden touch on the teenage Ronettes, producing a series of innovative smash records. He made Ronnie lead singer, and cowrote lovingly childish nonsense lyrics like "Da Do Ron Ron" for background harmonies.

Then he slowly weaned possession of her from Mama, and married her. The last time her mother came from Harlem to visit, Phil led her into the catacombs of their Bel-Air mansion. There he proudly presented an empty glass mausoleum he had built in Ronnie's honor, to enshrine her should she die before him. Mama was mortified.

Phil ended Ronnie's performing and recording career and kept her sequestered on the estate. Barbed wire and an electrified chain-link fence went up around the place.

"But he made me a star," she often repeated. This, she felt, excused anything, earned him a ten-year license to abuse.

No men, especially dogs in the music biz, were allowed near her. "Once we met Elvis in Vegas. He eyed me over real good. Then Phil orders me up to our room, alone, for the rest of the trip, says he's busy with business. But he had no business with Elvis—he knew the only business Elvis wanted was with me."

The only male she had contact with was their masseur. "I had a secret orgasm during each massage. If Philip knew, he'd have had the guy shot.

"When he left for London, we would sleep together over the phone—not talking, but keeping the phone line open on our pillows all night, so he could hear me breathe. Once he paid off a doctor to put my leg in a cast, when nothin' was wrong, so I had to stay in a wheelchair for weeks. His jealousy got crazier as he became impotent. By then he had me in my little pixie Santa getup, crawling along the floor on a dog leash, makin' me bark on command."

A pariah in the very business in which he was lionized, no one would work with him. "Philip pulled a gun on Lennon in the men's room at the Record Plant, and fired into his toilet stall, fed up that John was stoned. After that, John was finished with him, finally realized what a sick motherfucker he was. Phil always wanted to work with the Beatles. But he realized deep down, no matter what he did, he could never be as great as them. That's why Brian Wilson went crazy too. Anyway, John escorted me down to court, for protection, the day the divorce papers got signed."

"Lennon, the bodyguard and attorney?"

"He took me there in a cab."

"Maybe John could write a song for your comeback album."

"That would be nice." She smiled, redoing her eyebrow pencil in a pocket mirror. "Could you call him?"

His number was not even in her phone book. Nobody's number was in her phone book. Her sister and cousin—the original Ronettes—were married, fat, raising kids, long out of the business. They never called. A million cousins never called. Ronnie had practically no friends, except for the gay set designer and this Svengali shrink, Nadia.

But I worry about Nadia, the "psychologist." Is a psychologist licensed to dispense medicine? This one does. I accompanied Ronnie to Nadia's "office." The walls were covered with Ronettes photos, album covers, and mementos. Everything but a psychology diploma.

"She's a fan. Damn, baby, you just jealous cause you ain't got fans."

"And you ain't got friends. Just fans."

One night she gets that lost-her-mind-onstage look in her eyes, spouting disco lyrics: "'Stayin' alive, stayin' alive, uh, uh, uh.' John Travolta is a definite fox!"

"He looks like a monkey."

"He's a fuckin' star, he's on the cover of the *Enquirer*. And that's where it's at, babe. When they follow you just to report what *clothes* you wearin'. You could be my 'Mystery Man.' Cause nobody knows who you are. Mr. Nobody."

My idol of the rock 'n' roll hipsters watches soaps, reads only gossip tabloids, and falls asleep smoking in bed. A mongrel Gidget. Her teddy bear was worn and chewed up. The first astonishing thing I noticed in her apartment was the absence of any music. No albums or stereo, not even her own records. Cassettes arrive from chick songwriters, pitching songs written just for her. Tapes from Deborah Harry or Patti Smith, who idolized her in junior high and still carry a torch.

"Leave it for the maid," Ronnie shrugs. Unplayed tapes end up in the trash, personal letters unanswered.

"Let's hear a few," I plead.

"What's da use? Nobody can write for me like Phil did. When he was your age, he was a millionaire, a hit maker." Suddenly, she knocks cassettes, along with her take-out lo mein, off the counter, and heaves her pink princess phone to the floor.

"Just leave it for the fuckin' maid."

Twice a week, an old black cleaning lady lets herself in, bringing fresh flowers, then making her rounds until the whole place is orderly again. I never saw Ronnie pay her.

Then, during a drunken tantrum, she throws me and the maid out, and I'm shocked when the maid tearfully reveals she is Ronnie's mother. We compare notes. Ronnie has never drunk so heavily since returning from Philadelphia, where she shared Rayden's private limo. I sensed Rayden had done something terrible to her, something *nostalgic*, though she won't talk. (A few years later, Rayden would be found dead in a car trunk.)

We hear "Be My Baby" and "Walking in the Rain" careening out of apartment windows, car radios, TV sets, in elevators. We never stop to acknowledge it. It's just part of the air, in perpetual frequency around the planet. But on some days, all of a sudden, it's an issue:

"You jealous."

"I am not. I'm proud."

"You ain't proud, it's killing you. You can't stand it, hearing my records all the time. You never say anything, never tell me I'm great."

"Baby, it's time for a new album. Show 'em you're still great, get off the oldies bus."

"Ugh! You said it again, goddamn you—you said I'm old! Well, I may be the oldest woman—and the biggest—you'll ever fuckin' meet in this life. You young and stupid. Tellin' you to your teeth."

Hark: The Ronettes Boyfriends hear applause. Our womenfolk are returning. Both studs share a hairbrush, slap on cologne, ready their gold cigarette lighters. But for me, the moment of truth approaches. It's storming outside as I clutch my pathetic umbrella. I worry how the fuck I'm going to walk her those two blocks back to the hotel.

—1997

Label Stable: Over 50,000 forgotten tapes from the publishers above lay moldering on
Regent Sound's 5th floor.
(Author's collage)

CHAPTER 4

Adventures at the Bottom of the Music Trade
Regent Sound Studios, 1974–1976

Regent Sound Studios, at 24 West Fifty-seventh Street, was my alma mater. What began as a lucky summer job, fresh out of high school, became a two-year hitch. I dropped out of NYU that fall to maintain the job. It was my entrée into the music business at age eighteen—which never did really open up, shark that I'm not.

Many of the recording industry's major studios were in midtown Manhattan, within walking distance of the Brill Building on Broadway. They were secretive inner sanctums, their names familiar only from the backs of records: the Record Plant, the Hit Factory, Columbia Studios, Atlantic, RCA, Bell Sound, Media Sound. If you worked at one, you were privy to all, going beyond the reception areas when transferring tapes or equipment.

I lay claim to the vague title of "assistant engineer," but was never granted one album credit as such. Maybe I never asked. My job did entail being assistant floor waxer, handyman, gofer, and mic-setup man. Everyone took me under their apprenticeship—janitors, elevator men, and engineers. I was never certain whether the future they were grooming me for was musical or janitorial.

Many of my afternoons were spent in an isolated fifth-floor warehouse where fifty thousand musty tapes were stored in disarray. This wasteland of forgotten reels, dating back to the 1950s, was put under my stewardship. As tape librarian, I was instructed to organize them over time.

I arrived each morning at the crack of dawn to open Studio A. I followed a daily chart, positioning mics, chairs, music stands, and ashtrays for that morning's big band or orchestra session. I'd break down at the end of the session. But before I lifted a finger, I always began a ritual—having a fried egg on a roll from a greasy take-out on Fifty-sixth Street, followed by an exquisite hot coffee and cigarette. For just a few minutes as I kicked up my heels on the console, reclining in the plush black leather producer's chair, I indulged dreams of recording my own albums. To me, the most romantic lighting in New York was the glow of a studio console at midnight. It was a soundproofed, windowless sanctum, dark but for the red VU meters and faders—like the inside of a musical jet cockpit.

Musicians streamed in at 9 A.M. like factory workers. I never heard these hardened Local 802 musicians discuss the aesthetics of music. They only talked money. How much they'd logged at other sessions, overtime, residuals. But the elite double-scale guys—like Fathead Newman, Ron Carter, Steve Gadd, Cornell Dupree, Chuck Rainey—they seemed above the battle, smoking pipes, dressed like squires, flying in from Newport and Montreux jazz festivals.

Blind jazzman Rahsaan Roland Kirk entered the studio followed by his tribe of "black classical musicians." They shuffled down the halls like a fighter's entourage entering the ring. Kirk swung a mojo cane, scattering all in his path. The novelty aspect of Kirk was that he played three horns at once in his mouth, sometimes including an African nose flute. I wasn't sure where to place the microphone for this arrangement, and called him by his first name, Roland.

The entire tribe froze: "Don't *ever* call him that," one sideman threatened.

"His name is *Rahsaan*," came another.

"Or you can call him *Ra* for short," said a third.

Kirk recorded three pretentious double albums for Atlantic while I was at Regent. *Prepare Thyself to Deal with a Miracle* was one, for example. "Black classical music" is how he termed his jazz, espousing a jazz-victim philosophy, while hating rock and the white man's music. But the tribe let down their guard in the wee hours of the night in the warm glow of that studio console. Their bravado diminished and you could see they were just poor musicians. Ra's valet-percussionist confided the following pastime:

"Ain't nothin' I prefer more than buyin' a gallon of chocolate ice cream, then sit top the toilet, eatin' and shittin' all night. Ain't no better party in town. Diarrhea is the *po' man's pleasure*." He then admitted a soft spot for Tony Orlando & Dawn, curling an eyebrow when I mentioned that the songwriter's demo for "Tie a Yellow Ribbon 'Round the Old Oak Tree" was on the fifth floor.

Joel Dorn was Kirk's producer, as well as that of dozens of other singular jazz and pop musicians. His offices were entwined with Regent's on the third floor. Dorn was a brilliant con man/raconteur, a switchblade-toting hipster, whose career began on Philadelphia jazz radio as "the Masked Announcer." His forceful radio voice entranced dozens of artists who put their recording career in his hands.

"If I need a little blue palette," he might say, "I'll call Fathead Newman. If I need to add a little red to the canvass, I call in Hank Crawford." In each musician he saw a unique "coloring," a different "brushstroke."

"You remember the fuckin' group of people that came through that place?" says Joel Dorn today. "It was like a twenty-four-hour aural circus, chock-full of unicorns. I had the wheel. If you tied yourself to the front of a ship and just went headlong into the wind—and just screamed and yelled—that's what it was like."

Dorn had been a staff producer at Atlantic jazz. He scored in the pop world with Roberta Flack hits like "Killing Me Softly."

Dorn did surreal records, avoided big stars, and began to drift farther from the center of the record business. Among a hundred albums he did at Regent were the debuts of Leon Redbone, Bette Midler, and Peter Allen, as well as albums by Steve Goodman, Dory Previn, Yusef Lateef, and Don McLean.

I remember watching Peter Allen during a break between takes from his first album, *Continental American*. He sat before the TV impassively as news of his divorce from Liza Minelli came through on screen.

Don McLean's fourth album, *Homeless Brother*, was done at Regent. The Dorn-produced LP only furthered McLean's descent, but it did contain two overlooked gems: "Wonderful Baby," a ditty on par with anything Irving Berlin wrote (Fred Astaire later recorded it). And "Sail Away, Raymond," a sea chantey by George Harrison, which he apparently sent to McLean.

McLean was a bit schlubby and melancholy, and did not fit the romantic image suggested by "Vincent" and "American Pie" just a few years earlier. He recorded in Studio A every day, breaking to watch Nixon's resignation. "The critics don't understand me," he would say with genuine angst. I purchased a few of his brilliant earlier LPs at Woolworth's, which were already in the remainder bin. I ignorantly showed them to McLean, Woolworth's remainder stickers still affixed.

"Oh, God," said McLean, recoiling. The stickers depressed him.

Dorn lost all hearing in his left ear overnight during a childhood case of mumps. Because he couldn't hear stereo, many of his records were done mono. One of Dorn's artistic trademarks included adding aimless sound montages to albums, the noodling of a pothead. Another brainstorm involved his dream to record a duet between John Lennon and Kate Smith. This never happened.

Kenny Vance, originally of Jay & the Americans, was one of Dorn's right-hand men. They would sit stoned long into the night, doing dozens of mixes on some deep track from say, a Lucy Simon (sister of Carly) record. They'd imagine they heard some tiny noise or imperfection deep in the mix, crack open expensive virgin reels of Ampex tape, and do endless remixes, one indistinguishable from the other.

"I wanted to puke," recalls legendary Atlantic boss Jerry Wexler today. "Dorn wasted tons of our money."

Wexler himself was a master of the rollback: "If there's twenty bad takes, roll back to the best one and fix it. I've made a few records, and my heavy hand as producer is on them. I could change a record. Dorn would stop a take, and tell them to 'just try something different.'

"My ultimate definition of a producer," Wexler concludes, "is someone who can change the music, the tempo, syncopation, hum out a bass line. You don't have to be a musician."

Dorn worked almost exclusively with engineer Robert Lifton, Regent Sound's owner. Shortly after I arrived, Lifton took me up to a fifth-floor warehouse. He left me alone with the key, instructing me to organize a whole junkyard, and someday present him with an inventory. Regent would eventually return tapes to any rightful surviving companies.

I was left alone with fifty thousand musty reels of tape. A wasteland of forgotten master reels dating back to the '50s, from record companies, Tin Pan Alley songwriters and music industry publishers with dozens of subsidiary labels and shell companies that seemed like so much gibberish at the time: Coral Rock, Aeolian, Shapiro-Bernstein, Screen Gems-Columbia Music, the Wes Farrell Organization, ATV-Kirshner.

Publishers were the secret financial barons of the music industry. No one could explain exactly what they did other than collect money. The office of Aaron Schroeder International, for instance, was the penthouse of our building, 24 West Fifty-seventh Street. "Backside Schroeder," the guy with all the shitty Presley B-sides. He owned publishing rights on Elvis and, somehow, even some Beatles stuff. A bona fide crook, he often had lawsuits leveled against him for stealing money. I never saw the shadowy Schroeder in his office, only his hot blond receptionist. She got locked out one Friday evening when I was working late. She was the first, maybe the only, girl to ever step into my fifth-floor enclave. Her pocketbook and keys were stuck inside the top floor, and we spent hours trying to break through windows and fire escapes. Wilbur, the crusty old black night super, caught us. He took me aside and shook his head. "If you got dat broad naked, boy, you wouldn't know what to do with it."

After two years spent dusting them off, I still see faded box labels in my sleep. Amid chaos I would slowly reunite scattered tape reels with labels like Limón Dance and Beacon Hill or Phillips Productions. Shapiro-Bernstein had some two hundred dusty reels, each plucked from mountains of disorder to be filed numerically from 1961 to 1968. Endless quarter-inch reels of *Search for Tomorrow* soap opera cues, produced by Elliot Lawrence downstairs in Studio B. If you ever wondered what the 16-½ speed was on your old record player, it was for these huge, tire-round acetate records, once used on military radio. Hundreds lay moldering, playable only on long-obsolete industrial-size record machines. The machines themselves lay in ruin in this audio junkyard.

Robert Lifton was one of a handful of pioneer recording engineers, behind the scenes of rock 'n' roll records in the '50s and '60s. He was a man of tape, of studios, who rarely saw the light of day and had an alabaster studio suntan. A workaholic, devoid of personality, he was nevertheless a decent man and a fair boss. He always wore rumpled jeans and boots, and smoked four packs of Camels a day.

More importantly, Lifton kept personal musical opinions to himself during his round-the-clock sessions. He could handle some bubblegum idol in the morning, then be the consummate engineer for a jazz record by night. He only once revealed a personal music taste. Lifton sent me out to Colony Records for a new Rev. James Cleveland gospel album, which he cracked out of the cellophane like a teenybopper.

"He wasn't one of those engineers who had the kind of sound that producers chased after, like Phil Ramone or Rudy Van Gelder," says Dorn. "But he was such a basic engineer. He could get a very black-and-white, very mono sound, but a cinemascopic black-and-white sound. He understood what I said. A lot of other engineers didn't wanna hear my bullshit, would look at me like I was nuts. But Lifton would listen and pull it off."

Lifton was the first to ever achieve a 32-track setup, synchronizing two 16-track Ampex MM-1000 machines. Other engineers could never do it. Lifton was a science club member in high school, one of those guys who could make a tape recorder out of a Dixie cup and string and two pieces of iron, a wizard of sound. He sank all his profits into cutting-edge video equipment in 1974, foreseeing video as the upcoming boom of the future. Regent was the first recording studio in New York to do such. Lifton did live sound for Aretha at Radio City. He sent me and Jesus, the custodian, over to Rockefeller Center with loads of equipment one afternoon. It was for the first season of some new show called *Saturday Night Live.* He became *SNL*'s, and TV's, best live music sound engineer.

Lifton was revered by other engineers for his technical prowess. He was trained as a physicist, as were the other engineers he hired. He was an awkward guy in social situations when he wasn't behind the controls, and it was odd to see his smiling face turn up in trade magazine ads for Ampex tape, which he vigorously endorsed, leading the industry away from the mighty 3M Scotch company.

Scientists of sound, the three Regent engineers under Lifton could reconfigure the electronics of Ampex MM-1000 16-track machines. They could draft by hand perfect electronic diagrams. They could operate the Neumann lathe cutting machine in Studio D for acetate masters used to press the albums they engineered. They could troubleshoot any mechanical or electronic repair at 3 A.M., during a high-dollar, all-night session.

Engineers were the true wizards of production. Their trade was unsung, and more complicated than that of highly paid record producers—whom they felt honor-bound to serve as psychologist and technician. They often worked eighty-hour weeks and carried their burdens silently, so as never to worry the celebrated musicians, stars, and producers. Engineers Vince McGarry and Joe Ferla could read music charts. They had uncanny timing on tricky overdub punches. They often did the producer's job, but never saw the glory.

Before the days of computer editing, engineers performed daredevil tape splices, more delicate than circumcisions, where one hair off on a razor-blade tape splice could ruin the results of a ten-thousand-dollar session. Before the days of automated consoles, they performed master mixes with their own hands, memorizing dozens of knob tweaks, and fader levels for the final mix of a song. As assistant engineer, I might be required to push one or two faders up and down at the far end of the console, while the engineer did dozens. We might rehearse the moves an hour before going for a final mix. They were akin to seasoned fighter pilots, who could break down and rebuild their own planes from top to bottom. (I've never seen this level of professionalism at *any* recording studio today.) Though they took me under their wing as a raw engineering prospect, I gradually learned I didn't have the Right Stuff.

And so, one of my closest coworkers became Regent's custodial mascot, Jesus Rojas. The jolly, rotund custodian was cherished by rich music producers, who borrowed him on weekends to work in their homes. He'd come in with a team of fellow Colombian floor waxers.

Jesus was the first to introduce me to Forty-second Street's live peeps. He had no time for men's magazines, which didn't yet deliver the full-out goods. On lunch break he led me to a second-floor peep with curtained booths, where you could "see dee-licious poo-sey" on a revolving platform.

Another beloved Regent mainstay was "the most polite man in the world," Sam Vandivert. He was a portly, white-haired fellow in his fifties. Sam ran tape dupes and made cassettes, for which he typed out pressure-sensitive labels. He could do a miracle save on a damaged cassette. Sam was so organized in the "dupe room," we joked that his tombstone would have an arrow pointing downward. He remained jolly no matter how viciously he was berated by Bess, the bookkeeper. Sam never raised his voice to defend himself, but would meekly walk off bemused. "She's a rough ol' bird," he said, and choked when I suggested his presence threatened her virginity.

When I was new on the job, Sam introduced me to Jack Shaw. "He's a great guy," he kept telling me. "Wait till you meet him."

One day the elevator door opened and Sam wheeled Jack Shaw out. He was a crippled midget in a wheelchair, a human pretzel with a Svengali goatee. "Isn't he great?" came Sam, with utmost sincerity. And thereafter, Sam and Jesus were forever relieved of the task of wheeling Jack Shaw home from Dorn's sessions, where he was a frequent personage.

Dorn and Lifton helped support him and remained loyal as Shaw's health deteriorated. Shaw had once coproduced Fathead Newman albums with Dorn, and wrote under pseudonyms for *Tiger Beat.*

I was often sent to fetch Jack Shaw from his reeking West Fifty-seventh Street apartment. And there, disassembled from his oxygen tank, his apartment overflowing with garbage, was Jack, stranded in the middle of it, crawling over a trash heap like a deformed baby, the bones of his ass hitched up, his scraggly bearded face gasping for air. Soon I was shopping for his groceries (imitation "cheese food" his favorite). The poor guy needed more help than he got. When it was time to urinate, even in the studio, he would fumble out his disarmingly large pecker and piss into a bottle, oblivious to strangers.

A fellow Philadelphia jazz deejay with Dorn, he was then somehow able to drive. Shaw chauffeured Lenny Bruce to gigs in Philly. Jack described his wheelchair vantage point as "a crotch-eyed view of the world." I waited for some nugget of wisdom as payoff for all the errands I ran for Shaw on my own time. He'd contemplate my questions about jazz, or how I might advance as a studio guitarist. He'd twist his face into a wizened grimace, stroke his beard, looking heavenward, deep in thought as I waited for one kernel of crotch-eyed wisdom—but never got it.

Occasionally, Regent Sound went into some ridiculous high-security mode, and Studio A was declared off-limits. Once for a James Taylor–Carly Simon duet. Regent's mild-mannered security man, Fred, sat quietly in the Studio A reception area every night, unassuming, slightly built—but would pat the .38 under his jacket whenever I inquired whether he could really fend off an attack.

For a brief Raquel Welch visit, Joel Dorn ordered me, Jesus, and even Sam off the third floor. I would often retreat to the windowless fifth floor to be alone when my ego was wounded, and commune with the tapes as I slowly ordered them.

"What the hell does he do up there?" Bess the bookkeeper would always complain to whoever would listen.

That very week, Raquel Welch, with Shep Gordon, who also managed Alice Cooper, was in hot pursuit of my dad to write her authorized biography—a high-paying project that my father considered during a time of financial strain, though he wrestled with the humiliating subject matter. He did tell Welch that his boy worked at Regent, and to say hello. And so I stayed on the fifth floor waiting for an intercom buzz summoning me down at her request, so I could breach their pompous security. She never called. My father turned down the book the next day.

When Carol, the gorgeous Haitian receptionist, punched out at night, studio musicians and engineers would fight to sit upon her swivel chair while it was still warm. Her flanks were awe-inspiring. She transformed from prim librarian to bombshell by doffing her thick eyeglasses and releasing her hair bun, haughtily ignoring wolf whistles from janitors and elevator men. She never once visited me on the fifth floor, a dump she wouldn't dream of entering. She eventually married chief engineer Vince McGarry.

Bess would often complain about me or Sam to Carol, suspicious that my sixty-dollar-per-week salary was a waste, since they couldn't watch me upstairs. In fact, after endless dusty afternoons spent separating crusty, waterlogged tape boxes and deciphering their faded origins, I had whittled down the fifth floor, with only one small pile to go. My two-year odyssey was nearly complete. In a week or so, I could type up the master log and present a fully ordered library to my boss, Robert Lifton.

But then, suddenly, I was "laid off." Lifton mumbled something about "unions cracking down" and regretted my departure, but ol' Bess, the wicked business manager, had convinced him the budget had to be cut. I was lowest man on the totem pole. I learned a basic tenet of business: I had no clients, brought no accounts into the business. "But the tapes!" I cried. My masterwork of inventory organization was nearly complete.

"Oh, those," said Lifton. "Don't worry, we'll take care of 'em."

Dorn's reign lasted but a few more years. "When you're just a pure artist, when you do what you want when you want—that doesn't lay well with business people. As long as you make them money, they'll put up with your nonsense. I had a fifteen-year run—it was unbelievable.

"What happened at the end of the '70s, early '80s, is when the corporate takeover of music in this country was completed. Now lawyers and accountants and non-in-the-street, non-late-night people were running the music business. They observed it the way businessmen do. They said, 'Let's see. This kind of record that sounds this way, goes on this kinda radio, sells at this retail, and pulls this audience at this venue.' They applied the laws of logic to art. And you can't. They changed the music business forever. The wildcatters are gone. These are all corporate folks. It finished it for guys like us."

Years later, I saw Dorn, wild-eyed in his claustrophobic New York apartment, surrounded by boxes of tapes and potheaded mixes, cramping his life. He'd summoned me to a meeting for some TV brainstorm. I brought along my brother Drew, who was supposed to bring a friend who was a scholar of old movie posters. At thirty-five years old, the friend was living at home with his parents and didn't show. Reached by phone from Dorn's office, he said he wasn't allowed to come—he was being "punished." Then Dorn was summoned to a hospital by a friend having a heart attack. Meeting and TV show ended right there.

But Dorn's visionary hoarding paid off in the '90s, as he reinvented himself. Rhino/Atlantic CD box sets revolutionized the biz, and Dorn repackages lots of his old productions.

Lifton moved Regent to the Brill Building. He died of lung cancer around '86. Four packs of Camels daily. Regent's space is now part of a famous art gallery building.

I still see those tapes in my dreams, just out of grasp, a week from completion. I ran into Regent's beloved janitor, Jesus Rojas, many years later. "What happened to all the tapes—*my* tapes?"

"Thrown out, I theenk," said Jesus. "Years ago."

—1999

Unmasked: The Masked Announcer, Joel Dorn, in one of his last photos.
(Courtesy of Hyena Records)

CHAPTER 5

Joel Dorn
The Masked Announcer Strikes Again

L abel M, on West Twenty-third Street in Manhattan, is chaotic, but Joel Dorn sits detached from it all, slumped back in a chair filing his nails. Like Cadillac salesmen, old-school music executives always did benefit from a well-manicured handshake. Hundreds of aging quarter-inch tape reels are stacked on the floor of his office. My one-year-old daughter grabs one.

"Don't touch that!" says Dorn. "It's an unreleased Stan Getz."

I recognize these tapes—an obsolete format—from my two years at Regent Sound Studios. His offices have always resembled the aftermath of a storm. He's there to work records, not decorate. Dorn began when Renaissance Italians and Jewish hucksters ran the business.

"Pat Martino had some mobster in Philly get in touch," he bellows to one of his promo men standing at the door. "He warned me to lay off. Lay off? I told 'em, 'I'm the only one who released his fuckin' albums!'"

Dorn, a youthful sixty, resembles a ruggedly handsome, switch-blade-toting rabbi. He is one of the last active record men from the days when mobsters and telephone booth Indians—Bud Abbott types who operated from public phone booths in the Brill Building lobby—plugged records behind the scenes. "Don't give me that 'Hey, baby' shit," I've heard Dorn warn slick upstarts who suck up to him. "I invented it."

"I can tell you all the guys who are still making records from when I started forty years ago. Arif Mardin, Tommy LiPuma, and Phil Ramone. Hundreds of producers, some who were giants for eleven months, are gone. Hit records are a young man's game, and I fell outta the game—but not out of the quality game."

Dorn nonetheless now has a hit album with twenty-four-year-old jazz chanteuse Jane Monheit. He discovered her "at some dump." A certain bell goes off in his head on those rarefied occasions when he hears someone he wants to sign.

"We're moving ten thousand copies a week," says Dorn, of the album *Come Dream with Me.* "To think, after all those years—to have a hit record again. They come out of nowhere."

Label M, his current imprint, is a producer's vanity label. *Songs That Made the Phone Light Up* and *Back in My Disc Jockey Days* are repackaged compilations that commemorate Dorn's beginnings as an early 1960s jazz deejay at WHAT-FM in Philly. Then a nineteen-year-old junior at Temple University, he became known as the Masked Announcer. *Jockey Days* includes Dorn's opening radio theme, "Hard Times" by David "Fathead" Newman, along with tracks by Hank Crawford, Les McCann, Roland Kirk, and Yusef Lateef—all of whom Dorn would come to record when he became an Atlantic staff producer under Nesuhi Ertegun. He was the only boy who ever wrote fan letters to a producer—that being Nesuhi when Dorn was a boy. Years later, the Masked Announcer boosted his favorite Atlantic records into jazz hits—at least in Philadelphia.

"You broke a record one city at a time. In those days, they were city-states, like Sparta or Athens. A local compilation of doo-wop groups could sell fifty thousand records in Philly alone, and never be released outside Pennsylvania."

Dorn made inroads into the music business by convincing Atlantic he knew public taste in jazz. "We had a phone in the studio that listeners called in on," he writes in the liner notes. "It gave us instant access to what they liked, didn't like, what worked, what didn't, and why. That, along with spending five nights a week in Philly's jazz clubs, checkin' out audience reactions, taught me who to sign and how to record them."

Had the labels promoted Dorn's choices in other city-states, he's sure they would have been national hits. The Kennedy years were a ripe time for mainstream jazz. The pop charts then included records by Ramsey Lewis, Gloria Lynn, Nina Simone, Ahmad Jamal, and Stan Getz.

"Roland Kirk, before he became Rahsaan, called me one morning and said, 'I got somebody for you to sign.' It was a girl named Roberta Flack, his bass player's wife. I said, 'What does she sound like?'

"He got nuts and said, 'She sound like a *colored* lady!' then slammed down the fuckin' phone. So I never followed up. Then Les McCann called. He said, 'I got someone for you to sign. Roberta Flack.' That's two times in a row from two guys like this."

Dorn went to see her at a club, feeling she was too good to be commercially successful. "When I signed Roberta Flack, we put her in the jazz category. A chick who played piano and sang in jazz clubs. But we started making pop records. You might get a hit by mistake, like Etta Jones got with 'Don't Talk to Strangers.' And Roberta got one with "First Time Ever I Saw Your Face.'"

Dorn followed up with "Where Is the Love" and "Killing Me Softly," making him a hot property in the early '70s, when he copped his Grammys. His mentor, Doc Pomus, used to say, "Always stick with originals who have world-class ability." Pomus introduced Dorn to Bette Midler, a girl he'd been coaching as a singer. She was playing to an audience in the gay bathhouse below the Ansonia Hotel in Doc's neighborhood. Dorn produced Midler's debut, *The Divine Miss M*, in 1972.

"When you have million-sellers and Grammys together, that buys you years of people takin' a shot with you. I must have bought myself five or six years beyond when I was actually making hits."

Studio A and Studio B at Regent Sound Studios, on West Fifty-seventh Street, were booked round the clock with Dorn's projects. He would produce up to five albums at once—the likes of Steve Goodman, Yusef Lateef, Peter Allen, Joe Venuti, even one track on the Allman

Brothers' *Idlewild South.* Bette Midler in the morning, Lou Rawls at lunch, and Rahsaan Roland Kirk in the wee hours. And he would pair them up on each other's albums.

A conceit of Dorn's was to pair Kate Smith on a duet with John Lennon—presumably because it amused him, not for any legitimate musical reason. But Lennon didn't think it was amusing enough.

"I couldn't get Lennon," says Dorn "so I got Dr. John instead. I think Mac [Dr. John] is America's premier musician. If you just think of him as Dr. John, you're missing the whole trip. He knows how to adapt to any island you drop him on."

Dorn produced Don McLean's fourth album, *Homeless Brother.* Not long after McLean's massive hits, "American Pie" and "Vincent," Dorn released a piece of fluff for the single, called "La La Love You," which I remember being remixed hundreds of times, with nary a difference from one mix to the other.

"I fucked up 'La La Love You.' Chased the jacket and the slacks more than the body of the song," admits Dorn. "It should have been more like a white-guy rock 'n' roll song."

The real hit on the record was "Wonderful Baby," an Irving Berlin–like ditty that entered high for a few weeks on the easy-listening chart.

"But McLean's manager, Herb Gart, had a fuckin' knock-down, drag-out screaming match with the guy who ran United Artists [McLean's label], who killed the record to teach him a lesson." A slight consolation for McLean occurred when Fred Astaire recorded "Wonderful Baby," inviting McLean to London to hang during the session.

Sometimes Joel Dorn is too hip for the room. When he refers to "the Birds," he means the Dixie Hummingbirds of gospel legend—not "the Byrds." "The Swans" are short for Swan Silvertones, the most sublime spiritual group of their era. Their 1959 gospel standard "Oh, Mary, Don't You Weep" with the Rev. Claude Jeter's improvised line "I'll be a bridge over deep water" supposedly inspired Paul Simon's "Bridge over Troubled Water." Dorn produced a cover of "Bridge" for Roberta Flack, with the Newark Boys Choir and Cissy Houston behind her.

"At the very end Roberta holds a note while the choir sings over it," remembers Dorn. "At that time Claude Jeter was recording for

Scepter, a pop label with Dionne Warwick, B. J. Thomas. I wanted Claude Jeter at the end of the record, in his falsetto, to shout that line, "I'll be your bridge over troubled water!"

"Would have been a nice touch," I say.

"No shit," comes Dorn. "I wanted to document just *one line* at the end. So I called the guy who was producing Jeter's records. We were making a lot of money then—I wanted him bad. I told this gospel producer at Scepter, 'Listen, I'm a record producer, I'm producing Roberta Flack, we just recorded "Bridge over Troubled Water."' First, he didn't believe I produced Roberta Flack. I said, 'You want my number? Call Atlantic Records.' So he did; then he asked, 'Well, how much will you pay?' I said I'd give him a thousand bucks just for that one line, a lot of money in those days. Union scale was only fifty to a hundred dollars. And the guy said, 'Just a minute, what do you think I was born yesterday? Nobody's gonna pay that much.' I said, 'Tell me where you are and I'll walk the thousand over now.' He said, 'No, I don't think so. This is some kind of trick.' So I couldn't get Jeter. For fifty bucks, I probably would have gotten him."

Dorn, who loved pairing old showbiz legends with current artists (Frances Faye with Peter Allen, Mac and Kate), had a similar experience on Leon Redbone's debut.

"Lemme tell you who the ultimate American singer of all time is. You couldn't guess in ten fuckin' years. Harry Mills. The *easiest* singer I ever heard. He could never sing poorly. The 1930s stuff is breathtaking. I tried to get the Mills Brothers during the Leon Redbone album."

"Would have been a perfect match," I say.

"No shit," snaps Dorn. "There were three of them left—Harry was alive. So I tracked them down to Boston. Can't get through to them, but I got their guy. Slick white guy. Can't get past him. Told him I'm Joel Dorn, recording Leon Redbone, blah, blah, I'll give 'em two grand, whatever they want. Guy just laughed. I said I'd fly 'em in. They don't want to fly. I said I'd come up to Boston, rent a studio, it'd be simple. This guy Redbone's real hot right now, it could reactivate their catalog, focus attention on them. The guy said, 'Listen. They've worked with Al Jolson, Louis Armstrong, Bing Crosby, Frank Sinatra, Ella Fitzgerald.

They don't need to work with Leon Redbone, okay. They're tired.' And ya know, he was right. What the fuck did the Mills Brothers need with Leon Redbone to cap off their career?"

Dorn began at Atlantic Records at the height of its powers. Mom-and-pop by corporate terms, Atlantic nonetheless was home to Ray Charles, Big Joe Turner, Bobby Darrin, the Coasters, the Drifters, Otis Redding, Aretha Franklin, John Coltrane, the Allman Brothers, Cream, and Led Zeppelin. Atlantic was sold in 1967 to the Kinney (Parking Lot) Corporation for what turned out to be a massively under-priced amount—$17.5 million. (Kinney then turned over to Warner Bros.–Seven Arts, then Warner Communications, then Time-Warner, ad nauseam). Nevertheless, the heavy hitters—Jerry Wexler and the Ertegun Brothers—remained at the helm.

"I had complete freedom from Nesuhi Ertegun to do whatever I wanted," says Dorn. "As I started to get more successful, then I wasn't just Nesuhi's boy at the company. Because I had hits, they felt com-pelled to come in and help. I had developed somewhat into a spoiled brat. When I lost Nesuhi's protection, I had to interact with other peo-ple at the company. So I left Atlantic."

Dorn continued playing out a fifteen-year run in the fast lane. "Then things went bad for me for several reasons," he says. The hits ended as his records grew more stylized and esoteric.

"There is an old record business and a new record business," Dorn explains of the fundamental change. "The old record business was run by a combination of insane, fanatical music fans who had to make their own records. Guys with exquisite taste who specialized in a certain kind of jazz or folk or pop. Hustlers, tough guys, gangsters. If you had any credibility, you could walk into someone's office and say, 'Listen, I got a girl who can sing.' Then in the mid-'70s those guys started selling their companies off or dying. The record business became a real *business*. It had been this magnificent cottage industry from its inception—all of a sudden, music became a part of *everybody's* business. Now there were lawyers walking around in fuckin' Nehru suits listening to the Grateful Dead, with Trans America, Warner–Seven Arts, Gulf & Western buying up all these properties. Instead of buying a copper factory or a steel mill, they'd buy a record company and run it the same way."

Dorn's last stand came when Doc Pomus hipped him to the Nevilles. He went nuts after seeing them at the Bottom Line. "The same bell rang, I ran backstage. It took a long time, but I finally got them signed to A&M. Nobody wanted them. Three of the four brothers had done time, so they had a reputation as tough guys. We recorded *Fiyo on the Bayou.* I thought it was the best record I ever made. A&M hated it, didn't do a thing. Some idiot there said, 'You can't get on black radio with this.' I said, 'It ain't a black act.' He said, 'What are you talking about, everybody in the band is black.' I said, 'Yeah, but they play clubs with white college kids.' I said, 'Take a look at Leontyne Price and Jimi Hendrix, my man.'"

That was it, Dorn burned out, he couldn't do it his way anymore. He quit.

When Dorn tried to return to the industry a decade later, he couldn't get phone calls returned. He was humbled by record executives who didn't know his name. Dorn had four growing boys who he says were rich kids for a while—then they weren't. So, he "did shit. I'll tell you what I want to tell you. I did some security work for a while. Nothing illegal."

Then came the arrival of CD technology. Everything old was new again. The vast archive of two-inch Ampex tapes Dorn had stored in a New York apartment suddenly yielded gold. He went to the cutting edge of the reissue biz, supervising jazz compilations for Rhino and Sony. Repackaging became his stock in trade.

"All of a sudden they needed guys for box sets," says Dorn. "You could get a chimpanzee to say John Coltrane recorded the following six albums and here they are in a box. But we started coming up with unreleased material, pictures you'd never seen, alternate takes, lost sessions, and live stuff never heard. Documentaries."

Coltrane had been dead for years, the Atlantic Jazz vaults sucked dry of his every note. But the story wasn't over: "I'm floatin' around this pigsty warehouse in New Jersey," says Dorn, "and there's water dripping down from the roof onto some tapes in the back. I figured if there's gonna be something valuable, it's gonna be in the wrong place. I'm sure Debbie Gibson's tapes were encased in lead. So I ask the custodial guy, 'Hey, what's over there under the water,' and he goes, 'Ah, that's just some slop, shit.' I said, 'Good, I'll go over there.' Water was dropping onto the shelves, and I walk over to it and it's all Coltrane. Boxes of outtakes of *Giant Steps*, with studio conversations. We could actually trace all the developments of *Giant Steps*. There's a reason most unreleased stuff is unreleased—cause it stunk. But I found shit that was incredible. Not just alternate takes. Breakdowns of the stuff, Trane talkin' to all the musicians. It was released as a ninety-nine-dollar set; we sold 100,000. We made it into something, there was a whole story. While I'm in the warehouse, I'm at *C*, near *Coltrane*. So I wondered, 'What's at *D*?' The first tape I pick up is Bobby Darrin, a demo of 'Dream Lover' recorded at a Seattle radio station. I gave that to Rhino for their Darrin compilation."

Label M's contributions to society also involve repackaging jazz balladeers in their twilight—like Etta Jones and Little Jimmy Scott. Female jazz vocalists patterned their styles after Scott in the '50s. But his best records were continually withdrawn from release by court order. Savoy Records, run by a tyrant, tyrannized Little Jimmy Scott's career. Dorn produced a Scott album for Atlantic in 1969, also pulled from the stores—but just repackaged on Label M. In the new liner notes, Dorn writes: ". . . Through most of the fifties, Jimmy Scott was under contract to Savoy Records, a label owned and operated by one Herman Lubinsky, a hemorrhoid of a human and close personal friend of The Devil, whom even the worst record business golems of the era shunned. . . . For decades, Jimmy Scott waited in the wings for his ship to come in while singers who couldn't carry his throat spray took their turns in the spotlight."

Scott was "rediscovered" at Doc Pomus's funeral in 1991, when he brought down the house during his turn to sing. Jerry Wexler attended Jimmy Scott's record release party. But Little Jimmy had long since lost his fastball.

"All these young Hollywood record execs were suddenly singing his praises," says Wex. "I felt like having cards printed: 'It's not necessary to be hip.'"

Dorn continues to strike a few blows for the old record biz. And occasionally, as in the case of Jane Monheit, score in the new business.

"What I do for a living, my man, is spot talent," says the Masked Announcer, kicking his feet up on his desk, manicured hands folded in his lap. "I pick out a good butcher, a good tailor. That's my gift."

—2002

Note: *Joel Dorn died unexpectedly in December 2007.*

Big Mac: New Orleans's top funksterator, tricknologist, and mu-jician, Dr. John.

(Henry Diltz)

CHAPTER 6

Dr. John
King Creole

With each passing year, it becomes more evident that Mac Rebennack, aka Dr. John, is America's premier roots musician. This is not negotiable. He is the national treasure trove of New Orleans music history. An artist whose physical constitution is so strong, he appears, at fifty-nine, indestructible. Misunderstood? That too, but so are all great artists. The gris-gris Night Tripper act of the Woodstock era was no act. Dr. John is a true-blue *holy man* of music, and the Mardi Gras outfits were mistaken for psychedelia. "We presented a show that was a New Orleans traditional thing," says Mac. "That added to some confusement. And you're so far removed from what you do on a gig to what is reality. People adds mystique in their head. But I'm just some regulation kind of guy."

The Dr. John namesake was an admired, though much-feared, nineteenth-century New Orleans hoodoo conjurer. And these folks were no joke. A lot of modern medicine is based upon the once-dubious root and herbal cures of witchcraft and voodoo. Thus, the cover of Dr. John's album at this moment in 2001, *Creole Moon*, is a painting of the original Dr. John of the 1850s. For a song concerning one local witch doctor, his liner notes proclaim she's there "to cure your sorry ass from all that ails you. She knows about herbs, costs less than a croaker, and is sorta like your local HMO without all the forms to fill out."

Four of the tracks were cowritten with Doc Pomus, who partnered up with Mac for almost fifteen years. Their collaboration yielded some four hundred songs, many of which lie in a trunk, yet to see the light of day. Mac is demoing them up. Some consider the finest Pomus/Rebennack composition to be "There Must Be a Better World Somewhere." A blues standard now, the 1981 record copped a Best Blues Record Grammy for B. B. King. It was based upon an old hymn, "This Earth Ain't No Place I'm Proud to Call Home."

Dr. John puts his own embellishments upon the Queen's English every time he opens his jaw. On page two of *Under a Hoodoo Moon*, he describes his 1994 autobiography as "a testament to New Orleans funk—to funksterators, tricknologists, mu-jicians, who got music burning in their brains and no holes in their souls. . . . You can't shut the fonk up. No, the fonk got a mind of its own."

He also speaks in "gumbo-izms"—*vines* are clothing, *squares* are cigarettes, *screens* are sunglasses, and *legalizers* are lawyers. However, when Jerry Leiber first heard that N'awlins-Brooklyn accent, he thought Mac was Jewish and that his father was a tailor.

During the making of *Gumbo*, Dr. John's 1972 classic, Atlantic producer Jerry Wexler couldn't get the drummer to play a proper second line. "This was Mac's favorite second-line drummer, Freddie Staehle, and he was rollin' around on Mac's favorite number," recalls Wex today. "I just wanted a backbeat on the two and four. So I went out on the drum kit to demonstrate."

Mac walked up to Wex and said: "I don't know what wrong wid the motherfucker. The motherfucker used to be some kind of all right, but since he join Scientology, he won't play right no how."

Even more to the point, Wexler remembers a moment at Duane Allman's funeral: "We gave some cub reporter from *Rolling Stone* a lift on the [Atlantic Records] company plane. We're all standing around in

Phil Walden's backyard, and the kid explains to me and Ahmet, 'Look, Mac has his own talk, you see. You have to learn to *understand* Mac talk.' So Mac walks up to him and says, 'Man, can you lay a square on me, I wanna cocktail my doobie.' The reporter stood there apoplectic."

Hoodoo Moon was written with Jack Rummel at a time when Dr. John was under duress. He never read the finished book: "I went into rehab, came out, the IRS reneged on a deal with me, I couldn't make damn payroll. The only way I could make my nut was come up with this book. Three doctors put me on lithium. While I'm writing this book, and for about a year after that, I'm suffering from lithium poisoning. Three doctors, and each one thinks the other one is monitoring my dosage. I coulda sued all three. I had rehab-itis in the brain."

Under a Hoodoo Moon should probably be taught in college music curriculums. It would scare some kids away from a music career, thus saving them a lifetime of pain and paying dues. Its also bears witness to New Orleans' "tragic magic" dope scene of Mac's youth. Back when he ran a bullshit pimping operation, boosted from stores, and got the shit kicked out of him by cops. He did hard time in Lexington and Angola. At one off-the-charts gig, he worked for an abortionist, dumping fetuses (wrapped up, natch) into the Seventeenth Street drainage canal. Years of nightmares followed, in which he saw babies floating to the surface. During his stretch in Fort Worth—in which he missed the original British invasion—he volunteered for jailhouse medical experiments. There he saw one of his jailhouse partners stone dead on a morgue table, his body still trembling like a leaf. All part of a musical education.

The book, whether fact or fiction, is a powerful memoir of one musician's journey through life, so I recommend his own book to the Doctor. He says maybe he'll check it out someday. He only has a Japanese edition.

When he was twenty-two, Dr. John remembers hearing the Beatles when the 1963 Vee-Jay disc was released in advance of their huge Capitol Records debut: "I tell you what, I was in New Orleans when Wayne Shuller [Vee-Jay Records] walked into Joe Assunto's One-Stop Record Shop on South Rampart Street in New Orleans. Me and Earl King and some guys was hanging out. He put this record on the turntable and said, 'This is gonna be the next number one record in the United States.' Me and Senator Jones, Whirley Burley, Earl King, started *rolling* on the floor. We said, 'Nobody dances to nuttin' like dis, whataya crazy?' That was my first impression. The groove, everything about it sounded outdated to us. . . . But then, he was right."

On the Stones, Mac says, "It didn't connect early on, 'cause they were coverin' a lot of songs of friends of mine that was goin' down the terlit behind it. Like Benny Spellman's 'Fortune Teller,' that went down the drain with the Stones cover. Bobby Womack's record "It's All Over Now' went down the terlit with the Stones cover, on and on."

Mac revised his opinions, having played with various Beatles and Stones over the years. "Those weren't my first miscalls. I thought Elvis Presley'd never make it either. I got a track record of callin' 'em bad."

It's easy to see how a musical repository like Dr. John might hear things differently than the rest of the world. In the 1950s, while still in high school, Mac Rebennack hustled his own tunes to the New Orleans office of Specialty Records, and had some recorded by Little Richard, and Art Neville's group, the Hawkettes. He doesn't particularly remember which songs, or what they may have been retitled. It just represented pocket money, and thirty or forty bucks per song wasn't bad for a high school kid. He played in a local group called the Spades. They once did a talent show at Jesuit High, when the band was loaded, and their R&B material enraged the priests. His next band was a "loose tribe of musicians" that changed its name weekly, but was mainly known as the Night Trains. They adapted their style for any occasion. Juke joints, tourist dives, roadhouse grocery and hardware stores. At strip joints, the girls danced with customers between sets. The Night Trains provided a groove for every dry hump or belly rub.

At Cosimo Matassa's legendary R&B studio in New Orleans in the 1950s, young Mac Rebennack began to get hired as a session guitarist—before taking a bullet in the hand, ending his guitar career: "All of my guitar teachers had different influences that affect my piano playing. When Papoose [Fats Domino's guitarist] early on sent me to sub on some sessions with Paul Gayten, he said, 'Watch the piano guy's left hand, and the chords he's playin' so you don't mess up on the date and make me look bad.' Well, I got in the habit of sittin' right next to the piano player at Cosimo's studio for years on all the dates. I got to watch all of them piano players, whoever was on the session. I wound up playin' with wrong fingerings, but that's the way it was."

Mac's switch to piano was one of the better things to ever happen to piano. Dr. John has the mightiest left-hand rhythm I've ever heard: "In New Orleans in the '50s," he recalls, "until electric basses came in, a lot of bands didn't use a bass 'cause you couldn't hear a standup—the piano player played the bass with his left hand. We'd rather put a baritone sax or horn in there—adding a bass was dead weight. Until electric bass came in."

Dr. John may be too hip for the room, but he makes his case on piano perfectly. In twenty albums under his own name, he personifies all the great New Orleans pianists mixed to perfection, and then some.

"Alla what I do," says Dr. John, "is some mish-mosh of Longhair, Huey Smith, Allen Toussaint, Art Neville, Tuts Washington, Charles Brown, Lloyd Glenn, Ray Charles, James Booker. My shit is a huge mixture of alla that. But Booker's separate, because those other guys were strictly piano. But Booker, when he was with me, was a *killer* organ player and arranger with the band."

Among hundreds of too-good-to-be-real hustlers in the Crescent City musical underworld, the late James Booker was probably the most eccentric, if not respected, of all New Orleans piano men. His style seemed to defy classification, an enviable trait mainly to musicians.

Once, Jerry Leiber obtained the services of James Booker to give his then nine-year-old son Jed some piano lessons. Booker arrived at Jerry's front door straight from the hospital. He had a patch over his newly lost eye.

"Hey, man, what happened to you?" asked Jerry.

He put out his hand and presented himself: "James Carol Booker the Third . . . one eye later."

Considering his rep as a nut job–junkie-faggot, Booker inquired, "You trust me with Jed sittin' in my lap?" Jerry did. He had Jed lay his hands over Booker's hands on the piano while Booker played "Good Night Irene." He remembers seeing his son light up while getting a unique ride on top of New Orleans stride. Jed's hands danced over the keys on top of Booker's long skinny fingers, feeling the rhythm and the groove like no one else ever did.

One masterpiece of radiatin' the 88s is *Dr. John Plays Mac Rebennack*, a 1981 collection of instrumentals on Clean Cuts. Then there's "Fess Up," the Professor Longhair tribute off 1992's *Goin' Back to New Orleans*. A pianistic mindblower, "Fess Up" is the meanest, cleanest gumbo of New Orleans barrelhouse and boogie-woogie one could ever imagine. The jazziest piano Dr. John ever recorded—another side of the coin—is best demonstrated on the track "Bye-Ya," from producer Hal Willner's 1984 Thelonious Monk tribute album, *That's the Way I Feel Now.*

"Hal [Willner] says he's got thirty takes of me doin' that song in different bags. Me, Ed Blackwell, Steve Swallow, and Steve Slagle. When my father sold records in New Orleans when I was a kid, I always thought 'Bye-Ya' was done by a New Orleans band, with Art Blakey's drumming." He hadn't known it was a Monk tune, and followed advice of one of the elder jazz players on the date: "He said we oughta cut this the way the Indians woulda did it. I'd like to recut that song and do a tribute to Monk one day, a completely other take on anything Monk did."

Dr. John just about hit the high point of his career with the concept albums *In a Sentimental Mood* and *Goin' Back to New Orleans*, in the '90s. He also produced *Dreams Come True* for the Antone's label in Austin. An instant classic in Texas, the album was a natural union of Austin's three blues divas, Angela Strehli, Marcia Ball, and the great Lou Ann Barton. It took years: "I liked them girls," says Mac. "Listen, you throw that many bitches together, you're gonna have some ups and downs. Almost slapped Lou Ann's ass a couple times, she come off to me with some smart-aleck shit. Fathead had to call me down after I said, 'I'm gonna take this motherfucker out in the hall and kick her ass in a minute.'"

Dr. John's first release in the twenty-first century, previous to *Creole Moon*, was *Duke Elegant*, a funky tribute to Ellington. Some of the melodies are scaled down to mere blues progressions, quite unlike his

Monk interpretations. You imagine the composer wondering, 'Where's my song at in there?' His current backup band, on both albums, is called the Lower 9-11—a seemingly cryptic reference to Lower Manhattan on September 11—but the name was in place long before.

Dr. John, uniquely American himself, recorded a single with that 1940s symbol of over-the-top patriotism, Kate Smith. The old chestnut "Smile, Smile, Smile."

"I remember meetin' Kate and her bodyguard," says Dr. John. "I'm thinkin', 'This three-hundred-pound bitch needs a fuckin' bodyguard?' They should bring Kate Smith back right now, let her sing 'God Bless America' in her own inimitable style. That was her shit, man. She was ahead of the times."

—2001

The Sage of Tippo: Long Island's most prominent son of Mississippi, Mose Allison.

(Bill Phelps)

CHAPTER 7

Mose Allison
Allison Wonderland

Mose John Allison, Jr.
That's the way it's written in the book
Don't call me Moss, don't call me Moose
It's not some made up show biz hook

You can call me Mosé
But only if you come from down Mexico way

I approached Mose Allison after a 1997 show at Poor David's in Dallas. Some mook from the audience cut ahead, tugged Allison's shirt, and patted him on the back with deadpan sincerity: "Hey, you got an interesting way with lyrics. Very original."

I cringed on the spot, but Mose cordially nodded his head, though his eyes stared out a million miles away. (Imagine tugging Sinatra's raincoat to tell him he had an interesting way with phrasing.) Next, I made the mistake of asking Mose if he had any CDs for sale. Allison looked at me like I was nuts. Humiliation is part of the game, Mose has said, something that motivates him to endure. An artist selling his own records from the stage was once beneath dignity, and Mose is of that old school. Only during the past decade has it become de rigueur. Musicians rely on the extra bread, and their fans enjoy the satisfaction of handing cash directly to the source, skipping all the middle men.

Although Mose Allison won't sell his own CDs any more than Sinatra would have, he did something more unusual that night. According to Poor David's bartender-manager Jim Hicks, Mose returned part of his advance—even though the box office passed Allison's guarantee.

"It was the first time in twelve years I ever had an act return money," said Hicks, who was stunned. The great American sage of blues-jazz, Mose Allison, felt he should have had a larger crowd. Well, so does everybody.

Since he first recorded in the '50s, each decade of Mose Allison's twenty-five-album career gets better. There is no reason he shouldn't be ranked alongside Johnny Mercer, Hoagy Carmichael, Thelonious Monk, or Willie Dixon. As a matter of fact, he is. His sense of irony and rhyme is unique and remains sharp as a razor at age seventy. His last four CDs, on Blue Note Jazz, are good enough to make you wanna slap your mama (*My Backyard*, in particular). Among his standards: "Your Mind Is on Vacation (But Your Mouth Is Workin' Overtime)," "Parchman Farm," "I Don't Worry About a Thing," "Young Man Blues," featured on the Who's *Live at Leeds*, and "Everybody Cryin' Mercy," recently covered by Elvis Costello and Bonnie Raitt.

Judging from these songs, one assumes Mose Allison might be Mississippi's hardest-livin' streetwise hipster. But don't assume anything. "I could answer almost any question you wanna ask me by quoting one of my lyrics," he claims, huddled upon the couch in his Smithtown, Long Island, study. Allison does all business from the desk phone in this study. Like Chuck Berry, another stoic independent, he books his own tours. His energy goes into the music—not into being charming, not into being recognized, not into hanging out or late nights on the wrong side of town. He is a loner. Amazingly, there is no acoustic piano in the house, no practice room anywhere. The study looks like the lair of an Ivy League professor emeritus. The shelves are lined with hardcover American lit and science volumes. Peterson's *Field Guide to the Birds* sits on the table. There are no music books or LPs.

The science boils down into song, such as "Your Molecular Structure," or "Hello There, Universe." Allison sifts through weighty titles piled on the table, stopping at *Equations of Eternity: Speculations on Consciousness, Meaning, and the Mathematical Rules that Orchestrate the Cosmos.* "That one is really far out."

Mose Allison is not a loud man. He is accomplished at being a noncelebrity. "For the first twenty years, nobody here had any idea what I did," says Allison, who moved to Smithtown with his wife, Audre, now a retired eleventh-grade English teacher, in 1963. "But I like it that way. I hardly ever get recognized around here in the grocery stores. Don't mind that at all."

It wasn't until Allison's appearance on a PBS program, opening for Bonnie Raitt at Wolftrap, that neighbors recognized him. Even Long Island's esteemed paper, *Newsday*, was always negligent and never wrote him up until the 1990s. Allison's bravado manifests only in his songs, not his personality. He is not the first great American artist whose work is more literary than literal. Yet no one can presume to guess what insanity he witnesses along the road. Allison's secrets are private; only his songs are public.

In a recent composition, "This Ain't Me," Allison, a fit seventy, who jogs two miles and bicycles, sings of pictures on his wall: "That's me on the high school team, just another second-stringer, lost in the dream. Th' gray haired geezer that you think you see, this ain't me, this ain't me." In another, "Dr. Jekyll & Mr. Hyde," he asks, "Do I worry about the ozone layer, about terrestrial suicide? Or do I love my new hair sprayer? Dr. Jekyll & Mr. Hyde."

Allison's most prolific years were from 1961 to 1976 on Atlantic Records, under the late jazz chief Nesuhi Ertegun. Mose declined Atlantic superproducer Jerry Wexler's offers to make a pop record— not so much as one. Hypothetically, what would have been so bad about going down to Muscle Shoals just once, during his fifteen years with Atlantic, to let the great Wexler demonstrate his magic touch as producer?

"There are two things," Allison explains, with almost too much logic. "If it was a hit record, then I'd have to do that again. If it had become a hit record and made money, the only thing they'd want from me would be another. On the other hand, if it had flopped, that would have been bad. It would take me a long time to recover and get people back listening to what I do."

Former Atlantic records producer Joel Dorn, who produced several 1960s Mose Allison albums, describes him as "the most interesting abstraction of the blues I've ever heard. The blues is a language where most people speak the same dialect. But he has another way of sayin' the same things. The Delta meets the Village. He was a fixture in Greenwich Village when people who were diggin' anything hip were diggin' Mose."

Allison's Prestige album covers of the 1950s depicted rural scenes. One had an old weathered door on the cover. His second album, *Local Color*, pictured a Southern landscape, though the picture was actually taken on Staten Island. But there were no photos of Mose on the albums. "They didn't want to let the news out," says Mose, that he was white.

When Dorn first saw Mose live, around 1960 in Washington, D.C., "this fuckin' English teacher walked out. The difference between who he is and who you *think* he is gigantic. The first thing with Mose is everybody thinks he's black. When they find out he's white, it's the same thing as Charlie Pride, he's like the reverse. But he's a *regular guy* who comes up with this world-class introspection. A master of instant, dispassionate irony."

If Allison is hard to categorize—what bin is he in?—between jazz and blues, there were even some who classified him as a "folk artist." Phil Elwood, with the *San Francisco Examiner*, described Allison's piano style as "chromatic funk." On *Retrospective*, an early '70s Columbia LP, Morgan Ames's liner notes follow: "To Mose Allison's dentist (presuming he has one), he might be Cavity in Lower Right Molar. To his laundry man, Mose might be No Starch. . . ." But to his booking agent "Mose Allison is a man with a reputation for showing up on time for the gig, for paying his union dues, his agent's fees, and his sidemen. . . . He arrives with two neatly copied books of his arrangements, one for the bass player and one for the drummer."

"Nobody's been able to characterize me in a capsule comment," says Allison of this enigma. "Any one thing you say is gonna be wrong. You say I'm a blues person, that's wrong. Because I'm not strictly blues, I'm influenced by the blues and learned from the blues players. You say I'm a jazz man, you're gonna miss a great portion of what I do."

Who's in, who's out, who's gonna tell us what it's all about
Who's hot, who's cold, who's turning garbage into gold
Let's all get excited about th' party to which we're uninvited

This inability to fit neatly into a narrow marketing niche wreaks hell on careers. It's a corporate world of industrial music merchandising. If you're innovative or an original in the 1990s, forget about it, brother, move to France.

"I guess you gotta find somebody who has some power who's determined that you get across," says Mose, one of the last holdouts of major labels maintaining a "prestige artist" on their roster. "My daughter's havin' that same problem, just because she's got an original sound." Amy Allison, his second daughter, released a country album, *The Maudlin Years*, and now has her own group, the Maudlins.

If it weren't for the fact that Allison's albums are recorded like traditional jazz—that is, quickly made affairs, live the in studio with a small group—he might not have such a prolific discography. Even in the 1950s, his first deal with Prestige was for six albums in two years, for which he was paid only $250 per. But taking care of business quickly in the studio suits Allison.

"Records are just shadows," he believes. "They're how you felt that day, when material was new. Albums should take no longer than two days."

He is prouder of his live shows than any of his albums. "To me the whole thing is in performing. You have a chance to warm up, get a continuity and spirit going that you seldom get in a studio. Albums represent how you were able to put that material across *that day*. They [record companies] want new material, so a lot of it you haven't played much. After a year, you might be doin' it completely different. You gotta come to the club to really hear what I'm doing."

Record companies have rarely let Allison release instrumentals either, just songs, which is why live shows remain so crucial. Chromatic funk aside, each song contains a mandatory piano solo, which comes from the jazz side of Mose Allison.

"My dad played stride piano, a ragtime sort of thing, Scott Joplin–inspired, Fats Waller. He was semiprofessional, he played some jobs with a band when he was young. My dad taught himself to play by watchin' a player piano. I started taking music lessons when I was five, but once I realized I could pick things out by ear, I refused to learn to read music. I'm not a good reader now," he reveals.

> *I been so far*
> *I must be back*
> *Airline highway railroad track*
> *Won't you tell me where we are*
> *I been so far*

Mose John Allison Jr. was born on the edge of the Delta, fifteen miles from the hills in Tippo. He attended high school in Charleston, Mississippi. Mose's dad was a merchant and planter who became a store owner. "I came from a stable family background," insists Mose, and you tend to believe him. Allison's brother still has farmland in Tippo.

Renowned as the spawning ground of blues guitar, the Delta produced but a handful of renowned barrelhouse pianists: Sunnyland Slim, Pinetop Perkins, Memphis Slim, and Roosevelt Sykes, the latter two from Helena, Arkansas. Though Clarksdale, Mississippi–born Ike Turner was primarily a guitarist, his importance can't be underestimated on piano (among his many piano achievements was "Rocket 88" in 1951, considered the first rock 'n' roll record). Mose doesn't recall seeing any of the aforementioned live during his youth, or any famous guitarists for that matter. Just local guitar players around Tippo whose names he can't recall.

Allison worked weekends at his dad's general store, across the street from the gas station. The Tippo Service Station was the town hangout, and actually featured a country-blues nickelodeon. "I used to go over there three or four times a day. They sold beer. It was sorta integrated; there was an area up front where the white guys shot craps. Then there was a back room where the black guys shot craps. But anybody could go in and listen to the records."

It was at this gas station in the 1930s where Mose heard 78s by Tampa Red, Big Bill Broonzy, Memphis Minnie, and Roosevelt Sykes. A bit later he became entranced with the Buddy Johnson Band, which had great vocalists, including Allison's favorite, Arthur Prysock. "I came up in a Southern blues thing, with a Southern pace. The big band that exemplified that pace was Buddy Johnson, out of South Carolina. Very talented guy, wrote songs, played piano, and his big band was the epitome of that slow-drag, laid-back Southern style of playin'. It started with Louis Armstrong, you know."

Blues balladeer Percy Mayfield was another unique influence. Mayfield's band had four saxophones, for whom he wrote a lot of thirty-two-bar blues, a stylish departure from standard Mississippi stuff. Allison recorded three Mayfield songs, which he still performs—"Life Is Suicide," "Stranger in My Own Hometown," and "Lost Mind." Allison tried unsuccessfully to get into a Percy Mayfield show at a black club in Jackson, Mississippi. But whites weren't allowed.

Like Doc Pomus, Mose Allison was one of a handful of white blues singers in the early '50s. They couldn't play the chitlin circuit. The reverse term *Crow Jim* would have applied. In the South, whites *legally* couldn't attend black clubs—except on the sly. Black friends would sneak Mose into the Blue Moon R&B club in Baton Rouge, where he sat in. Mose was tight with Bill Harvey, B. B. King's first musical director, who'd sneak him into the horn section, where Mose played trumpet. B. B.'s first bass player, Sheeny Walker, had Mose over to his house for jam sessions, and snuck him into other gigs on Beale Street in Memphis, like the Mitchell Hotel. The R&B bands on Beale Street rarely used horn charts or written arrangements—everything was done by ear.

Allison remembers no ill will directed his way at Negro establishments. He was a musician, he came in connected. Only whites gave him a hard time. Once, a couple of detectives in Chicago ran him out of a black club, warning he'd get his throat cut in there.

Mose and Audre Allison moved to Dallas for a few months in the early '50s, to be near a good friend, drummer Bill Patey. Audre got a job at the Adolphus Hotel. Mose played gigs in Waco and Longview, Texas; Jackson, Mississippi; and Louisiana. He never worked for Jack Ruby, but worked a strip club in Odessa. "That was like the other side of the moon. Lotta oil money. The strip club was run by the sheriff. 'Night Train,' that's all you had to know for the strippers, it was easy. I was there a couple of weeks and they had three murders locally. So the sheriff had to keep leaving the club."

Allison took eight years to get through college, beginning at Ole Miss, with an eighteen-month interruption for the army at the end of World War II. He played trumpet with the 179th Army Ground Forces Band, here in the states. Finishing with an English major at LSU, Mose wrote a few short stories in college. He recalls a literary magazine's rejection letter from the late 1940s. It said his story showed promise but didn't *flow*. "It was a bunch of vignettes about Tippo, Mississippi. It wasn't supposed to *flow*." This single rejection stopped him in his tracks and he never tried his hand at fiction again.

Allison first came to New York in 1951, the only destination for an aspiring jazz player. "I played with Brew Moore, a real good tenor player from Mississippi, one of my favorites of all time. He knew everybody in New York. There were lofts where you'd go around for jam sessions. Hardly anybody was working during the summer of '51. All these people I'd been readin' about were standing around scufflin'. Miles Davis was workin' only an occasional Monday night at Birdland. Gerry Mulligan was workin' only an occasional night out in Queens."

Allison's point man in New York was jazz player Al Cohn, who set him up in Manhattan. "When I came back to live there in '56, it perked up a lot. I'd met Al's wife, a singer named Marilyn Moore, while playing down in Galveston. She sat in, liked what I did, and said if I ever came to New York to call, and gave me Al's number. Al picked me right up, had me and my wife out to dinner, and referred me to people. He was writing arrangements for everybody at the time. He and Zoot Sims started playing a lot, and Al got me my first record date. Al and Zoot swung hard, they had fans among everybody, there was no racial thing."

The 1960s were golden years when labels like Atlantic could afford to have so-called prestige artists—musicians who brought respect to the company without necessarily racking up profits. Respect alone, and all its abstract benefits, was actually worth something. This line of thinking is alien today.

In the early '60s, Atlantic might sign someone like Solomon Burke or Mose Allison within minutes of them merely walking through the office door on Columbus Circle in New York.

"I lost contact with Nesuhi in the last few years. I just walked in and he signed me to Atlantic. I said, 'Look, I just got released from Columbia. I was with Prestige, which was too little, then Columbia, which was too big. I'd like to talk to you guys.' They were a midsize independent."

Columbia released Allison after putting the squeeze on him to release more commercial stuff. Mose has resisted this pressure consistently throughout his career. "As long as I can make a living doing what I want, I'm gonna do it. I didn't get into this to make money or become famous. I did it hand-to-mouth down South for years. So when I came to New York, I was overjoyed."

> *My backyard*
> *Is a factor*
> *Where an actor of note*
> *Can take off his coat*
> *No need to pretend*

When Allison moved to Smithtown in 1963, there were thirteen acres of woods behind the backyard. A decade ago, development encroached.

"I could go for walks in those woods," he says, as we repair to the back-yard. "This is one of my favorite spots." There are four wooden chairs in a circle, each with a backward slant that somehow grounds one with the earth.

So, do you want to be buried on Long Island or in Mississippi?

"I intend to be cremated. I'm gonna leave it up to my kids to scatter my ashes. One possibility would be the farm I was born on in Mississippi. It's fallin' down, but the ruins of the old house are still there. I go down once or twice a year."

Allison retains his Delta drawl and Southern sensibility. Even after raising four children on Long Island, now in their thirties, and being married forty-eight years to Audre from St. Louis. He's one of the last blues musicians who picked cotton as a youth.

"The word *memes* just got coined a few years ago." He refers to another science book, *River Out of Eden: A Darwinian View of Life*, by Richard Dawkins. "Genes are biological, the stuff in our physical makeup from birth. *Memes* are what we pick up culturally. There are scientists who say memes are not valid. But I think you pick up stuff from the culture you're born into. The idioms, your thinking."

"The William Faulkner of Jazz," is a cheap compliment often lev-eled at Allison, simply because both men hail from Mississippi. Yet they *look* like brothers. We tour Allison's living room, where paintings from friends hang. Cowboy etchings, a painting of bulls, a portrait of Albert Schweitzer. A painting of Mose by an El Paso artist depicts him with no eyes, looking look a blind man who sees everything.

With each shingle in place on this house, it is a monument to stabil-ity. In the garage, every single garden tool, including Mose Allison's lawn mower, is perfectly hung in its place on the wall. Can this really be the res-idence of the Sage of Tippo? Or a staged setup at some straight friend's place? It's like discovering Miles Davis in Scarsdale, a PTA member in good standing with a golf club membership.

Allison swims, but only "when the wind is southerly, one hour past high tide—that's the best swimming in the Long Island Sound." His jogging regimen is down to two miles now that he's seventy. He recently debuted a John D. Loudermilk number, "You Call It Joggin', I Call It Runnin' Around."

Mose does several songs by Loudermilk, the wandering songwriter responsible for classics like "Tobacco Road" and "Windy and Warm."

"I think he's written five hundred songs. He's got a trunk full of them, a lot unrecorded. A friend told me that line, 'You call it joggin', I call it runnin' around.' I said, 'Man, I gotta have that.' I wish I'd written that myself. I played at the Bluebird Cafe in Nashville, and he came in one night. He's one of these guys that knows *all* the songwriters, Johnny Mercer and people like that. I hear he spends his time just traveling, doesn't have a home."

Allison himself averages 130 road dates a year. "That's comfortable, that's enough." In the 1970s he was doing two hundred nights a year. "A lot of one-nighters, and that takes it out of you. I try to limit the one-nighters now and try to get as many weekend or three-night clubs. I just came from a place called Jazz Alley in Seattle. That's one of the few places outside of New York or London that has a six-nighter. I work there once a year. I'll be doing sixteen out of eighteen days in London."

Being a musician's musician, Allison has always relied on other musicians to spread the gospel. "They've helped me to survive. The rock 'n' rollers who've done my stuff over the years have brought in new audiences."

He claims to have never heard of the Cactus or Johnny Winter versions of "Parchman Farm," perhaps his most covered song. The Who did "Young Man Blues" on 1970's *Live at Leeds*, something you imagine made Mose Allison hold his ears in horror—yet it was impossible not to appreciate the recognition and the initial seven-thousand-dollar royalty check. Edgar Winter's debut album from 1971, *Entrance*, had uncanny Mose Allison–like vocals.

"People are always tellin' me, 'You know, so and so did such and such.' I'm the last person to find out about it. I always say, 'Man, I don't care what you do with my material just as long as you give me credit.' As long as the business is taken care of, which isn't always done. I've missed out on a lot of money, man, by not gettin' credit. The Kingston Trio, who was sellin' millions of records, did 'Parchman Farm' and claimed it was public domain. Then the Clash did one of my tunes, 'Look Here,' and they put my name on it. But some company in London claimed publishing rights, so I ended up with a small fraction of what I was supposed to get."

> How does it feel to be
> Born wealthy
> All you gotta worry 'bout
> Is staying healthy
> When you're born wealthy

Another factor making this musician's career long and stable is being married to a high school English teacher. "Mose was very steady, responsible, reliable, that way with the children at home," says Audre. "If I call him on the road, I know exactly where he'll be at what time. Now he's eating breakfast, now he's exercising, now he's taking a nap. That keeps you sane, right?" she asks her husband.

Allison has also written his share of don't-tread-on-me songs, like "Your Mind Is on Vacation," and more recently "You Can't Push People Around," and "Somebody Gonna Have to Move." So who's been pushing this man around, who seemingly has a charmed life?

"It's temperament," says Allison. "When I was younger I considered myself an example of what might be called *the resistant strain*. I resisted being told what to do. Whatever the prevailing social mores were where I was living."

He was angered by a British interviewer's question asking how he "stole the blues." Responding to the blues police, he wrote the lead-off song on *My Backyard*, "Ever Since I Stole the Blues."

"I'm not concerned with that anymore. I just do my work. I don't care if people call it blues or jazz. My whole thing is gettin' to the gig, playin' the gig, and gettin' home."

Mose recently told John Lee Hooker that it looked like he was doing the "bohog grind" on *The Tonight Show*. "He knew exactly what I was talkin' about. You have to be a country boy to visualize the bohog grind. It's the male hog sexual encounter, the way he proceeds. If you lived as close to a barnyard, as I did, the first few years of your life, you see that."

Hooker took it as a great compliment.

—2001

*Pachuco Low-Down: Texas's baddest-ever bassist, Keith Ferguson, laid
down a swinging elephant trunk of bottom.*

(Geoff Winningham)

CHAPTER 8

Keith Ferguson
The Beautiful Loser

"I have to admit, there's a guaranteed future in dirty dishes, which there ain't in blues," Keith Ferguson concedes. "I seem to be the only one who regards himself as a professional musician. Our lead singer's a dishwasher in the back of some restaurant. If he put half the energy into booking our band that he puts into scrubbin' dishes, we'd be fartin' through silk. But he'd rather do dishes."

Keith Ferguson—Austin's once-reigning blues bassist and ulti-mate hipster—is out to pasture. His pasture is a rustic wooded estate in the hills below downtown Austin. His voice is a dead ringer for that of William Holden narrating *Sunset Boulevard.* Some won-der whether Keith's fall from grace was conspiratorial, orchestrated by the blues nazis who run this town. But prison wisdom dictates that you don't fuck with an old wolf. Hear Ye Whomever Keith Has Offended: He offers no apologies or regrets.

Keith welcomes me to his front porch, the center of his uni-verse. His current band is the Solid Senders. Fronted by the singing dishwasher, they rarely work. And Keith will only play cities south of Austin—or Amsterdam. Sane drug laws, hardly any cops, crime, poverty, or AIDS, Amsterdam is a tailor-made utopia. The Solid Senders did a blissful tour there. Keith pines to return.

"If I hustled up some job washing dishes in Amsterdam—hell, I'll supply the Palmolive—we'd be back in a shot."

Ferguson, forty-nine, was founding bass player of the Fabulous Thunderbirds and the Tail Gators, and played with a dozen Texas virtuosos in their formative years, including Johnny Winter, Stevie Ray Vaughan, and Junior Brown ("He's a cracker's cracker, thinks that Waylon and them are commie fags."). Keith Ferguson keeps a band honest. When he departed the T-Birds, that band was ready to compromise, play the pop charts.

No bass player ever layered so much bottom. Ferguson's trademark wasn't licks, riffs, slapping, or thumb-popping—just a swinging elephant trunk of bottom underneath the song. This deceptive gift earned him a lower pedigree than "musician's musician"—itself a poverty-stricken but honorable curse. Keith Ferguson is a bass player's bassist.

But now, he is grand host of this dark, sun-proofed crash pad and halfway house for down-on-their-luck friends. Sweet old hippies and beautiful losers recline on his front porch to chew the fat, bird-watch, discuss the weather. Not that he wants them here—people sort of just move right in. Many who visit this front porch—be they from the dust bowl, the barrio, or the music biz—regard Keith as *numero uno*.

Inside, walls are covered by roadside artifacts: South-of-the-Border Sammy and the Fabulous Erections are sneaking across the border for One Night Only. Club posters from the Tex-Mex frontier circuit—LOS ALEGRES DE TERAN! LOS TORNADOS DEL NORTE! LOS CASTIGADORES!—Keith knew them all. His words contain sudden accents of caló—street language of the pachucos he grew up with, a sort of Mexican Yiddish.

A few years back, the house became knee-deep in such hipster compost, burying him alive in coolness. Live-in archivist Liz Henry led a mercy mission of volunteers that bulldozed through. All his worldly possessions were thus organized into three archival categories: "Negro," "Mexican," and "other."

Ferguson whips out his huge vintage Gretsch bass. "It's called the John Holmes model. It's loud." He's healthy, proud, and fit in 1996, but reduced to playing the meat-rack clubs on Sixth Street. Still, some consider this miraculous. A few years ago, cats in Austin were predicting the end of this man's career, even his death.

Flashback: 1992

Ferguson paces his pastoral porch, hunched backward, scratching, chain-smoking, downing one cup of Kool-Aid after another, looking like an old Indian. His body ails, his tattoos have worn out their camouflage. A rooster claw adorns the front door, like wolfsbane. "Gotta keep the neighbors pacified." Next door lives a bookie for cockfights; a few doors down, an unlicensed bad-debt collector. A Mexican Day of the Dead skeleton stares through his window, with a sign:

La Plaza—Closed—Call Again.

The Ferguson estate is verboten, like Castle Dracula. Few musicians in Austin will have anything to do with him. I always make this road stop after my gig in town. A festive trio of German blues fans have also made a pilgrimage today. But no music plays in this household. Keith's basses are all in the hockshop. Horst, Otto, and Gretchen are starstruck before Texas blues royalty, as Keith signs a few Fab Thunderbirds albums. The left-handed '52 Fender Precision bass that Europeans remember him by is long gone. He's a normal 180 pounds on the Chrysalis Records covers he signs, compared to 130 now.

Keith soberly inspects the festering tattooed arm of a young Chicano, nodding out on his couch. "Gotta clean out that abscess," he advises, shaking the fellow. "You can die."

Old hombres, in tank-top undershirts, are always present. They slink in and out, from another zone. Retired bullfighters, he tells the tourists. The old men study a black phone. They sit and wait. And watch. Then the phone rings once. Keith disappears with them in a supernatural eyeblink. No one says good-bye, ever.

Musicians avoid the Ferguson ranch for fear of having their car commandeered for a barrio run. During one visit, it is my job to drive him to some urgent destination. Though banished from the Antone's blues community, Keith is highly received in the Mexican ghetto, like some kind of shaman. He was raised in the *Sexto*, or Sixth Ward, a barrio of Houston. The odd Anglo in a Mexican gang back in San Jacinto High, class of '64. Our ride, through dusty roads, conjures up childhood.

Summers were spent with his grandmother in San Antonio, totally gaucho. "It was great in the '50s, pre-Beatles, before everybody had bands. There were only about eight bands in the whole area. Doug Sahm & the Pharaohs, Sammy Jay & the Tifanaires, Eddie Luna. You had Mexicans, blacks, and whites in the same band, which was unheard of."

Electric guitars were rare and exotic sights until the mid-'60s. "I remember hearing Dino, Desi, and Billy do 'Scratch My Back' on *Shindig*. Good, too. I was one of two left-handed bass players in all of Houston when I started in 1966—at the age of twenty."

Few musicians start so late. In high school, he had been tight with the best mariachis in town, heavy-duty lounge acts. A member of the Compians, Texas's leading Hispanic music family, taught him to play. Ferguson turned professional mere days after first picking up a bass. He soon played in a Chicano show band, where he danced the Sideways Pony with a tambourine on his hip. He worked the Suburban Lounge, the Polka Dot, Guys & Dolls, Houston blue-collar joints frequented by characters from the Overton Gang and the Laura Coppe Gang.

"They would rob places. They dressed like Mexicans, listened to black music, and hated both of 'em."

"Where was your father?" Keith directs me off the main road through dirt alleys. "My father was a bum. I hated him with a passion. He didn't live with us; I never saw him growing up. But he would be called whenever I was deemed unmanageable. Like hangin' out with someone with a natural tan. My mother would panic. 'You've *got* to talk to him, John!'

"Once, when I was fifteen, I was supposed to get a haircut but didn't. When he arrived, I asked him to get the hell out. He pulled me out of a chair by my hair. So I cut him with a metal rattail comb, the one with the end bent into a hook. Then I tried to get to my room for something better: my big Italian, spiked, carbon-steel switchblade. He managed to knock me out before I reached my room. My mother was shaking me, blubbering all over me when I awoke.

"It was a nasty scene. I'd cut him in the throat but unfortunately missed the carotid artery. I was a little off."

Keith escaped from his bedroom window that day to gang quarters, over an icehouse. A place where Mando, Mario, Ladislado, Alfonso, and Parrot could crash, drink, smoke, inhale paint.

"The side of my face was bent out of shape when I showed up. They decided to kill him. I had to talk fast. He was my *father*, I said, he didn't really come to discipline me. Don't kill somebody for that. 'Cause they would have been caught in a second. My father was a white guy—they wouldn't have stood a chance.

"They drafted the guys with a gang history out of my school into the marines. The other option was jail. They were perfect canon fodder, cause it was the ideal chance for them to become Americans, if they fought for their country. But they came back with one leg and were still Mexicans. Most of 'em got killed in the war. Idiots."

Keith was destined for Mexico, his spiritual homeland, not Canada, to evade the draft during Vietnam. A week before his draft board physical, he tore the cartilage in his knee during a fight in Laredo. He got his deferment.

"I didn't wanna be part of blowin' up one of the most beautiful places on earth, with tigers and elephants. Then land mines and Agent Orange and CIA operatives, just garbage. Anybody in a parade comin' back from Vietnam looked like they were walkin' down the street in a Bozo suit. It was ludicrous that they would come back any way but craven in shame."

It wasn't until Keith's midtwenties that he found out who his father was: John William Ferguson, concert pianist with the Chicago Symphony. "I never even knew he was a musician."

"You *asswipe*," he told the maestro during their next encounter. "I've been beat, ripped off a thousand times playin' clubs. There's *so much* you could have taught me."

After the Thunderbirds tore up the Houston Juneteenth Festival, being the only white band there, they received a four-page spread in the *Houston Post*. From then on, Keith's father began showing up at Thunderbirds gigs.

"He would point me out to his friends—my son, the rock star. He picked up girls at our shows. Johnny Winter and ZZ Top sent their limos for him to attend concerts. After I left the T-Birds, I never heard from him again."

Keith directs my car through the barrio. Somewhere in these hills beneath Austin remain the last of the old pachucos. Time-honored Mexican families who dealt heroin to Texas hill country junkies for decades, in relative peace. Until the era of crack arrived. The old-timers were overwhelmed, their quaint Norman Rockwell–era heroin days over. Colombians moved in with machine guns.

Keith describes the current transitional wars, directing me through a Mexican shantytown. We finally reach a tin shack. Keith has been summoned to visit an old friend's dying boy. At least that's what I'm told as I wait outside in a spanking new white Honda Accord.

Sure enough, fifteen minutes later, Keith emerges. A worried *madre* and *padre* follow, gratefully embracing him for paying his respects. This is Texas, not Mexico. Why wasn't the boy in a hospital, I ask.

"They prefer their own *medicina*," he says.

Back to the Present

"This is about the only thing my dad gave me as a kid that I saved." Back on the front porch, Keith shows me a cherished, yellowed 1945 paperback by madcap cartoonist VIP. "This and a few old records.

"People would kid me about my large collection of blues records. That's all I listened to, I was fanatic, that and Mexican stuff. Like in sixth grade, people would bring 45s to parties, but they never wanted me to bring my Otis Rush or John Lee Hooker records."

Johnny Winter moved from Beaumont to Houston when Keith was in high school. "Since blues was all Johnny liked, these local musicians thought it would be hysterical if we got together: 'Let's put these two freaks, these two mutants together.' Johnny flipped out—he never saw that many 78s in his life. He had records too, but I had more."

Keith Ferguson began backing Winter at small lesbian bars, like Club L'mour. Ferguson was dazzled by Winter's virtuosity—it was "alarming," he says now—and often had to tell himself not to stop and stare at his fingers in the middle of a song. "We used to call him the Stork. Nobody messed with him. One night he knocked out an off-duty cop for callin' him a girl. I saw Johnny Winter fight many times, he was real strong and mean. Whoever was botherin' him became everybody that ever bothered him in his life—he could redirect it with intensity. Just defended himself against some jagoff who wanted to beat on a skinny, blind, albino freak. He'd hit somebody like a lead pipe. Johnny didn't see very well, just put his sonar on the attacker. They usually had to be told later what happened to 'em."

Ferguson made Austin his home in 1972. He moved because the aggressive Houston police force made him uncomfortable—and he wanted into the Storm, Jimmie Vaughan's old band. After a brief stint, he joined up instead with Stevie Ray Vaughan and Doyle Bramhall Sr. "Nobody wanted to hear us," Ferguson recalls. "Nobody." In 1975, Kim Wilson left Minnesota to play with Jimmie, and Ferguson rejoined. "We couldn't get arrested either, but we were doin' a helluva lot better than me and Stevie and Doyle did, locally.

"It was the 'Cosmic Cowboy, Willie-Waylon-and-the-Boys' outlaw town then. But *we* were the outlaws. People wondered how we survived: 'Well, they never work.' We were so hard-core [blues], nobody knew what to do with us. But Antone's came along, sort of saved us—at least we could get some food. They served lots of po'boy sandwiches.

"Muddy Waters heard us at Antone's. We fried him. We were told we sounded like his best band from the '50s, with Jimmy Rogers. We weren't trying to, it was innate. He went back north ravin' about us, and Jimmie started gettin' calls. So we got in our little van from Austin to Boston, nowhere in between. We started openin' for [Kansas City jump-blues revivalists] Roomful of Blues. Then it got to where they were openin' for us. People seemed astonished by us."

The Fabulous Thunderbirds were the first white blues group that didn't look and play like hippies. The T-Birds took it back twenty years. Jimmie Vaughan exorcised all the rock guitar innovations—as if Beck-Hendrix-Clapton-Winter-Bloomfield never existed—and threw it back to a spare '50s Chicago groove that had been long abandoned. More authentic than early Stones. Countless guitarists took heed. Kim Wilson applied no fake rasp to his voice, no black affectations, no phonetic imitations of slurred words. He sang it straight.

The Fabulous Thunderbirds spearheaded a reanimation that stabilized the course of blues, spawning back-to-basics bands that proliferate to this day. Blues cognoscenti began to emulate Jimmie Vaughan's slicked-back hair and open-collar, 1950s rayon shirts, newly designed and imported from India by Trash & Vaudeville in New York's East Village. Keith's transparent *camisas* tripled in price at Austin clothing stores. "That's just the way we dressed in high school," says Keith. "The fashion of pachucos and thugs, who've long since died—or gone double-knit." Keith was also probably the only man cool enough to wear women's perfume and come off masculine.

"Pretty soon everyone up in Boston wanted to *be* us," Ferguson recalls. "We still couldn't get arrested here in Austin, but we went from floors to motels in Boston. Everyone in the band but me wanted to move to Boston. They followed the record company line—'You guys are fine, but all you have to do is change.' They think blues is a stone to step on to get somewhere else.

"You'll notice each one of our records got more expensive to make, and more diluted, as far as I'm concerned. I thought we should have held out for an art subsidy, 'cause there wasn't anybody else out there doin' it except Roomful of Blues. But we were more primitive, playing like skeletons."

Tuff-chick/hick blues shouter Lou Ann Barton—the best female blues singer in Texas—was in the T-Birds for a spell. "We got married in Rhode Island. She told people she and I could be happy in a pile of shit. She kept a good house, for a white girl her age. Since I was always gone, and she was fixin' to be, marriage would give us some sort of stability. But it worked just the opposite, blew us apart."

It's whispered that the T-Birds were the only white blues band that intimidated the Stones—whom they opened for twice at the Dallas Cotton Bowl and twice at the Houston Astrodome during the 1981 tour. But the T-Birds were too hip for the room. Eighty thousand people at the Cotton Bowl booed so loud, the Thunderbirds quit and walked off-stage. A vicious experience. But pussy flowed, more abundantly than for any mere blues group ever. "I'm the only one in the band who actually *talked* with girls, too."

The T-Birds played a bit worse when whale-watching the audience for pussy. They all suffered from herpes; like females menstruating in unison, when their collective herpes flared up, it slowed down their onstage performance.

Ferguson played bass on the essential first four Thunderbirds albums, as well as the *Havana Moon* collaboration with Santana. He was fired in the mid-'80s, around the period they switched to CBS Records and began scoring big on Top 40. Keith leveled a lawsuit at the T-Birds, refused to settle, and was trounced in court. To this day there is acrimony and scorched earth.

Jimmie Vaughan and Kim Wilson would not discuss Keith Ferguson for this article. Clifford Antone says nothing for the record, other than swearing, "Jimmie Vaughan and Kim Wilson never did any-thing to hurt him. You can't guess at this—it's too deep. Don't even try."

Perhaps he was too bluesy, too primitive, too tattooed, the Illustrated Man, The Man with the Golden Arm. Couldn't cross bor-ders. Maybe he got so hip, he just hipped himself right off the planet. There were knock-down, drag-out shit-kicking fistfights between Keith and Kim. And these were distinguished, sharply dressed ambassadors of the blues. About Keith's playing during his last year in the T-Birds, drummer Fran Christina pronounced the ultimate insult: "It sounded like . . . *jaazzz*."

"They wanted somebody else," shrugs Keith. "That's what [Jimmie Vaughan] told me. Just wanted to do somethin' new. So I went lookin' for other work. I found it. Anyway, I quit drinkin' liquor when I left the T-Birds, and lost fifty pounds," he boasts, as if that fact made the departure a good health move. But it was fifty pounds he seems to need.

Nonetheless, Keith's replacement was the brilliant upright bassist Preston Hubbard, fresh from Roomful of Blues. Who happened to be a most presentable pretty boy, helping to propel the T-Birds into MTV power rotation with the multiplatinum "Tuff Enough." The Absolutely Fabulous T-Birds would no longer have to shoulder the burden of a tattooed, heroin-shooting, tour-hating blues purist. But it was sort of like replacing Ray Charles with Helen Keller. Unbeknownst to the rest of the 'Birds, Hubbard himself had embarked upon his own eighteen-year heroin journey. Ferguson's replacement later revealed that he "shot well over a million dollars into my arms," eventually collapsing the veins in his hands, arms, and neck. Then Hubbard became Austin's most elite dope dealer—in his own words, "selling twenty-dollar *pesetas* of *pura chiva*—pure tar heroin," and "cookies of primo rock," which were ounces of coke cooked up to resemble sugar cookies. Hubbard did two years in a Texas prison and thankfully recovered.

Break for ITT Tech commercial. A long-haired dude stands in a recording studio and preaches his testimonial: "I'm not a musician. But I work in rock 'n' roll."

"No shit?" mutters Keith Ferguson. "I'm a musician, and I don't."

The legendary out-of-work bass player arises another day to click on *Real Stories of the Highway Patrol.* Commissioner Maury Hannigan, our host, represents *the man*—every man empowered to break Keith Ferguson's balls. This fatherly, mature voice of law enforcement embodies everything that's ever kept Keith down—a sprinkle of absent, abusive father, perhaps a dash of 1960s draft board, a few shakes of burr-headed gym coach. The customs officers who make Keith miss planes, the Austin cops who ticket local musicians unloading amps on Sixth Street. Narcs who've interrogated and beaten him, who could give a shit how many landmark albums he played bass on. They all form a composite of this brown-uniformed, hair-dyed, showbiz cop.

"Look, they're on a roll," observes Keith, as state troopers hunt down some truck driver's roach. The next segment has New York's Finest surrounding a maniac, about to toss the Net—a humane method to capture PCP freaks. Keith sits transfixed as the maniac flails, rendered helpless.

"That's nothin'," comes one of Keith's roadside cronies. "They got a blanket called the Wrap for smelly winos, so's not to befoul the back of the squad car."

Commissioner Hannigan's back on-screen, with contempt for everything Keith Ferguson stands for. For the seventeen individual lizard tattoos snaking up and down his right arm, for his glistening *We-don't-need-no-steenking-badges* gold tooth, his born-cynical sneer. Such cops were put on earth to make life miserable for Keith, a once-studly rock star who now resembles a withering Aztec Indian, a poster boy for ethnic suspicion.

Avoiding the Highway Patrol is one reason Keith doesn't drive. You want the legendary Ferguson on your gig, gotta come fetch him. "I was drivin' alone in 1970 and this big voice came outta nowhere and said, 'When you get to where your goin', you need to quit, or you're gonna die.'"

Don't cop shows give him nightmares?

"No. We get stopped, pulled over, and humiliated for real." Keith was jailed en route to a gig with the Excellos, several blues bands ago. He'd moved a roadblock on Sixth Street to avoid a construction detour in front of the club.

"Cops were staked out there, waiting to fight crime. They fucked with me the whole ride to the station about how I look. Textbook Batman-and-Robin pigology: one bad cop, the other pretending to be reasonable. Some little booger half my age, heavily armed, baiting me while I'm handcuffed. Tells his partner, 'Would you mind takin' *this* down to the station?' Then he tells me, 'I don't know why you're pissed off—you're makin' seven hundred dollars a night.' He thought it was a riot I only had sixteen cents.

"Austin is the live music capital of America. So what do the police do? They prey on musicians who work on Sixth Street, where all the tourists come for live music. Let's eat ourselves. They had a meeting with musicians and club employees and said, 'All you gotta do is put a card in the back of your car stating which club you work.' Then they towed off and ticketed each car with one of those cards. We're the live music capital, but you can't unload your equipment."

Why are Austin cops so tyrannical, why do they harass innocent citizens?

"Because there haven't been enough of them shot. That would slow 'em down."

I ask him if he has picked up any tips from *Real Stories of the Highway Patrol*.

"Yeah," he responds. "Move, leave the country."

"Do you hate the French?" inquires Ms. Legere.

"Only their gendarmes," answers Keith.

On another day's visit, I drop by the porch with New York rock diva Phoebe Legere. She straps on her "squeezy-gut" accordion, about to launch into "La Vie En Rose." Keith lies on the hammock. Sweet Liz Henry, who organized his house, is slumbering on the couch. Others lie across the porch in various zones of consciousness.

Keith opens one eye. Then the next.

"Oh, I like your smile," Phoebe says.

"Cost me two hundred bucks," Ferguson answers.

At the very last note of the waltz, absolutely on cue, the transformer near the top of a tree that intersects the roof begins to explode. Showers of sparks rain down on the porch. Hippies scurry from all points into the front door.

Liz and Keith offer permanent residence to Ms. Legere. Some other fellow eyes the squeezy-gut, wondering how much it might fetch downtown at Rockinghorse Pawn.

Ethnic musicians have a tendency to serenade Keith Ferguson, if only to watch his spectacular, gold-toothed smile. When the Tail Gators toured with Los Lobos, there was the unforgettable image of Los Lobos circled round Keith's hotel mattress one evening to awaken him for the stage. Each had his conjunto instrument—the *bajo sexto*, the *guitarrón*—like mariachis harmonizing in Ferguson's beloved Spanish.

It has been a few years since Ferguson sojourned to the guitar-making town of Paracho, in the pine-forest mountains of Michoacán.

"I never had any trouble with Mexican customs. But America's convinced everyone's bringin' back tons of dope. Don't ever say you have a plane to catch. Believe me. You might as well just arrest yourself," says Keith, offering one more reason he now shuns touring. "When I came back on Christmas through Houston, I brought a custom-built bass. They took me in the little room in handcuffs, just hopin' I had a plane to catch, which I did, then went through all my stuff and got smart with me. They were dyin' to incarcerate someone on Christmas Eve, but they couldn't find anything."

These days Ferguson prefers watching the Mexican soap opera *Calienas De Magura* [Chains of Bitterness], starring Daniella Castro, five days a week. It's set in San Miguel de Allende, his favorite town.

Ferguson formed the Tail Gators with Don Leady in 1984. The next five years would be his favorite stretch in a band. He cowrote "Mumbo Jumbo," the title track to their best album. "I loved every minute of it. I made more money with them, you could trust everybody, you *got* your money, a lot of it. Don was always writin' new songs. He'd play it for us once, then we'd cut it. That's the way we did records. We worked our asses off, the physical labor of playing all night onstage. I'd be happily replete, drained, each night. Then seven hundred miles to the next gig. We never had a roadie. But after a while Don fixed it to where I carried a bass, Mud Cat [Smith] carried a snare and symbols, Don carried a guitar, and the clubs would furnish everything else. We'd fly to Boston, rent a car, and drive to Maine. I didn't have to pay any other creatures."

Yet, Ferguson says, he receives no royalties from his acclaimed albums: "Not enough to get cigarettes. I got a big check the other day. Three dollars and twenty-two cents from BMI. Then I got a letter from [Nashville publisher] Bug Music sayin' I owed *them* money. It's surprising how niggardly everyone connected with the music business becomes over money. People tell you you're important, but apparently not important enough to give you money you've earned."

Be it former Tail Gators manager Scott Weiss, or former T-Birds manager Denny Bruce, Keith would kill them if he could "get away without doing thirty seconds of time. They're to be pitied and stepped over, like shit." And then, he feels the weight of banishment from the entire Antone's blues community. Hubert Sumlin, Howlin' Wolf's old guitarist, asked Ferguson to back him on a record slated to appear on Clifford Antone's blues label. Ferguson insists Antone won't release the record because Keith is on it.

"[Clifford] just hates me," says Ferguson. He told somebody once he can't meet a girl anywhere that doesn't like me, and it pisses him off. He redid that book, *Picture of the Blues* [Antone's Press], just to get me off the cover. Me and Kim and Jimmie and Muddy Waters. They redid the cover just to get me off of it. They couldn't get me out of it, just off of it."

"Keith is a real musicologist," says Clifford Antone. "What made us friends was his love for the most lowdown music that existed." Antone denies that the Sumlin record was unreleased because of Keith, denies omitting Keith's mug from the second book cover, but will discuss nothing on record about their bitter relationship. The Austin music community tears down its stars but provides a cottage industry for its faded and fallen. There are lots of beautiful losers, like Roky Erickson, Evan Johns, and all those generic dropped-from-labels women folkies who gravitate here as if part of a support group.

So all Keith's got now is this woodsy refuge surrounding his old front porch. His reclusive mother and grandmother have other homes on the grounds. No matter how much his profession shuns him, like all

Texans, he remains patriotic about the land. He loves the hawks flying overhead, the snakes that fetch rats, the ecosystem.

"I kept hearing someone screaming, 'Fuck you, fuck you,' deep inside my walls. I thought I was having a nervous breakdown the first few weeks."

Keith released several gecko lizards under the house, for insect control. "I'd be shaving, and suddenly from within the wall something would shriek, 'Fuck you, fuck you!' I'd whip around and cut myself. . . . It was the geckos!

"They emit this uncanny shriek that comes out as 'fuck you' in English. They're indigenous to Laos and Cambodia. Freaked out our boys in 'Nam who thought they were Cong, cursing from the trees. '*Fuck* you, *fuck* you!' But they eat roaches, rats, mice, and do an amazingly efficient job. Don't leave over anything, no blood or tails. They breed like Catholics, grow up to twenty inches over the years."

"Aren't they also a delicacy in Southeast Asia?" asks a porch hippie.

"*Delicacy?*" comes Keith. "Doesn't that word usually mean something on a stick that shouldn't be there? Something's balls or brains?"

Keith Ferguson's closest allies are his grandma and a beautiful old pioneer woman, Mrs. Alberta McKnight, across the road. Keith and the two ninety-two-year-old girls form an unlikely alliance of environmental defense against land developers and the erratic behavior of Keith's mother.

His mother, the reclusive Margaret Ferguson, lives in a little house on the estate, behind the trees, which gives off the aura of the Norman Bates home in *Psycho*. What's that like, living with Mother?

""Hell," says Keith. "She's been trying to evict me for eight years. She knocked down the whole garage because there was a hornet's nest inside," he says, citing pointless acts of destruction his mother implements. "Didn't tell me, I just woke up one morning to a wrecking crew. She had our natural bamboo all torn out, which was worth thousands."

Ma Ferguson files surreptitious complaints against Mrs. Alberta McKnight, one resulting in a citation that forced her to cut back her shrubbery. Mrs. McKnight has lived on her own property since 1910. Her family arrived by covered wagon. Local developers are out to get her remaining five acres, so she strung barbed wire around her land. She resists real estate goons, who've tried to convince her the land is better suited for a strip shopping center. They showed up at her door carrying axes. Once, when some particularly aggressive developers intruded on her property, she came out on the lawn with a twelve-gauge shotgun and fired. Keith heard the shot and ran to her aid dressed as an Indian, wielding a machete. "I saw the smokin' shotgun in the crook of her arm. She rigged up the barbed wire so it would boomerang viciously toward whoever stepped through. There were chunks of clothes, skin and blood all over the fence. 'Guess that barbed wire did the trick,' she cackled."

Keith loves his grandmother, Effie Lou, who was born in 1900. He spent idyllic summers in San Antonio with her as a boy. It's feared Ma Ferguson may be in collusion with the land cannibals and would sell these pastoral woods—Keith's last refuge and bequest—if she could remove Mrs. Alberta McKnight, Keith, and his grandmother, Effie Lou. She wants Keith to inherit and preserve the property. "But my mother keeps her in a vegetative state," says Keith, pointing to another small house, off-limits to all. "She keeps her locked inside, feeds her one soft-boiled egg a night. That's all. Tells her if she leaves the house, gangs will get her. My grand-mother finally signed a huge stack of legal documents making my mother legal executor. And my mother's top priority is to evict me.

"My mother will disappear, without notice, for two weeks, to California or somewhere. I try and shake my grandmother out of it. 'What color vegetable are you today?' She'll come back alive after a real meal, her wits are strong. Then my mother creeps back, always late at night. Grandma suddenly goes back to vegetable land."

Bats hang upside down in a tree box Keith built. Hard-luck animals, as well as people, find solace on the Ferguson estate: "I was in the market for a sick cat without a tail. So I got one. A female named Bill." Sure enough, a dog with one eye strolls over to play with Bill.

"Cats began disappearing in our neighborhood," adds Keith. "And I eventually noticed one of Mother's cats disappeared. Then late one night, I saw my mother stuffing another cat into a box. As the cat was fighting to get loose, a walking stick comes down across her back and knocks her to the ground. It was my grandmother: 'If'n you ever put that cat in a box again, I'll whup this across your face.'

"Them two been doin' that shit for years, before I was born. It scared the hell out of me, but I've heard other old mothers and daughters do that to one another. It was a relief to find out. They fought each other all the time, tore each other to pieces. And they used me for a football."

Keith was amazed his grandma still had it in her.

"They call him Chago."

He sits on his porch, beatific over *bajo sexto* player Santiago "Chago" Almeida—on a scratchy Narciso Martínez *conjunto* record from the 1930s. It's simple folk music, but Keith rides some low wave underneath, inaudible to most human ears. "*Listen* to that tone."

He leads me into his bedroom to show his new *bajo sexto*. Though he's hesitant to fess up, it's a Keith Ferguson model. Built on his design, he named it the Rodando. "This is the cheesiest one of the bunch that were made. Keith Hofner owns the company. A Mexican luthier now makes 'em with truss rods and contours. No two are alike."

Bajo sextos please Keith Ferguson immensely. But they are transient, like visitors to the house, or old girlfriends. For years, Austin players have spotted his bass guitars sadly hanging in hockshops.

"I always got 'em out myself. Or else I left 'em. I don't know where people get the idea you gotta play the same bass forever. One guy bought my '52 Fender Precision, took really good care of it. I borrowed it for that Solid Senders tour to Holland, then gave it back. I brought it to watch people's reactions. It freaked 'em, because they remembered the bass, but they never seen me lookin' like I do now."

Keith Ferguson does the only sensible thing when an old tattoo fades—he gets a new one over it. A feathered serpent Aztec god adorns his left elbow to wrist. The seventeen lizards, resembling Escher prints, run up his right arm.

"I got most of 'em so I'd remember where I'd gone. I used to play so many different cities, everyone was so screwed up and tired, they wouldn't know where we were. But I remember gettin' each tattoo, where I was at the time, 'cause that's the thing that lasts, innit? You look down at your arm and think Spokane or Atlanta or Toronto or Seattle or Austin. . . ."

—1996

Note: *Keith Ferguson died April 29, 1997, at the age of fifty.*

Lightning Struck Twice: Tommy Shannon (right) accompanied both Johnny Winter and then Stevie Ray Vaughan (left) from obscurity to fame.
(Clayton Call)

CHAPTER 9

Tommy Shannon
Cry Tough

K eith Ferguson died the day before this interview. Austin's other
legendary blues bassist, Tommy Shannon, is deeply shaken.
He can't even attend the wake on Sunday—his new band,
Storyville, is booked on the road. Shannon donated five bass guitars to
Ferguson in recent years. Each bass got Ferguson out to a few gigs. Then,
like all of Keith's instruments, they ended up hanging in Austin hockshops for dope cash. Shannon arranged Ferguson's first and only stab at
rehab. The defiant Ferguson withstood only three days of such nonsense.

Ferguson was bassist to both Johnny Winter and Stevie Ray
Vaughan, immediately before Shannon. Though Ferguson's career
may have disintegrated by way of his allegiance to heroin, he remained
savagely witty, cool, a bittersweet sage among plentiful admirers.
Shannon never possessed such charisma, and bottomed out harder
than Keith ever did.

Tommy Shannon and his wife, Kumi, are currently raising four elegant
horses—three of them Trakehners, an athletic European breed—on
their Austin ranch. This land, where the Shannons have recently

settled, spills out into unspoiled hill country. With just a bit more land-scaping, it will resemble the American dreamscape befitting a humble musician who's overpaid his dues. No kids are planned. "Just horses and cats," says Shannon, at the corral. "We just got that black mare over there. Her name's Deja, she's being bred tomorrow. They're sending sperm down, the vet's gonna squirt it in, and she's gonna have a baby."

Two eleven-year-old cats stroll the turf. The Shannons eye them poignantly, since both were presented as kittens by an old friend who died yesterday. The friend was Keith Ferguson, the only other Austin blues bassist whose importance—and struggles—rivals that of Shannon's.

The interior of the ranch house bears testament to Shannon's allegiance to another dear, departed comrade. Shannon was Stevie Ray Vaughan's musical partner for a decade. Gold records and Canadian platinum discs line the hallway. Four Grammys sit atop the piano, awards given to Vaughan and Double Trouble. "I'm so proud of these," Shannon says. The most recent arrived in 1996, Best Blues Instrumental for "SRV Shuffle," from a televised tribute concert. Another commemorates the 1984 Montreux Pop Festival. "Seven people booed us, but it sounded like a thousand," recalls Shannon of that night. "We left the stage brokenhearted, crushed." For the live recording of the evening, *Blues Explosion*, Stevie Ray Vaughan and Double Trouble copped a Grammy—karmic payback for the encore they never received.

Encores continue as the SRV legend grows. Vaughan justly provided Shannon points from album sales, and even on merchandising—an extremely rare arrangement for sidemen. And, like that of SRV, Tommy Shannon's ego remains modest in light of his legendary past. His special place in music history boils down to the uncanny fact he was the primary bass player for both Johnny Winter and Stevie—Texas's two most celebrated rock guitarists, during two distinct and separate eras. He accompanied both from obscurity into their prime—in the case of Vaughan, through his entire recording career.

"I'm glad to be fifty years old," says Shannon, who now plays bass in soul-rock band Storyville. "I was born the perfect time. I witnessed the birth of rock 'n' roll, I went through the whole revolution of the

'60s, and I got to participate and live it. There's no way you can explain to kids today how great it was."

It's also hard to explain Shannon's plunge from budding '60s rock stardom into a hell of unending addiction and multiple jail sentences, followed by years of hard labor as a bricklayer—which to this gifted and sensitive musician was no different than being on a chain gang. Then Shannon teamed up with an obscure Austin guitarist named Stevie Ray Vaughan. Lightning struck again, a generation later, as Double Trouble took flight, with Shannon at Vaughan's side for nine years.

The months before and after an artist's breakthrough—the elusive transitional period known as "making it"—are often their most urgent artistic moments. That Tommy Shannon happened to be there for both guitarists may not be sheer coincidence. The tall and humble— Lincolnesque, you might say—Shannon's rise, crash, and resurrection seem orchestrated by angels.

Born in Tucson in 1946, Shannon moved to West Texas at nine, growing up primarily in Dumas, where there existed no black folk. Not even a wrong side of the tracks. "They simply weren't allowed. I guess I never gave it much thought back then, I was only fifteen. If they drove by, the cops would escort them through town. You'd hear some Jimmy Reed and Sam Cooke on the radio. But since there were no blacks in Dumas, I had little exposure to black music."

He'd thankfully gotten his first blast of rock 'n' roll in Tucson. "I'll never forget, when I was a little kid, someone picked me up after school and 'Good Golly Miss Molly' came on the radio. It shot electricity through me, the hairs stood up on me."

Shannon began "makin' a living playing music" when he was in high school. Like most bass players, he began on guitar in a local Dumas band of fifteen-year-olds called the Avengers. On Shannon's bedroom dresser, beneath glass, is a show card for a 1962 Avengers gig at the local picture show, along with *Where the Boys Are*. They played Ventures, Duane Eddy and "The Limbo." They loved twang guitarist Lonnie Mack but felt his repertoire was above their heads.

Shannon moved to Dallas after high school, joining soul music cover band New Breed in 1966. They played now-forgotten discotheques where go-go girls danced in cages, with names like Phantasmagoria, the Four Seasons, and the Fog. "Back then you were expected to play soul music at every club. I tell younger musicians today you gotta get out and play what everybody else has already done, draw from different influences in a big melting pot—it's the best training.

"So I discovered good soul music in Dallas—especially Les Watson and the Panthers, an all-black band that did Motown. Their bass player was Willie Weeks, my favorite bass player in the world. We became friends. I'd sit there and study him every night."

A funk/R&B session musician in the '70s, Weeks played bass on *Donny Hathaway Live at the Bitter End*, an elite musician's favorite, which Shannon calls "one of the best records ever made. Stevie and I used to listen to that for hours. The rhythm section is perfect." (Today, Willie Weeks plays on Vince Gill and Wynonna Judd records, nearly half the country hits coming out of Nashville.)

New Breed was managed by a gangster whose name Shannon still prefers not to mention. Uncle John Turner, the brilliant drummer with whom Shannon would team up for his next three bands, was in New Breed. "Our band soon changed to the Young Lads, a pretty stupid name. Our manager owned an East St. Louis club called the In Crowd. Really low-down and funky bars, integrated, side by side in the Gaslight Square district. I got robbed one night for fifty cents at gunpoint— that's what the guy asked for, just fifty cents. Across the street from us was a band called the Almond Joys—which was the original Allman Brothers, whom I met back then."

The long-forgotten Fog was the Dallas site of the two most significant meetings of Shannon's career: First, when he met Winter, and then—a decade later—where he met Vaughan. "Johnny sat in with the band and I was blown away. I thought he was beautiful, he came in with long white hair, incredible stage presence. I'd never seen an albino before."

Uncle John had known Winter since childhood in Beaumont, and he left New Breed to get with Winter in Houston. As soon as they needed a new bass, Shannon moved to Houston. He had no idea from whence the blues came until meeting Winter. "I'd heard Cream, and saw the name Robert Johnson or Albert King under the song, figuring that must be a friend of theirs. I had no idea until I joined Johnny Winter, whose apartment went wall to wall with blues records. He sat me down and played me everything, all the way back to field hollers—which we did in one of our songs ["Fast Life Rider" on *Second Winter*]." Thus began the seminal power trio that became the Progressive Blues Experiment in 1968. "To survive, we were playing cover songs, with Winter singing 'By the Time I Get to Phoenix,' whatever was on the charts to make a livin'. Then we started doin' more Hendrix stuff. Jimi Hendrix changed me forever, the biggest influence of my life, period.

"The best concert I've ever seen, to this day, was Hendrix in Houston. Johnny, Uncle John, and I sat out there in the audience like everyone else. He was so graceful, kind of like he was less than a god but more than a man. On the first record where you hear all that stuff backwards—he was doin' it live and makin' it work. Johnny kept sayin', 'Nobody could be this good.' It was like seein' some angel."

Shannon keeps a bass in the closet that Hendrix played twice, and although Winter later jammed with Hendrix often, Shannon says, "He's the one I never got to play with. Played with Jeff Beck, Eric Clapton, Albert and B. B. King, Muddy Waters—but not Jimi.

"We started playin' more covers of Hendrix—and we were doin' it real good, too. It was almost blasphemy back then to attempt Hendrix, you had to have a hell of a lot of balls, like walkin' through sacred burial grounds. Just like Stevie could, Johnny could get tones out of his amp that were intuitive, and play the shit out of it. People take it for granted now, but back then it was a shock."

Shannon wore Nehru shirts and beads, was immersed in hippie culture, playing the Love Street Light Circus in the Montrose district, which was Houston's Haight-Ashbury. "We played this gay club, all guys. They hired us cause they liked our roadie, this little blond-haired, good-lookin' kid. They hated us."

Winter's bassist before Shannon, Houston-born Keith Ferguson, recalled that "the lesbian places went wild over Winter—which beats the hell outta me. They loved hard-core rhythm and blues. But the gay bars thought he was ugly. Not your average boy next door."

Ferguson once explained that Winter "came from the straightest of straight backgrounds. His parents were real genteel old South. They had the house with white pillars and the whole nine yards in Beaumont." Ferguson himself held his own on the streets, but was nearly as awed by Winter's savage street-fighting ability as by his guitar prowess. Shannon remembers, "Winter was fearless, and you didn't want to make him mad."

The trio had a calling higher than playing covers. "We'd be in a motel room after a gig doing blues, what we liked to do. And Uncle John said, 'Man, we oughta *just* play blues. Look at all these guys who can't do it."

Shannon was turned off by most rock bands, like Canned Heat or Quicksilver Messenger Service: "They weren't worth shit. And Johnny'd sit there playing, one of the greatest slide players who ever lived. Uncle John had to talk Johnny into it, because Johnny was afraid we wouldn't get any work. Which at first was true. Uncle John and I were sleeping on floors. Johnny at least had a girlfriend with a job and an apartment."

Winter's liner notes on 1986's *3rd Degree* reunion album proclaim that if it weren't for Uncle John and Shannon, and the sacrifices they made during six impoverished months, he would never have emerged. They practiced at Uncle John's mother's beauty shop. "Those guys, if they hadn't done that, nobody would ever have heard of me or known that I was a blues guitar player," wrote Winter.

Uncle John was the thinker in the band, naming them the Progressive Blues Experiment. "It was Uncle John's idea, and Johnny'd tell you the same thing. He was the brains," Shannon confirms. "Mean Town Blues," Winter's finest composition/shoulda-been hit, reflected hard times in Dallas. Several of Winter's songs of this time contain bitter lyrics about his home state, which he left forever in 1969. Take the solo National Steel guitar piece, "Dallas":

> *Goin' back to Dallas*
> *Take my razor and my gun*
> *So much shit in Texas*
> *Bound to step in some*

The *Progressive Blues Experiment* album was recorded for some huckster named Bill Josey, now deceased, before they even had a record deal. A bona fide masterpiece, it was recorded live in two afternoons on a 2-track machine at the Vulcan Gas Company, a psychedelic ballroom in Austin. Nothing happened, says Shannon, it just sat there. But Josey sold it a year later, after Winter had been signed to Columbia. "We never made a penny off of it to this day. Johnny has no rights to that record, not even publishing, to my knowledge."

A tiny article in *Rolling Stone* somehow appeared, attracting New York entrepreneur Steve Paul. A wealthy New York bon vivant, Paul owned the trendsetting Manhattan club the Scene. He also managed Tiny Tim, another effeminate-looking male parody, who like Johnny Winter, experienced his first taste of success at lesbian clubs. The idea of an albino superguitarist prompted a trip to Texas, where he signed Winter in early 1969.

"It's so strange when you hear about overnight success. But literally overnight, Uncle John and I packed our footlockers, everything we owned, and caught a plane the next day to New York. I was twenty-one and moved to a big mansion [in] upstate New York set up by Steve Paul, one of the weirdest people I ever met."

"I remember getting off the plane in New York," continues Shannon, "where two beautiful girls were waiting, Eleanor and Jenette. They were big-time groupies, girlfriends of Jimi Hendrix and Led Zeppelin. They would have nothing to do with anyone who wasn't a musician. So here we were, these three hicks from Texas—which is what we were, man. I ended up with Eleanor, she became my girlfriend for a while. They showed us what clothes to buy, like bell-bottoms, and got us shag haircuts. They laughed at our twang, but it was their mission to develop us, let us know what was hip."

The groupies smoothed the path into rock society. Keith Ferguson came up to live at the mansion awhile, shacking up with Jenette. Within weeks Clive Davis signed Winter's power trio to Columbia for $600,000—the biggest record signing in history to date. "They signed it in my bedroom in the mansion, Johnny and Clive Davis, smiling with these papers in front of 'em."

Johnny and Steve Paul got their cut of the advance, while Shannon and Uncle John went to five-hundred-dollar-per-week retainers, with clothing perks. "It was such a magical time, everything fell together perfectly. We started playing big concerts as the record came out. It was the era of the Great Guitar Player, and this Texas albino who could play the shit outta guitar and sing great was gonna be next."

The first Columbia record, *Johnny Winter*, made the Top 40, but Imperial Records released *The Progressive Blues Experiment* at same time, confusing people. Winter scored no Top 40 singles, as had immediate predecessors like Hendrix and Cream.

In 1969, most major cities had huge pop festivals: "We did that whole circuit and Woodstock was one. It was just another day on tour, nobody could have realized the significance at the time. We had to come in by helicopter. I'll never forget this ocean of people, as far as you could see, from this bubble helicopter. You get down, there's babies being born, it was like a city. We stayed high most of the time."

Edgar Winter joined the band at Woodstock, where they plugged into amps already onstage, no sound checks. "After we did *Second Winter* [the only three-sided vinyl LP in history—the fourth side remained blank], Johnny had a hard time writing songs," Shannon says. "Steve Paul also managed the McCoys ["Hang On Sloopy"], who had another house on the same property as us, where they practiced. Rick Derringer, Randy Jo Hobbs, who's dead now. They had material. Steve Paul pressured Johnny to get with the McCoys. A blind man coulda seen it comin'. Johnny'd start goin' over there, jammin' and stuff. Johnny'd said things earlier like, 'We gotta do a new record, but I don't have any new songs, I'd hate to let y'all go, I hope we can pull this all together.'

"Uncle John and I were let go. It wasn't so much a shock as a very big disappointment. I was madly in love with this girl Susan, real high-class girl from Buffalo. I had all this success around me. She wasn't even a groupie, that's what I dug about her, she was an executive with Neiman Marcus. All of a sudden I wasn't a star and she dropped me, which hurt as bad as losing the gig. It was a devastating double-whammy."

Shannon and Uncle John were dismissed with two thousand dollars apiece compensation. Winter's new band, Johnny Winter And, featuring Rick Derringer, became one of the hottest concert tickets in America, often touring with Edgar Winter's White Trash, soon to be even bigger. Meanwhile, Shannon and Turner joined a minor San Francisco–area band called Krackerjack. "It hurt a lot, considering I suffered through the hard times. But I love Johnny to this day, we're still tight. Johnny and Edgar are geniuses, as musicians and in IQ."

Upon his dismissal from Winter's comet, Shannon's life began a dramatic plunge. He feels no need to keep it secret. In Krackerjack, "we starved our asses off out in California, so we moved back down to Austin. That's when I started shooting crystal meth. A polydrug abuser. And here comes the hard part of my story. In a year and a half, I got so screwed up and pathetic, I lost enough weight to look like a skeleton. I began missing gigs. I alienated myself from friends and all the good people in my life. Began hanging out with dealers and hard-core criminals who burglarized drugstores then came over to my place. It was the sickest time of my life."

Shannon briefly left Austin for Dallas. "I went back to my old stomping grounds at the Fog, where'd I'd first met Winter. And again, I heard this incredible guitar player. I looked onstage and there was this little fourteen-year-old kid. It was Stevie. He was so humble and meek. All these older musicians blew him off, and I'm saying, 'God, he's better than all these guys.' Him and I hit it off and I told him, 'Man, you're great.' Stevie has said in a lot of interviews he remembered that night, 'cause I was the only person who talked to him." For a moment in the early '70s, Shannon and Vaughan briefly played in a band called Blackbird, living in the same duplex. "We talked about spiritual things, got high together, all that shit."

But then things got worse for Shannon. "I'd stay up five days without sleep. I remember one night getting ready to play. So I did a shot and just blacked out. They found me with the rig hanging out of my arm. I didn't wake up for three days, while friends shook me. None of us thought we could die back then. But I got busted and thrown in jail, ending up with two years probation."

As a provision of probation, Shannon spent four of the most humiliating months he'd yet experienced in a San Antonio rehab center, where he was treated with Valium. "Nowadays you hear about rehab every day on TV, it's accepted. Back then it wasn't, it was a disgrace. People looked at you like you were pathetic, had no willpower. Even people who were doing drugs looked down on me."

Shannon kept rotating between short jail terms and probation, failing urine tests, unable to remain straight. For a while he held down the bass for an Austin group called the Fools, but not for long. His next jail term released him to a halfway house for four months, where he was introduced to AA, whose methods he at first rejected.

"I was young, I got lost, I didn't mean harm to anybody," he says. "But who really helped was an old, gray-haired AA man named Don Herwick, who saw some goodness in me. I owe my life to this guy. He spoke to judges, and they'd give me another chance. Then I'd get busted again. Once for pot, spending sixty-six days in jail, the whole time being told I'd be in for ten years. My probation officer said, 'I'm fed up with you, you're the worst person in my caseload out of a hundred people.' I was in Travis County Jail—this windowless iron tank with killers, rapists, armed robbers. I used psychology to avoid fights, only got beat up once. But I got by 'cause people would say, 'Man, you really played Woodstock?' There was an article in the *Austin American-Statesman* about my downfall, which inmates read."

Shannon's brokenhearted parents were then living in Amarillo, clueless as to Tommy's whereabouts for years. "I eventually ended up on this 'farm' out in Buddha for over a year, where derelicts were sent. Halfway houses wouldn't have me, considered me hopeless. I was the only young guy amongst all these old guys they'd find under the bridge. It was hell."

Coming from hippie culture, Shannon could relate to no one— the generation gap stood firm even amongst dust-bowl derelicts. He'd pour concrete, pull nails out of wood. He had no money, lost every friend he'd once had, couldn't even buy candy or cigarettes at the commissary. No girls, no music, no drugs. "I'd had my '62 jazz bass, which Hendrix had played, out there at the farm for a year under the bed. I only pulled it out once, looked at it, broke down and cried. But I didn't kill myself."

When Shannon was freed from the farm, his probation stipulated he couldn't join a band or even *play* bass—the court automatically associated music with drug abuse. Shannon's bricklayer cousin took pity on him, teaching him the trade. He laid bricks and rocks for a year and a half. "It ate at me every moment of my life that I wasn't playin'. My hands had mortar sores all over 'em. I'd go to the clubs to see my old friends and they'd ignore me. I went a couple years without bein' with a girl."

After seven years at rock bottom—laying rocks without playing—Shannon finally picked his bass back up at the age of thirty. "Try to imagine," he asks. "Back in them days, you were considered too old to play music, unless you were somebody established like Johnny Cash."

Never formally religious, Shannon forged his very own vision of spirituality. Shannon's ranch library is chock full of books on Buddhism, Christianity, sociology, psychology. "I try to live a spiritual life, and it's real hard. When I look at my whole life, I can see there's a thread that runs through it which is, to me, the will of a power greater than myself."

Finally, his callused hands bleeding, Shannon laid down his trowel in 1977. He told his cousin he was going back to music and walked off the job. He went down to Ray Henning's music store and posted his name on the bulletin board: "Played with Johnny Winter."

"I was no longer of the status where I could ask for a gig in Austin. People laughed at me and made jokes, as if I couldn't feel or hear 'em. But with my name on the bulletin board, I got into a couple of rinky-dink bands. I was basically homeless. I was still on probation, but they'd gotten off my back by then." Shannon got a call from Rocky Hill, brother of ZZ Top's Dusty Hill, moved to Houston to play with him and Uncle John—and then onto a higher-paying gig with Allen Haynes.

Shannon hadn't seen Stevie for years—until one night in 1980, when Vaughan was playing Rockefellers in Houston with Double Trouble—him, Chris Layton, and bass player Jackie Newhouse. "I'll never forget this. I walked in and had a revelation. That is where I belong, I knew it. After their set, we hugged, and I told him, 'I belong in this band, I belong playing with you.' Normally, that's not the way to approach somebody. You just don't go up and say, 'Fire the bass player [Jackie Newhouse], let me play.' But that's how strong I felt, I had no shame. So I sat in with Stevie and Chris Layton and it sounded great. I sat in a few more times in Houston. Then I got a phone call and joined Double Trouble in 1980."

Starting at two hundred dollars a week, traveling the country in a milk truck, Shannon spent nine full years with Vaughan, till the day he died. "You'd think I had enough of it, but Stevie and I were doin' cocaine and alcohol. Yet good things started happenin' for us. We met Jackson Browne, who was blown away, the night we did the Montreux Festival. He gave us his studio free to do basic tracks on *Texas Flood*. David Bowie was there, whom Stevie *almost* played with. That shows what kind of person Stevie was. We'd made our record, but hadn't yet sold it. Stevie had this incredible opportunity to go from ridin' around in a milk truck to limos with Bowie. He was pushed into it by management and said okay. They rehearsed, but the night before leaving, he said, 'I just can't.' He chose to stay with his band."

The Bowie tour was to be a year. Chances are, had he done it, he would have never become *the* Stevie Ray Vaughan. Vaughan was soon signed through the good graces of John Hammond, history's greatest A&R producer, who actually answered his own office phone, taking calls from both power brokers and unknown musicians. "Working with him was the greatest honor. He talked Epic into signing us—they didn't want a blues band. They only did it because John Hammond said, 'There's something here.' Then the record took off. I'll never forget, we were touring around in our little milk truck. All of a sudden, out in California, there was a line of people around the block at the club, after *Texas Flood* came out. And all this stuff started mushrooming. It got to a bigger level than Johnny Winter. I had everything back. Even more than before. All the girlfriends I could want, traveling in nice buses, free dope and alcohol. Like coming out of hell, I had everything back that I wanted."

The main difference in groupies, according to Shannon, from the Woodstock era to his second shot of stardom, was that in the '60s, girls didn't mind being called groupies. By the 1980s it had a bad connotation. "Nonetheless, when I was playing with Stevie, there were lots of groupies. They just said they weren't."

Shannon and Vaughan seemed to be made out of Texas cast iron. "We had fun for years, somebody babysat us. But him and I both started getting real sick from over-coking and drinking. We were doing it all night and all day. Best way we figured to never have a hangover was to never stop." They eventually reached meltdown. "One night in a hotel room, we had a big ol' pile of coke. He drank Crown Royal, I drank vodka. We knew we were in trouble. We couldn't stop. We'd isolated ourselves from everybody 'cause they thought we were getting too high. Chris Layton and [keyboardist] Reese Wynans would indulge a little, then the next day have a little bit of a hangover and want nothing more to do with it. But they couldn't make me and Stevie stop. And this night we both got down on our knees and prayed together for help to stop. We knew instinctively we were violating the laws of human decency. We got back up and did some more cocaine."

Addiction is addiction. As Shannon describes his descent back into nonstop indulgence, an ashen, shell-shocked expression comes over his face. But he once again set himself up for salvation.

"When I met my wife, Kumi, I didn't realize for months that I was in love with her. I'd go out and meet a girl, be with her one night, forget about her. But I kept remembering Kumi. I didn't pick her up like I did other girls. She comes from a military family. Never got high or drank or smoked or any of that stuff—just amazes me. She didn't like the drugs and alcohol, but she seemed to like me. Thank God she could do that. She's the best thing that ever happened in my life. Stevie was best man when I married her in 1986. Shortly after that, Stevie and I got cleaned up."

The band was in Europe. "Stevie started vomiting blood. Two days later we were in his room just drinking after a gig, 'cause you don't go out hunting cocaine in Germany. And we turned white, started sweating. He went to the hospital. And we knew that was the bottom. We canceled our tour. He checked himself into Charter Lane Hospital in Georgia. I checked myself into Charter Lane in Austin the same time. It'd never work if we weren't separated. We got clean and sober. Everything changed. It was a miracle."

Shannon recites the twelve-step program from AA, which worked for him: "You had to hit bottom, become totally powerless and helpless and full of despair before you could break through and find a life, a way out. Which comes from a power greater than yourself. Stevie was sober when he died. Four years of sobriety. We were playin' better, our ideas blossoming. I helped write 'Crossfire,' came up with that riff. I've got over ten years of sobriety now. I'd rehabbed on my own. Cops didn't drag me in."

Having defeated his demons, Shannon met disaster once again. He was on one of a convoy of helicopters flying back to Chicago from Wisconsin's Alpine Valley Music Theatre in 1990, where Vaughan opened for and played with Eric Clapton. "We got there first, and I went to my room, got a call about six in the morning that Stevie's helicopter had gone down, no survivors. The best friend I ever had in my life. Lost him and the career. But this time was different. It's strange, I had no desire to go drink or get high. Every year you get a chip for however many years you've been clean and sober. Every year I get my chip and I get him one too, and give it to his mom."

About five years ago the Stones called Shannon when auditioning for Bill Wyman's replacement. "They flew me up first-class. I played 'Start Me Up,' 'Brown Sugar,' 'Tumbling Dice,' about ten songs at S.I.R. studios in New York. This is the Rolling Stones, they don't have to bullshit nobody. Some of the bass players would come in and play only one song. I was there playin' ninety minutes. I had a blast, and you could see they were having fun. Even though I didn't get the gig, it was one of the greatest experiences of my life."

As with Uncle John Turner, Shannon forged a rhythm partnership with Chris "Whipper" Layton. After SRV, they both joined the Arc Angels with noticeably younger members Doyle Bramhall II and Charlie Sexton. "The idea was to play a few gigs around town. But people packed the clubs goin' nuts. So Geffen flew down an A&R guy. We did a lot of rehearsals, did our record." The process was a bittersweet experience; Shannon cites "internal conflicts" as having destroyed the rising band within eighteen months. "If we stayed together, we'd probably be rich by now."

At present, Shannon and Layton are like road warriors in twilight, trying to make Storyville ignite beyond its fanatic Austin base. Thirty years after playing with a white albino, Shannon finds himself playing in a band fronted by black albino Malford Milligan. "I don't like being on the road anymore," declares Shannon. "Been there, done that, seen that, so to speak. My whole idea of enjoyment is different. I'd like to do studio work. But I'll never quit playin' as long as I live, that's like breathing."

His foundation comes from the '60s, when music shaped people's lives the way World War II did the previous generation: "It breaks my heart, I feel sorry for young kids today. Music is so disposable now, so totally *oversaturated*. It's just business. People have totally lost touch with what it's really all about, the love of music."

Still, when Shannon acknowledges a young guitarist—like the adolescent Stevie Ray, the young Winter—people should perhaps take heed. Shannon and Layton recorded an album with Kenny Wayne Shepherd. "He's nineteen, this guy Jonny Lang is sixteen, another guy in town here, Guitar Jay, I think he's sixteen. He's incredible, I first played with him when he was seven years old at Ann Richards' inaugural ball. Give 'em a chance, what do they expect of 'em at this age?" Shannon says, still taking young gunslingers seriously, when few other professionals will.

"I also got to play with Clapton, the Stones, Jeff Beck, Little Richard—can you imagine that?" he marvels, like some provincial musician. I point out something that seems to elude Tommy Shannon:

They also got to play with him.

—1997

*Reigning Bassist: Perhaps no man has played bass on more hit
records than Chuck Rainey.*
(Courtesy of Chuck Rainey)

CHAPTER 10

Chuck Rainey
Glory and Injustice

Asked if anyone in history has played bass on more sheer numbers of successful records than himself, Chuck Rainey shrugs, "I don't think so." He's all over the essential albums of Aretha Franklin, Steely Dan, Quincy Jones, King Curtis, the Rascals, Jackson Five, Marvin Gaye, the Crusaders; an eye-popping mélange of movie and TV scores (*Midnight Cowboy, Lady Sings the Blues, White Men Can't Jump, Maude, Good Times, Hawaii Five-O, MASH*, ad infinitum). . . . You might safely figure that for every ticking moment for the past thirty-five years, half the world is listening to *something* on which Chuck Rainey plays bass.

The man deserves to take a bow, except for one fact: He ain't workin'. At least not in his home territory, Dallas–Fort Worth.

"I'm fifty-six years old, and I've played in a *lot* of cities. And this is the only place on the planet where club owners have asked, 'Do you have a tape, what kind of music do you play, do you have experience? Not just everybody just can come in here. Do you have a *following*?'"

Rainey's blood pressure rises as the chips fall. Well, *does* Chuck Rainey have a following?

"He is the godfather of Fender bass," says Will Lee, veteran of a thousand albums, and permanent bass player on the *David Letterman Show*. "Without Chuck Rainey, I would not have a career. He is a source of constant inspiration, and I try to listen to everything he does."

"There is only one person in Dallas with whom my reputation preceded me," continues Rainey, "and that was a guy named Lynn Smith, who booked Greenville Bar & Grill in the '80s. I was floored. I went to White Rock Lake to jog every day, get my weight down, bein' happy. I said, 'Wow, I didn't even have to sell myself.'"

That was the last steady gig this renowned musician enjoyed in his adopted hometown of fifteen years. The record books rarely contain the gospel according to session cats like Rainey, whose bass weaves through decades of music heritage. As a double-scale, work-for-hire studio musician, Rainey suffered the poseurs, fakers, users and no-talents who sometimes come out big winners in the music industry. He often cites heroes who "fell through the cracks."

"From 1967 to 1975, I spent a large part of my life on Sixtieth and Broadway [Atlantic Studios]. Or at [Atlantic's sister studio] Mastersound on Forty-second Street. Recording with Solomon Burke, the Rascals, Aretha, Roberta Flack, Donny Hathaway, Don Covay, the Fugs, you name it. There was a three-hour *History of Atlantic* special on TV, and of all the hits recorded there, they made not one mention of those two studios and all the New York musicians. Except for Ben E. King and Don Covay, who talked about how great Atlantic was. The program talked about all the Southern musicians and Muscle Shoals [Atlantic's studio in Alabama] and Stax [Atlantic's Memphis acquisition]. And how it hurt them when Ray Charles left them—you oughta hear Ray Charles talk about their ass. Even with Aretha—they talked about her only at Muscle Shoals. This hurt my feelings—I don't understand how you could forget all those New York musicians and artists."

King Curtis and the Beatles '65 Tour

Chuck Rainey, raised in Youngstown, Ohio, was a college brass major who switched to bass at age twenty-one. The only guy in Cleveland in 1961 with a Fender Precision bass, he joined an upward succession of bands, capped by jazz pianist Big Jay McNeely. From there, Sam Cooke, Etta James, Jackie Wilson, and the Coasters rotated on his schedule as touring bassist.

But it was King Curtis who Rainey bonded to. A New Yorker for ten years beginning in 1962, Rainey joined Curtis the next year. Curtis was *the* definitive rock 'n' roll studio saxist of the entire 1950s. "Whether it was a Top 40 gig, cocktail jazz, or a big band situation, we did it well. The three years I spent with King Curtis I was never out of work. *Never.* Six nights a week."

"Chuck was part of one of the greatest rhythm sections I ever worked with—King Curtis and the Kingpins," states Atlantic Records producer Jerry Wexler, with warm reverence. "Chuck's feature was those sliding tenths that he used to do. It put such a beautiful sound on record." The backbone of many hits on Atlantic, they were later canonized as Aretha's band: Chuck Rainey, Richard Tee on Fender Rhodes, Cornell Dupree on guitar, Bernard "Pretty" Purdie on drums.

"Everyone in Curtis's bands ended up being a studio musician," says Rainey, "'cause that's what *he* was. New York was a small community once you got a foot in the door. Nobody in those days used their own live band when they recorded." The Curtis band also became "family" to whomever they backed up on tour—the Supremes, Patti LaBelle and the Bluebelles or the Coasters.

As bandleader, Curtis was "the perfect dad" to the young Rainey. "He'd kick your ass when you needed it, and he'd love you when you needed it."

The King Curtis All Stars played, then backed up the American groups during the ten-city 1965 Beatles tour, kicking off with Shea Stadium: "We had a police escort by car from New York to the Philadelphia Spectrum, maybe seven big buses. It was like a parade along the route between the cities, people waving and screaming, trying to figure which bus the Beatles were on. The Beatles weren't even with us on that trip, but people didn't know that. We always stayed in the same hotels as them. I remember explicitly: George and John were great. They hung out on the airplane with our band, played gin rummy, joked, real people, they never stayed in their part of the plane. We never saw Paul and Ringo, and when we did, they had their nose in the air, aloof—or so it appeared."

Rainey felt the Beatles tour—unlike those of other stateside groups, whose egos took a beating before mass hysteria for the Beatles—was "handled real well, and the kids were listening." The entire show was two and a half hours, with Curtis's band backing up now-forgotten American opening acts who had big records at the moment: Cannibal and the Headhunters ("Land of a Thousand Dances"), the Manhattans, Brenda Holloway. The American bands did only two numbers each; the screaming didn't start until the second half of the show, when the British bands appeared. "We liked the Hollies," remembers Rainey, "but none of us in Curtis's band were familiar with the Beatles' music until the third show, when we realized the magnitude of people. We'd been playing jazz, we were more into what we did."

"King Curtis was known as a rock 'n' roll saxophone player. But during the years I was with him, he did four or five jazz records. At our matinee shows, he would play all the jazz standards. People like David Newman, Willis Jackson, Red Prysock, Illinois Jacquet, Ben Webster, came to his gigs to get him, to kick his ass, to show him up. Because he'd once been a jazz saxophone player, who now played rock 'n' roll, and they said he'd sold out. But to their shock, Curtis ran everybody off the bandstand with his horn. Every living tenor saxophone wished they could play like that and have his tone."

In the late '60s, Curtis was the Hendrix of saxophone. Or maybe Hendrix was the King Curtis of guitar. In the year Jimi Hendrix himself spent in Curtis's band, there's no telling how much the young guitarist learned. Curtis used a wah-wah pedal on sax, and pioneered the funky octave-divider sax effect (as featured on the Quincy Jones *Sanford & Son* theme, which Rainey played on). Before the days of digital rack mounts and LED foot pedals, Curtis defied the gods of electricity with his own hands:

"'Soul Serenade' had an echo that could only be achieved live by him rewiring the PA," says Rainey. "Every club we played, Curtis had his little toolbox, and he'd rewire the house mic with a soldering iron, then wire it back before we left."

Chuck Rainey's mentor was stabbed to death by a junkie on his Upper West Side doorstep in the summer of 1971. (Legend goes, Curtis pulled out the knife and stabbed the attacker back). "He slipped through the cracks," says Rainey, bemoaning the full musical knighthood that eludes King Curtis's reputation today. "If he were alive, I think everything would have come full circle."

When asked who were his bass role models, Rainey reverently bows his head before the only poster hanging in his home recording studio— that of Motown bassist James Jamerson. His eyes light up over mention of Doug Rodrigues, whom he played with in the Voices of East Harlem in 1970: "Greatest rhythm guitarist I ever heard in my life! He also fell through the cracks."

Rainey no longer leads the charmed gypsy life of an elite New York/L.A. session player, cabbing from Joe Cocker to Perry Como to Van McCoy to Paul Simon to Lena Horne, studio to studio, coast to coast. Rainey left L.A. for Texas in 1982, after he split Ricki Lee Jones's band to tour with Hank Crawford. Colleagues like Cornell Dupree and Fathead Newman kept homes in the Dallas area, and after Rainey met his new wife there, he decided to settle.

Rainey supports four kids. His oldest son, by his first wife, is twenty and weighs 365 pounds. Married to Susan in 1982, Rainey is now raising three young kids and a new puppy in a mainstream American household, in the bland heartland of Bedford, Texas, far from the fast track. The great bassist becomes most animated over his son's seventh-grade football games. Rainey would like his children to become great athletes. They are several generations removed from the hit records their daddy has graced.

Aretha and Jerry

Rainey played on several of Aretha Franklin's dozen low-profile Columbia albums, before she hit big at Atlantic under Jerry Wexler's tutelage. "As a matter of fact, King Curtis was responsible for bringing Donny Hathaway and Aretha to Atlantic, when he was head of A&R," says Rainey.

Curtis himself fronted her live band, with Billy Preston, Cornell Dupree, and Bernard Purdie; Jerry Jemmott was on bass at the time. At King Curtis's funeral, Aretha hired Rainey as her touring bass player. "It was a tuxedo gig," says Rainey, recalling that the band also carried six horns, a local string section from each city, and ever-changing conductors on keyboard: "We had an awful time when Bernard Purdie was conductor. A drummer conducting an orchestra didn't work out, plus Purdie's an egomaniac, so he didn't last long.

"When we did Aretha's *Amazing Grace* album, there was a song, 'Oh, Mary, Don't You Weep.' We did it live in church, where the band builds with the intensity of the audience, and there's a reason why you arrive at the last verse. I remember them taking that track back at Atlantic. They wanted to build it up quicker, so they took out the second verse and made it the fourth verse. I observed Aretha straightening out those people quite a few times. 'Can you sing this song? I've been singing this song all my life. So this is the way I'm singing this song. I don't tell you how to sell records or push buttons. Don't tell me how to sing the song.'

"But when she wasn't there, she couldn't prevent them from splicing out verses. When we listened to *Amazing Grace*, it was almost sacrilege, almost disgusting."

Amazing Grace recently became the only Aretha Franklin album to go double platinum. But incredibly, Rainey claims that the legendary Atlantic team behind the making of so much music history—producer Jerry Wexler, engineer Tom Dowd, arranger Arif Mardin—was "not needed at all, it was just politics, someone from the company to be a boss over musicians."

At Atlantic's Criteria Studios in Miami, Wexler flew down his musicians and housed them in a North Miami Beach mansion, with a swimming pool, several cooks, and chauffeurs.

"Atlantic did do certain things," acknowledges Rainey. "One morning when the car picked us up to take us to Criteria, the only guy there was [assistant engineer] Gene Paul. We [rhythm section Cornell Dupree, Bernard Purdie, and Richard Tee] were elated no one else was there. And Aretha played 'Rock Steady.' We were always trying to get our heads clear so that we would have that *thing*, before the interference would come. Aretha is like Roberta Flack, Laura Nyro, or Ricki Lee Jones. When they play it the first time, the one-thousandth time later is gonna be the same way. By the time they [the aforementioned Atlantic crew] got there, we had it and had laid down a reference. Eight hours of bullshit later, thirty takes later, we went back to that original reference take. That's what became a hit, the first take, before they got there."

Semiretired at seventy-nine in East Hampton, Jerry Wexler feels no need to defend his stature on music's Mt. Rushmore. Producers were usually not necessary for the likes of Miles Davis or traditional jazz records, he says. "But pop and R&B records are a whole 'nother thing, baby. I'm sorry, they required somebody to be at the helm.

"First of all, I would be in the studio before they'd arrive," says Wexler, who produced fourteen Aretha albums, "and we'd hand out the chord charts. The whole thing was hiring great musicians and letting them play into the track naturally. Of course, they generated their own parts. If it ain't broke, don't break it, I'd let it play on and be a traffic cop. But there were many times I wanted to change something."

"Jerry Wexler and Ahmet Ertegun were great *businessmen*," Rainey maintains. "That company has taken a lot of credit for things that they have nothing at all to do with." Rainey dismisses even Tom Dowd, Atlantic's pioneering engineer, who pushed away office furniture to record Ray Charles and Joe Turner in the '50s, before Atlantic had its own studio. Dowd later engineered *Layla* . Rainey pins the credit on Dowd's assistant: "*Gene Paul,* man, was the guy. All Tommy Dowd did was maybe remix or bring something up. I thought he was a bullshit artist, always talking ethereal shit, like he was God's gift to musicians. By the time Tommy Dowd sat down at the board, Gene Paul had already gotten the bass and drum sounds.

193

"How do you write eight to the bar and a shuffle at the same time, like 'Spanish Harlem'?" Richard Tee, who played Fender Rhodes, would be asked to overdub two or three different parts on top of the track. Then Arif would turn around and arrange it for the orchestra. But it was *Richard Tee* who never got credit for orchestrations.

"But if I had to go through it again," Rainey wearily concedes, "I'd do it. Time heals all wounds. The end results were great, my reputation got greater, I got paid. Five years ago, I may have said, 'You dirty motherfucker, you ain't shit.' But today, I'd hug Jerry Wexler if I saw him."

Rainey does a solo act these days, which he calls "funky folk music, storytelling with my bass." He performed solo as Al Dimeola's opener on seven concerts. A recent Japanese CD compilation has two of his solo bass compositions. The CD cover displays gratuitous female butt. "That's disgusting," he says, with uncharacteristic prudishness. "I can't even show this to my family."

Both Alvarez and Ken Smith manufacture a Chuck Rainey signature line of bass guitars. His kids run in and out of the house as he plugs one of these basses into a floorboard rack of ten pedals. "Of course, they didn't have these effects when I did sound tracks like *The Pit and the Pendulum* [Vincent Price, 1963]. In his home studio, with a Eurodesk Console, Rainey demonstrates dramatic bass lines from the 1971 movie $ (Money) and a scene from *For the Love of Benji*, in which a little dog is hiding.

His fingers fumble before recalling some of his most famous Steely Dan parts. "Peg" has instruments playing simultaneously in different keys: "It breaks the law of theory, which jazz—and the blues—does do. On 'Peg,' you just have to not listen to it when you're playing it. I've had people try and analyze this in clinics," he says, finally hitting the riff, "and you just can't do it." He plays his remarkable bass parts from "Josie," which incorporate Rainey's trademark three-note bass chords, and tenths. The phone interrupts.

"A new book sale! Just sold my latest textbook," he says, hanging up, "called *Interval Studies for Four- and Five-String Electric Bass.*"

Steely Dan

Steely Dan, named after a dildo in a William Burroughs novel, became the premier studio "band" of the 1970s—perhaps the *only* major rock group that never toured during their entire era. The harbingers of digital clarity, they shied away from any attempt to reproduce their exquisite records in concert, at least during the '70s and '80s. But then, Steely Dan was not really a band, but the studio creations of Donald Fagen and Walter Becker, around whom revolved a court of session-cat royalty.

Chuck Rainey was Steely Dan's primary bass player on *Pretzel Logic*, *Katy Lied*, *The Royal Scam*, *Aja*, and *Gaucho*, and on Fagen's *Nightfly*.

"Let me tell you. When you listen to *Aja*, those are some *masterful* songs. Those things'll be around for a hundred years, man. Walter does not read music, neither does Donald. They came to the studio with full-blown demos. But the demos would sound like punk rock. You talk about credit—Victor Feldman and Paul Griffin [keyboards], Larry Carlton [guitar], Jeff Porcaro [drums]—those are the people who sat down and put the chord changes on paper and made a road map for us to play. As always, the good guys fall through the cracks. I may be going back even to *The Royal Scam* [1976]. They should be as rich as Becker, Fagen and [producer] Gary Katz. Paul Griffin was so good, they gave him songwriting credit for part of a tune."

Rainey doesn't suggest he ever earned a songwriting credit with the Dan (akin to owning original shares of *The Honeymooners*). Even though you hear their hits every day in elevators, supermarkets, weaving without barrier through divergent radio formats, the records still sparkle. Because of their sophistication, it's a pleasure to hear Steely Dan survive amongst the ever-dumb downsizing of the classic-rock canon.

"If you're not a musician, you'd think Donald Fagen's the world's greatest writer. But if you're a musician, you know that he ain't it. He writes good melodies, he can play a little bit of piano. But if it don't be for Walter Becker, there don't be no Steely Dan. Seriously."

But then Rainey concedes that Fagen's solo *Nightfly* album does sound pretty much on par with Steely Dan.

"It had the same producer and family of musicians. Becker and Fagen had a talent for voicing things in ways you never heard it before." But Rainey believes Steely Dan—after *Pretzel Logic* in 1974—modeled their style from a group in England on A&M in 1972. "A horn band, I can't remember their name. The times I brought this up, I was made to feel that I shouldn't by Gary Katz."

Rainey got paid double scale and he played on tons of sessions. While *Royal Scam* was cut in two weeks, it took three years each to produce *Gaucho* and *Aja*. "They had budget up the yang-yang. I was very fortunate. For every song on *Aja*—with the exception of 'Deacon Blues,' which Walter played—as many drummers as are listed, I did the whole album through with that drummer. There were seven drummers, that's how many albums of *Aja* I did. I would do a month with Rick Marotta, then three months later do the same shit with Jeff Porcaro, and then Paul Humphries, then Bernard Purdie or Steve Gadd."

Steely Dan extracted favorite versions for final release.

After he arrived in Texas, Chuck Rainey gigged with former Blood, Sweat & Tears member Bill Tillman. "The best rhythm-and-blues band I've ever been in—and I'm sayin' a whole lot here—has been the Rodney Johnson Blues Band. Except he could not get more than $225 for his band." After a few years in town, Rainey claimed a prominent Dallas promoter began referring to him as "the uppity nigger from up north." He had screwed Rainey on a $1,700 contract as opener for a Herbie Hancock concert. "If he had gone down to four hundred dollars, I would have taken it, because my [three-piece funk] band wanted to work." Rainey saw his band advertised for the evening. Three days before the show, the promoter suddenly reneged his $1,700 guarantee, saying he only had two hundred dollars left in the budget. Rainey pulled out. "I told him, 'You owe me one. It's not a matter of me suing, I don't sue people. You don't go into a new area—I'm new—and sue a prominent person over some bullshit.'"

"After that I was only offered a coupla little gigs for what y'all call 'Juneteenth Celebration' [Texas holiday commemorating the end of slavery—news of which didn't reach Texas till June 1865]. I never hearda this shit till I came here. Juneteenth? Gimme a fuckin' break. That's the only time I would get action from three or four clubs. I been to one of these Juneteenth parades. Where I come from, when we have a parade, it ain't just a bunch of black people on horses."

Quincy Jones

"Quincy Jones is a great continuity director, that's it. He jobs out 90 percent of what he does musically. He knows how to get brilliant people. I have done six albums with Quincy. I've yet to see him write a note for me, or anybody in the rhythm section."

Behind the scenes, Quincy Jones farmed out a lot of his arrangements to the great arranger Billy Byers, his secret alter ego. Rainey imitates Q shuckin' and jivin' a rhythmic pattern, whilst recording the score for the film $. The Record Plant session included Lee Ritenour, Eric Gale, Harvey Mason, and Donny Hathaway.

"On everyone's music stand was a blank paper and pencil, which Quincy never touched. After five minutes, we all wrote down two pages of some kinda chord structure. But Donny didn't touch the piano. And Quincy stops the band for the fourth time, asking Donny what's the matter. And Donny says, 'Hey, Q, you don't have nothin' written here. The other guys can do this for you, but I am an arranger, producer, and writer. I'm not gonna do your job." So Donny sat out. He told me on the drive home, 'You guys are fools. He's making a whole living offa your creativity. When you work for me, I've got something for you to play.'

"I sit and listen to what me and Eric [Gale] did with $. Stuff nobody could write or arrange, just two cats gettin' down. Then you hear these trombones and tubas, horns, the whole thing written off of this thing. He's very smart. Like Arif Mardin, he doesn't create. They hire the people who create the parts, orchestrate into what you created, put their names on it.

"The right way to do it? Have a production company and give future royalties out.

"When I saw Miles Davis's last concert in France that Q did, Q almost had to force Miles to hug him onstage. Miles didn't respect him. Everybody's either had a lawsuit against Quincy or cause for one. I've had a cause for a lawsuit against Quincy, from *Guess Who's Coming to Dinner*. Me and Paul Griffin were writing partners, and we started fooling around on a song we wrote, during break. And Quincy comes in, says, 'Wow, man, sounds great, let's put this in the film.' So we trust Quincy, it's cool. Film comes out. The longest piece of music in *Guess Who's Coming to Dinner* is me and Paul's song. But when you look at the credits, everything belongs to Quincy Jones. And on the sound track, that song's not included. I had to go to that film three times to time when this piece of music comes up. We didn't chase the lawsuit. But Quincy is a crook, he's sneaky, sly, and full of shit. But he's the kinda guy who's sneaky, sly, and fulla shit, that you wanna be in his corner, 'cause he's successful.

"But one thing Q has done—every film that I did with him, my name is on the credits for playing bass. And I was always paid double scale, always. Hit records are very important to your career, to people liking you. If I could push a button and change everything? I would take whatever animosity, bitterness, or negativity that was in me at any time in my career and get rid of it. When I go to Germany, France, or Japan, whatever good happens on my bio, happens because of the Quincy Joneses, Jerry Wexlers, Arif Mardins, Charlie Calellos.

"If I had been [session bassists] Jerry Jemmott or Gordon Edwards, they'd say, 'Y'all stuff it. You got the wrong motherfucker here.' Get their bass and go home. I never would do that, my mother would roll over in her grave. As a consequence, I've been on more records, had more success. You can go in the backyard and bitch about injustice. But you go in the front yard, people are sayin', 'Hey, this guy played with Quincy Jones,' pattin' you on the shoulder, maybe one guy hires you for somethin' else."

Donny Hathaway

Jerry Wexler believed soul singer-composer Donny Hathaway was destined to stand equal with Ray Charles and Aretha. The troubled musician fell mysteriously to his death from a New York hotel room window at age thirty-three.

"Donny was not at all himself the last two or three years of his life. No one knows what happened, they weren't there, but you can guess what may have happened. Nobody pushed him. We all know that Roberta Flack had just left him—he did not like Roberta, very few people do. When he came to Atlantic he was forced to do duets with her [three hits, including "Where Is the Love?" Rainey was bassist for both artists]. Roberta had been his teacher at Howard University, in choir. He didn't like her then, and he certainly didn't like her as a pro. He was extremely overweight. The Essex House [in Manhattan] was an old hotel, had that chicken mesh between the glass. It may look sturdy, but you never know in an old hotel. Donny was always hittin' himself [demonstrates playing percussion on his body]. I'd witnessed him push himself against a wall, being mentally unbalanced. I'm thinking it probably was an accident, he made a mistake and put them four hundred–plus pounds against some shit that wouldn't hold him."

These days, Rainey has a penchant for playing prisons. Huntsville, Angola, Boys Correctional Institute in Shreveport. He doesn't get paid, but often fits in a nearby bass clinic. "I'm doing it as a service. I'm trying to get points for heaven, but I'm not a preacher. Kids in prison aren't grown, they listen. At Riker's Island last month, out of four hundred people who started out, fifty were left. Most of those guys don't wanna hear nothin'."

Chuck Rainey also does thirty gigs a year with Herbie Mann, and joins other all-star bands with his circle of fellow session players like Fathead Newman, Tom Scott, Ralph McDonald, Hugh McCracken, Cornell Dupree, and Les McCann. They tour France, Germany, and Japan. He has six bass guitar textbooks on the market, six widely distributed instruction videos, and does bass clinics around the country. He might headline the Majestic Theatre in Dallas as part of Herbie Mann's group, but he can't score a gig at Caravan, Terelli's, Club Dada, or the West End, joints where even amateur part-timers cut their teeth. The hometown gigs are a thorn in his side. Though he can't remember bass lines from the many hit records he's played on, he does recall every slight and unreturned call from local clubs. If Rainey was that hard to work with, he couldn't possibly have done decades of elite session work. It's the most delicate craft—like neurosurgery—in the music industry. His local jazz-fusion trio flies to resorts far out of town.

"I'm a player, so I want to play."

—1996

Last Man Blowing: David "Fathead" Newman is the last of the Big Texas Tenors.

(Gene Martin)

CHAPTER 11

David "Fathead" Newman
House of David

D avid Newman's Oak Cliff, Dallas, home contains a living room wall-of-fame—the "Fathead National Museum"—which is adorned with his twenty-eight album covers in chronological order. They date from 1959's *Ray Charles Presents Fathead* to 1995's *Mr. Gentle, Mr. Cool.* The tenor sax player's feisty old Aunt Freda runs his Dallas household. "He's got twenty-two albums on that wall . . . then he stopped doing records," she shrugs, pointing at the CD covers, "and made six of those little things."

Newman's *nom de sax*—Fathead—seems a total misnomer for this prolific, sweet-mannered maestro. A high school music teacher barked the name at him once after young David flubbed an arpeggio—and it stuck. But Fathead's never since missed a beat. Aside from his own twenty-eight, Newman estimates he's played on some four hundred pop, jazz, and blues albums as a sideman.

"I've been very fortunate, indeed," he says, in his living room, amongst his sons' golf and tennis trophies. Few jazz musicians at age sixty-three are so upbeat and fit. Newman himself plays tennis. "Music has changed over the years, but never to the point where I haven't been able to fit in."

David Newman is regarded as a perfect blend of bebop jazz musician and authentic blues/R&B player. "You never get lost listening to Fathead," explains his longtime producer, Joel Dorn. "He never solos past a logical thought or melody. I always think of him and Hank Crawford as guys who were singers that happened to play saxophone."

The recent two-CD career retrospective, *House of David*, on Rhino/Atlantic, demonstrates Newman's longevity. The set includes many Fathead-as-sideman tracks, beginning with Zuzu Bollin's local 1952 chestnut, "Why Don't You Eat Where You Slept Last Night." Then it rolls through seven Ray Charles classics, which prove just how essential Fathead was to Brother Ray. He was Charles's sax star and alter ego. In 1952, they both passed through Lowell Fulson's blues band in Dallas. Fathead became first pick for Ray's trailblazing septet two years later. The question arises as to why Ray Charles was referred to as "the Genius," on so many Atlantic album covers.

"I don't know about him being *a* genius," Newman considers, "but I do think he had a *stroke* of genius within his makeup. They started calling Ray 'the Genius of Soul' after we did a recording session in Atlanta. I think it was 'I Got a Woman.' He does a have a great mind, perfect pitch, he can compose and arrange instantaneously. He could write arrangements in Braille, but he preferred to dictate. The rests, notes, the key, tempo, everything."

Ray Charles' fabled charts, dictated to Fathead or Hank Crawford, made seven or eight instruments sound like fifteen. "I Got a Woman" hit number one on the Billboard R&B chart in January 1955, the innovation being that it was the first use of a sixteen-bar gospel chord progression in pop music. Many songs imitated this progression, but Charles took the slings and arrows from sanctified church folk for raiding the spiritual canon. Putting three black chicks (the Raeletts—an "amen corner") behind the band was another Ray Charles stage innovation, copied ad nauseam to this day. Credited with the "birth of soul," Brother Ray and Fathead were also there at the dawn of rock 'n' roll (which Atlantic Records first wanted to call "cat music" before Alan Freed christened it otherwise). But the Ray Charles Band never pandered to reap teen coin. They kept their themes adult—church music gone orgasmic (like "What'd I Say").

Dorn, who later produced eight Fathead LPs when on staff at Atlantic, was a teenage Ray Charles fanatic. "I was his most twisted, sickest, devoted fan." Dorn left school any time the Ray Charles band played within a few hundred miles of Philadelphia, crashing backstage. "I knew all the guys in his band, his road manager, his valet, the driver. I used to tell him, 'I'm gonna be a record producer.'" For his Philly radio show on WHAT-FM in '61, Dorn made Fathead's "Hard Times" the show's theme. "The record became a smash in Philly, sold thousands of copies a year in that town."

"Hard Times," from Newman's debut as leader, *Ray Charles Presents Fathead*, came to symbolize what aficionados termed *soul jazz*. The only money Newman sees today from his prolific output on Atlantic records—as sideman, and as leader on two dozen of his own LPs—comes from the all-important publishing royalties through BMI for writing compositions like "Missy," "Fathead Comes On," "Turning Point," "Shiloh," and "Children of Abraham."

"He was a *darling* child, beautiful—and so was his mother," declares Aunt Freda, poking her head in from the kitchen.

"They was just crazy about my mom, crazy about her cookin'. She worked for Jewish families all of her life," says Newman, whose self-tooled saxophone case carries the Hebrew inscription of his name, DA-VEED. As personal maid, his mom prepared kosher meals in the home kitchens of Neiman Marcus chairman Stanley Marcus, as well as the Sanger Bros. "I would eat the same things as the Marcuses or Sangers when I was a young kid," says Newman, raised on the same menu as the Coasters.

Kosher meals aside, Newman attended St. Peter's Academy, a Catholic school in North Dallas, through sixth grade. After graduating Lincoln High in South Dallas, Newman attended Jarvis Christian College, in Harkins, Texas, on a church scholarship, but didn't study theology. "I would have gone to a music school if we could have afforded it."

Jack Ruby's Vegas Club and the Silver Spur were dives that employed black jazz musicians in Naughty Dallas of the '50s: "The thing I remember most about Jack Ruby," chuckles Newman, "were the stag parties in his clubs. Whenever the striptease dancers came out, he'd want the musicians to turn our backs. 'Cause these were white ladies. He'd say, 'Now, you guys turn your backs so you can't see this.' But the strippers would insist that the drummer watch them, so he could catch their bumps and grinds. So Jack says, 'Well, the drummer can look, but the rest of you guys, you turn your backs on the bandstand.'"

Newman played bebop in Fort Worth with Ornette Coleman, and jammed Sundays at the American Woodmen Auditorium, a black insurance company on Oakland Avenue. "We knew every tune that Bird, Diz, and Miles would put out, note for note." R&B package tours came through Dallas, featuring T-Bone Walker, Big Joe Turner, and Lowell Fulson (with Brother Ray on piano). Buster Smith's Dallas-based ensemble, which Newman played in as a teenager, backed these package tours in town. "I'd listened to Charlie Christian before him, of course, but T-Bone Walker was the first blues guitarist to really impress me," remembers Newman. He had never heard a blues guitarist use diminished and augmented chords.

Dallasite Buster Smith had been to Count Basie what Fathead was to Ray Charles—an alter ego. Smith was Charlie Parker's teacher, as well as a mentor to Fathead. Since Newman led a tribute album for Austin's Amazing Records, forty years after his stint, he was a natural to play Buster Smith in Robert Altman's fascinating flop, *Kansas City*. The film's house band played counterpoint to the plot, with all musicians approximating roles of historical figures. But with little musical direction, the younger cats weren't true to their 1934 counterparts. Joshua Redman, as the Lester Young–based character, didn't play like Young, and Cyrus Chestnut didn't play like Basie, not being grounded in stride piano. Altman felt that commercial 78s of the time may not have reflected the experimentation during these Blue Devil jazz days. Thus, bebop riffs poke in and out of the solos. Ron Carter and Fathead Newman were the movie band's elder statesmen. Playing alto sax, Newman was thinking Buster Smith with every note. "I was a little older and knew about this from experience. Had I played tenor saxophone, I would have been able to imitate some of the Coleman Hawkins or Lester Young sounds."

Newman himself carries the mantle as today's preeminent Big Texas Tenor. The Texans who created this world-renowned sound came a generation before: Arnette Cobb, Illinois Jacquet, Buddy Tate, and Herschel Evans. Influenced by many, Fathead saw Charlie Parker only once, in 1954, racing down to Birdland after a Ray Charles Apollo gig in Harlem. "That was a big moment in my life."

Newman's albums sell big for jazz records. *Ray Charles Presents Fathead* sold 150,000 by 1960. *Bigger & Better*, which cost fifty thousand dollars to make in 1968, sold 200,000, and his last on Kokopelli topped the Gavin jazz chart with over 100,000 in sales. He never forgot local peers, like Marchel Ivery, with whom he cut a 1993 album in Holland called *Blue, Greens & Beans*. But Holland doesn't count. For a jazz musician, says Newman, "you have to move to New York or L.A. to further your career, be on the scene. You have to leave town, like the young Roy Hargrove, to make it."

Newman also cut two albums with recently deceased hard-luck story James Clay—one in 1960, and one recorded live in New York in '91, one of Clay's swan songs. Though Newman took Clay out on the road with Ray Charles's big band for two years in the early '60s, Clay's critical expectations fell short as he spent most of his career in Dallas jazz obscurity, perhaps the better to nurse his addiction.

"We used to believe you had to be high to play," Newman says of his days with Ray Charles. "Nowadays, we know this is completely untrue. I'm so proud of guys like Mac [Rebennack, aka Dr. John], now that he gets up in the morning, eats a nutritious breakfast, then gets to work."

The image of Fathead's close musical ally Dr. John eating a nutritious breakfast is somewhat unsettling but, fact is, he cleaned up his tracks and recorded the strongest records of his career—*after* thirty-four years of heroin addiction. Today's jazz players, Newman believes, are far more disciplined than those of his own generation. Young jazz musicians are today's four-eyed squares, who go to college, practice diligently—and eat nutritious breakfasts. (It is the MTV bubblegum groups who drown their sorrows in heroin.)

Though now based with his wife, Karen, near Woodstock, New York, which he calls "God's country," Fathead always comes home. This September he headlined the Second Annual Shirley McFatter Jazz Festival in Fair Park, Dallas. He emerged onstage to cries of "*Fathaid, Fathaid,*" shouted by old-timers who remember from way back. And there were cries of "Dino, Dino!" for his thirty-two-year-old son, on drums in the quintet. David Newman exudes style, in dapper vest and suit, an *un*show-off. But he conks you upside the head with his subtlety.

Newman wants to become an independent producer and work at writing lyrics. Eventually, the lip goes. "I intend to buy a Mac computer. I want to be connected to music beyond my playing years." Even though he feels rap has been "bad for the music industry," he thinks he'd make an interesting choice to produce in that genre. After fifty years playing his horn, he says, "The time has finally come."

—1996

Invisible Man: "Not many people read the backs of albums," shrugs Cornell Dupree.

(R. Andrew Lepley)

CHAPTER 12

Cornell Dupree
The Ultimate *Un*showoff

H e is the king of nonflash guitar, the guitar man on an estimated 2,500 pop and R&B records of the sort where you don't necessarily recall the guitar parts. Cornell Dupree himself can't recall most of his discography, save for some obvious credits: Brook Benton's "Rainy Night in Georgia," Aretha's "R-E-S-P-E-C-T," and King Curtis's "Soul Serenade."

Dupree has been first-string choice of record producers for thirty-five years, making him one of the most prolific R&B guitarists on the map. Flashy axe murderers are like hot-lookin' blondes in Hollywood—a dime a dozen. But subtle players who add snap, crackle, and pop, who complement a great singer's voice without eating the furniture—those are the rarest breed. Only a handful or two of these elite mystery guitarists—like Mickey Baker, Vinnie Bell, Eric Gale, Hugh McCracken, Elliot Randall, David Spinozza, and Larry Carlton—dominated the music industry for decades, at least until the onslaught of rap.

Dupree seems casual and far removed from his history. Each record was just a matter of doing his day job, punching a clock. His house, in North Richmond Hills, north of Fort Worth, could be that of an ordinary Joe in the civil service. There is nothing to indicate this is home sweet home to the man whose guitar graces a yellow pages of popular song by Aretha Franklin; King Curtis; Sam Cooke; Otis Redding; Joe Cocker; Ringo; Miles; Paul and Carly Simon; B. B., Freddie, and Ben E. King; Big Mamas Thornton, Streisand, and Midler.

"Not many people read the backs of albums—they don't know who the hell it is," shrugs Dupree. At fifty-four, he and his wife of thirty-five years are helping to raise their fifteen-year old granddaughter, whose beauty queen photos are tacked up throughout the kitchen. The den contains four gold records from R&B band Stuff (a fifth was stolen), Grammy nominations, pictures of the King Curtis All Stars in Montreux and a *New Yorker* "Goings On About Town" write-up.

Yet somehow, you sense Dupree's move back to the Fort Worth suburbs, after decades in the fast lane, is not entirely one he wished for. The industry in which studio lions like Dupree once prevailed is now beholden to rap and MTV, and those mediums have surgically removed those pesky studio musicians from pop culture. Though youthful, with thin frame and trademark goatee, and looking every bit as cool as his name—Cornell Dupree is old, by bottom-line corporate rock standards.

Dupree's last solo album, *Bop 'N' Blues*, in 1995, was his first foray into be-bop standards—though Cornell streamlines them into an R&B format. "I always try to make it plain and simple, so that everyone can understand it—mainly myself," says Dupree, who never felt comfortable playing jazz. Only on the first cut, "Freedom Jazz Dance," does the guitarist burn out some unconventional licks. The rest of the album patronizes the conservative "smooth jazz" radio format, like his Kokopelli label mates Fathead Newman and Herbie Mann.

Born in 1942, Dupree attended I.M. Terrell, Fort Worth's only black high school in the 1950s. King Curtis and Ornette Coleman were previous alumni. "The first person who made me want to play guitar was Johnny Guitar Watson when I was fourteen. A buddy of mine used to open the sodas at one of the concert halls. I went down to help and caught Johnny Guitar Watson. Oh, man, I had to have me a guitar. My mother got me one that Christmas."

As a teenager, Cornell played the honky-tonks along Fort Worth's Jacksboro Highway. The Jax was a volatile sixteen-mile neon stretch, where Carswell Air Force Base personnel, hay hands, gangsters and backroom gamblers brawled, drank and whored. Though many country musicians feared for their safety in these chicken-mesh beer halls, Dupree, who played in a black R&B band, came out unscathed.

"They was rough joints, but they always treated us well," he remembers. "We had no problem. We worked the weekend from midnight to five am, an after-hours club called the White Sands, seven nights a week. In fact, that top picture over there," says Cornell, pointing to a gothic blues photo of his young cherubic self holding a Les Paul Jr., "was taken at the White Sands, with Leon Childs and the Hightones in 1959. Rednecks and truck drivers come in, did their thing, I didn't mess with them, they didn't mess with the group. Truckers used to chew bennies like candy. Our band only drank, but I dropped a coupla bennies, it'd wake you up, man. All those truckers would hang there till the last note was played at five am."

Like fellow studio ace, bassist Chuck Rainey, currently Dupree's neighbor in nearby Bedford, Cornell's career mentor was the great King Curtis. They never met until 1961. Cornell was working with a local R&B band called the Red Hearts at Small's Paradise, whose owners were tight with Curtis.

"I don't think this club had anything to do with Small's Paradise in Harlem," he explains. "Just coincidence. Someone in Curtis's family had passed, and he came down to Fort Worth for the funeral, and he come by the club and sat in with the band. Before he left he said, 'Hey, man, you keep on practicing, and I'll send for you one of these days.' I was eighteen. A year to the day later, he called me. I played 'Soul Twist,' one of his hits, and 'Moonlight in Vermont,' over the telephone. He said, 'Okay, I'm gonna send you a ticket.'

At the age of nineteen in 1962, Dupree left Fort Worth for the first time, and moved straight into the apartment of King Curtis, at 100th Street and Central Park West. "I got there on a Monday afternoon, and we opened at Small's Paradise in Harlem on Tuesday. I was scared to death, didn't know anyone, only Curtis. He showed me the ropes."

From Small's Paradise in Fort Worth to Small's Paradise in Harlem—young Dupree withstood the culture shock and exceeded expectations. He advanced his chops hanging with Atlantic Records studio pros Eric Gale, Carl Lynch and especially Billy Butler. Butler had been Curtis's previous guitarist, who did the original "Honky Tonk" with Bill Dogget. After a few months in Curtis's pad, Dupree sent for his wife and moved into a little hotel for thirty-three dollars a week.

The King Curtis All Stars opened, and backed up the American opening acts during the ten-city Beatles '65 tour: "Very exciting, traveling in a private plane, whole floors in hotels, girls passing out and falling from balconies like they were hypnotized. One thing I can say about our band: We weren't hounds, we weren't like other rock 'n' roll bands, chasing after every little skirt. I was married."

In the mid-'50s, King Curtis was doing sixteen record dates a week, getting union scale $41.25 per three-hour session. To cut down the pace, he raised his price to a flat $100 per session, but demand for his honkin' tenor horn only increased. Dupree recounts the simple wisdom Curtis imparted on the essence of studio musicianship: "He taught me how to pay attention, how to listen, never overdo it. Less is more. Speak when you have something to say, otherwise stay in the background and don't interfere. Coming through his band, I look at it as my degree."

Jimi Hendrix also came up through the college of King Curtis; the year he was with the band Cornell covered rhythm. "There were jazz standards he just didn't mess with. Hendrix was definitely a stylist, a heavy blues player then. We'd bounce off each other, we'd do a little pickin', of course, supporting Curtis, playing along with the rest of the band, not sticking out.

"But he would always steal the show, just seemed to get all the attention. It didn't bother me, it was fun watching," says Dupree, who remained humble—an essential virtue of the star sideman. The two-guitar team of Dupree and Hendrix pitted the ultimate flash guitarist with the ultimate unflashy guitarist. His closest studio colleague became Atlantic session guitarist Eric Gale. "We never had to talk about what we were gonna play. It was just one, two, three, bam. We'd never clash. It would always match."

For years, the standard lineup at Atlantic Records called for three guitarists per session. Megaproducer Jerry Wexler, now seventy-nine, remembers the 1960s: "Eric Gale, Hugh McCracken, and Carl Lynch— those were the days I used to use three guitarists, because I wanted a lot of fullness. But it always created a problem about what parts each should be playing. 'Okay, you play four on the bar, you double the bass, and you play obbligato.' And they'd get in each other's fuckin' way. It used to be the worst part of my recording career. Then Cornell Dupree and Steve Cropper came along. The two magicians who established the ability to play rhythm and lead at the same time. Cornell Dupree, man, covered all of the shit, so we could dispense with three guitarists."

Gale and Carl Lynch may have lost work due to Dupree's flexibility, but Cornell still teamed with Hugh McCracken on countless sessions. "Again," states Dupree, "we also could pretty much just play without discussing what we were gonna do, and never get in each other's way."

"Whatever Cornell didn't cover, Hugh McCracken put down. The two guys would ham-and-egg it," says Wexler.

"Cornell was definitely the Professor," says Hugh McCracken, who was sixteen when he played guitar on King Curtis's 1959 record, *Trouble in Mind*—before Dupree *or* Billy Butler played with Curtis. "I used to call him Professor because of his demeanor—all-knowing without boasting, an amazing coolness. He wasn't just creating guitar parts, he would hear the whole thing."

Dupree began his decade as Aretha Franklin's full-time guitarist in 1968 (songs like "Rock Steady" and "Day Dreaming"). His anecdotal memories are dim, but he recalls Muhammad Ali going out on the road with them, warming up the audience. According to Jerry Wexler, Aretha turned down "Let It Be" and "Son of a Preacher Man," both offered first to her (she recorded them years later, when it hardly mattered).

"Maybe she just didn't hear the right tingle at that time," speculates Dupree. "She would hear certain songs that no one else would hear the way she could."

When off the road with Aretha, Dupree was top session ace at Atlantic's Fifty-ninth Street flagship studio in New York, as well as Jerry Wexler's two studios down south, Criteria in Miami and Muscle Shoals,

Alabama. "I was like a troubleshooter," says Dupree. "They'd fly me into Muscle Shoals for a week. I'd do some overdubs, some rhythm, whatever it called for to make the record good. I can't describe my style. I always listened to the vocal, supporting without interfering, always enhancing in a sense. I listened and replied. Blended."

When asked whether his musical sense comes from the head or the heart, Dupree replies, "Always from the heart."

Always in the public ear, not the public eye, Cornell can't recollect countless dates he did, but lists "Rainy Night in Georgia" as a personal favorite. "The whole arrangement was built around the licks I played, thirds, which I think made the song."

For a studio man, it's surprising that Dupree's three favorite albums, as far as his own playing, were live: *Aretha Franklin Live at the Fillmore West*, *King Curtis Live at the Fillmore West* and *Donny Hathaway Live at the Bitter End*.

Unlike most studio aces, Dupree cannot breeze through orchestrations like reading a newspaper. But he never felt intimidated, even with the clock ticking on high-dollar dates. "I can play a few notes, if they're not too close together. I do read chord charts, but I'm not a fast reader; I can usually figure it out in a couple of minutes. I could make out enough to understand what it was saying, and I *listened*, paid attention. Then, if they played it down a couple times, I'd get it."

Dupree was always surrounded by fellow Atlantic sidemen/Aretha band members like Richard Tee, Eric Gale, Bernard Purdie, and Chuck Rainey. Rainey claims the group would lock in the groove before the producer and arranger arrived at sessions.

Cornell Dupree's most famous spotlight outing was in the 1970s funk/R&B outfit Stuff. The concept involved merging New York's premier sidemen—Tee, Gale, Steve Gadd, Gordon Edwards, Chris Parker, and Dupree—sans vocalist or front man. Yet they still had to acquire management and be "introduced" to Warner Bros. as a group. Stuff released six albums, and "Foots," off their first, was the closest thing to a hit single. Contrary to popular belief, Stuff was *not* the original house band on *Saturday Night Live*. They guested several times the first season, and backed up Joe Cocker's appearances.

"One reason Stuff didn't get as big as they could have was we never really committed to the group. We were all doing sessions by day—we'd cancel Stuff gigs to do Joe Cocker or Paul Simon concerts." The players remained lifelong sidemen to the core. Guitarist Eric Gale died of cancer in 1994; keyboardist Richard Tee died in 1993.

Dupree has had a Yamaha endorsement for twenty years. The Dupree Jam is his signature-line guitar. "When I first went to Japan, I had my Telecaster. I had put a DeArmond pickup in the center. The Japanese people [Yamaha] saw it and constructed a few similar guitars, which I liked. They said, 'Okay, you play it, we take a picture.'"No longer manufactured, the Dupree Jam sold two or three hundred, by Cornell's estimate. Yamaha, however, builds better acoustics than electrics, and though still active, Cornell's endorsement is due for renewal.

"I have a problem with acoustic," says Dupree, who doesn't even own one. "I hum. And I hum louder than the acoustic. In fact, when they go direct from the electric guitar to the board, they pick up my voice. I have a bone—it's real freakish," says Cornell, whose Dupree Jam rests at the hip. "And somehow my voice comes through the guitar. So me and acoustic just don't get along."

Dupree has always kept a place near Fort Worth, even when he lived in New York City from 1962 to 1982. Then he moved to L.A. with his wife and two of his three kids (the youngest is now thirty-three) for three years. "I couldn't get into anything worth mentioning. In fact, when I was in L.A., I kept coming back to New York, doing more work, especially when the *Cosby Show* came out, which I played for."

His seventh solo album, on current label Kokopelli, will be called *Uncle Funky*, a nickname from saxophonist Hank Crawford. (The first under his own name was 1973's *Teasin'*, on Atlantic). "They don't play my own records on Dallas radio," Dupree shrugs. "The clubs can't afford you, and I'm not that popular here; they only pay fifty bucks. People don't read the back of albums, they don't know who I am. I've been gone so long, the people have forgotten me."

Like fellow studio icons Chuck Rainey and Fathead Newman, who have homes in the area, Dupree must take jets to his gigs. He often headlines New York's Bottom Line, Lone Star Roadhouse, and 2,500-seat venues in Japan. But he feels anonymous in Texas.

"I'm contemplating getting another place back in New York. It's too expensive to send for me, put me up in a hotel, and then pay me. I'd be much busier living in New York. My last big venture is the upcoming Tom Jones CD. All rhythm and blues, and he's kickin'. He's a hard-workin' man, I really admire him much more than before."

Yes, he would like to have a steady gig in Dallas–Fort Worth. However, excitement in his voice builds only over the prospect of being a sideman. Would he like to go on the road with Tom Jones?

"I'd *love* to," says Cornell Dupree.

—1997

Pretty in Pink: "Sweet Sammy" Myers, shown onstage in his "titty pink"
suit, wore his harp belt to heaven.
(Jeff Horton)

CHAPTER 13

Sam Myers Dusts His Broom

"How come none of the Meskins in this joint don't speak no English?"
—Sam Myers quoted on the dressing room wall at the Chesterfield Café in Paris, France

S am Myers, the finest Mississippi-born blues man in Texas, is at a crossroads. He moved here from Jackson, ten years ago this month, to front Anson and the Rockets on vocals and harp. Having just turned sixty, he's still not entirely sure he feels down home in Texas. "Most players here like to do copy tunes, rather than develop their very own style. You don't want to spend a lifetime doing that."

Aside from the copy tunes, Sam will often bemoan the state of vegetables compared to the old days. "You can't get proper mashed potatoes in Dallas," he says. "Now, in Mississippi, they know how to do mashed potatoes right."

He awaits the call to begin work on a tenth-anniversary album with Anson Funderburgh, but the project is stalled. "I've been in this business a long time," he says, wearily drawing from a Camel. "A *long* time."

In his space-age bachelor pad apartment are vintage 1950s LPs of Louis Jordan, Percy Mayfield, T-Bone Walker, and of course, his old partner Elmore James. An honorary life achievement award from the Sonny Boy Blues Society and three Handy Awards sit atop the jumbo TV. Being legally blind, he prefers old radio shows on tape, favorites from childhood—*Gangbusters, Captain Midnight, Sgt. Preston of the Yukon.*

Myers wrote about half the material that appears on five Anson and the Rockets albums. One of his Handys is for "Changing Neighborhoods," [Blues] Song of the Year 1988. The lyric, he explains, is actually a metaphor for changing your life.

"If you stay in a neighborhood too long, you start lookin' like the neighborhood. It start favoring you, you don't belong anywhere else."

For song inspiration, he tries to "catch it while it's hot." Myers recalls making a trip to New Orleans in 1959, only to find his friend wasn't home. "So I said, 'This has been another sad, sad, lonesome day.'" Time stood still when he spoke the phrase, and by night he had recorded a single at Cosimo's studio called "Sad, Sad, Lonesome Day," released on the Fury label. His 1956 Ace Records single "Sleeping in the Ground" was recorded by Clapton, Canned Heat, and Robert Cray.

Myers was born in Laurel, Mississippi, in 1936, a swampy terrain eighty miles south of Jackson. He attended Piney Woods Country Life School, a highly unusual integrated boarding establishment during the 1940s: "And it was a country life that you lived. It was a trade school; you could learn carpentry, brick masonry, dairy, or farming—whatever line of work you would like to obtain once you grew up, you could study. I started in general education, and joined the school band when I was seven. My trade was music."

Sam began on trumpet, then switched to drums, where he marched in a 139-piece band. He remembers visiting opera singers and big band concerts at Piney Woods. "We had musicians in school qualified to play banquets and social gatherings. Never had to send off campus for musicians from Jackson or New Orleans."

Sam's mother was a teacher and his father laid track with a section gang for the L&N railroad. On a four-year nondegree scholarship,

Myers attended the American Conservatory of Music in Chicago. He met Marian Anderson there in 1954, when he was already a working blues musician. A big-city cousin, who knew Anderson, arranged for concert tickets. "Never dug opera till I saw it live."

Sam's cousin took him backstage after the concert. The famous black opera contralto worried whether the audience understood the music. "'We are here for *you*,'" Sam remembers telling her. "She thought that was one of the greatest compliments." Myers didn't dare invite Marian Anderson to one of his chitlin club blues gigs. "But if she had stayed longer, some instinct tells me she would have come."

Elmore James came from Mississippi to Chicago in the early '50s. Sam caught him at a West Side club called Civio's. "Had Robert Johnson lived, he would have had to go electric. Elmore's style was unique, but he was doing what Robert Johnson would have done if he lived. The 'Dust My Broom' slide lick—that was Robert Johnson's creation. It became Elmore's trademark, but he electrified it, that's what the deal was on that."

Myers was introduced to Elmore on break. "It was a bunch of guys playing, just like they do on open-mic night now. He needed a band to hit the road with his group, the Broom Dusters. None of the drummers there could make it. Odie Payne couldn't get time off from the post office. S. P. Leary couldn't go cause he was contracted by Chess for some sessions. So I told Elmore, 'I'm just outta school, I don't know who you want, I've got a lotta free time. Mind if I sit in, tell me what you think?'"

Elmore was mighty impressed, and it didn't hurt that Sam was also from Mississippi. For the next decade, until Elmore James died in 1963, Sam Myers was his main drummer. And though session credits are somewhat cloudy on these landmark recordings, Sam Myers laid down some of the greatest blues drumming on record. Blues drumming is the ultimate support job, out of the spotlight. It requires the drummer to put his ego aside so the guitarist or singer can shine. But listen to "Madison Blues" or "Talk to Me Baby," and you'll hear grooves that helped convince the teenage Rolling Stones to choose blues as a career option. It's a style few white drummers have ever duplicated.

Myers explains it simply: "It boils down to a tight backbeat with a rhythm section—drums and bass locked together. When you got that, the lead player can go anywhere he wants, long as the guitar don't get outta tune."

"There's lots of snare roll when Sam plays drums," says guitarist Hash Brown, "almost a circus quality."

They used to call Sam "Schoolboy" back in the Chess studios, where he hung out at Willie Dixon and Little Walter sessions, sometimes as gofer. Since the session logs got lost through time, there's no telling how many "drummer unknown" credits were actually Myers or Odie Payne, the previous drummer with Elmore James and the Broom Dusters.

What exactly does "dust my broom" mean?

"That means you gonna leave. Get up in the morning, clean up your act, sweeping your tracks as you go. You gettin' out, leavin' town. It's an old saying."

In today's corporate culture, ol' Elmore might have landed an endorsement from Black & Decker or Hoover.

Sam cut his teeth on the Southern chitlin circuit—the low-paying black juke joints, no whites allowed. "We got to play more places than now, and got to relate to the audience more. The reason they called 'em chitlin circuit clubs was 'cause musicians played gigs for little money and some lunch—a plate of chitlins."

Yet Myers says the Broom Dusters averaged $125 per man each week, playing five to seven nights. "It was easier to live then than now. Rent was only twelve bucks a week. You had heavy drinkers and a lotta guys on drugs, same as now, but back then it didn't cost as much.

"I never discussed it, but me and Elmore had a side thing going. We made whiskey on the banks of the Pearl River in Mississippi. We never did get caught by Internal Revenue. The still was hidden in the woods. We made our own recipes from scratch. Some people come up and only want the first running we made—that's the first whiskey that you run off, wouldn't give it time to age or nothin'. That's what you call 'grade whiskey.' It would be clear in the jug. And we made rye. All of it was made from sour mash. We'd cull it with what we called 'charter chips'—we'd burn 'em till they get as black as that ashtray there, wash 'em off, then drop 'em in the jug with the whiskey, and the whiskey would turn out brown or solid red."

This was "quality stuff" he says, and at a mouthwatering one hundred proof, Elmore and Sam's moonshine could knock you for a loop.

"Since it's all over and done with, I'll tell you. We had an in with a couple of cops from Jackson. We sold around the black neighborhoods. Five dollars for the clear moonshine, seven dollars for the red whiskey, and that rye, we got ten dollars a gallon. The still was runnin' 250, 500 gallons a day. We used a Ford for deliveries. When we got off the road that's what we would do."

Myers says he earned more loot from whiskey than music. While the Broom Dusters toured, the burners were left off, letting the hooch age on its own. They gave up the still after four years, in 1959, when they nearly got caught.

"There was a federal man, name of Sam Newman, white guy, sent a lotta people to prison. He'd say, 'If you're sellin' whiskey anywhere in the state of Mississippi, I'm gonna catch you.'

"One night I said, 'Elmore, seem like I hear a cowbell ringin'.'

"Elmore said there was no cows supposed to be out in that pasture. Then I looked up and saw a light flash in the trees. And he said, 'Yeah, I hear the cowbell now.' I said, 'We need to turn off the boiler and get outta here. That ain't no cow. That's Sam Newman with a bell.' Him and his henchman, a black guy. I coulda picked him off with my Winchester, wouldn't nobody ever know it."

Myers, whose eyesight was much better then, spared the cow-impersonating Fed. Even though "a whole lotta people wanted to kill him," Sam says he died a natural death years ago. The henchman was killed in a crap game.

Like other elder statesmen, Myers bore witness to the extraordinary transformation of the blues audience from black to white. "It has been proven beyond a shadow of a doubt blues has no color barrier. But somewhere down the road, blacks [who are ashamed of blues] have forgotten their heritage. They've lost something. And what they have lost, that is what the white person has gained."

These days, when not on tour with Anson and the Rockets, Sam Myers is the most eminent regular at Dallas blues clubs. Particularly Schooners, which he walks to by himself, sometimes arriving in the afternoon. Many have witnessed his dirgelike trek from bar to stage when he's called up during a jam. Nonregulars who block the aisle or touch him risk getting elbowed upside the head as he clears a path. But suddenly, a local blues jam becomes world-class, the moment Sam Myers's deep, resonant voice welcomes the ladies and gentlemen.

Hash Brown, who runs the major blues jams in town, roomed with Sam for two years and considers Myers "my father, older brother, and uncle." He tries to pit Myers with the best players. If someone doesn't cut it, Sam will berate the motherfucker mid-song. "He's notorious for beatin' up on drummers. He's cantankerous because of his vision, but I don't blame him. A lotta people don't realize what he's done and who he is."

"There's a lotta guys never leave home, sit around and wait all day," explains Sam. "They're not pros, they never take their guitars out, never rehearse. But they come out for the jams. They think bitterly of me, because I won't play with them."

Last fall, Sam was jiving Cold Blue Steel guitarist Shawn Pittman at Schooners, telling him to "play your guitar, asshole." Pitman's cousin charged onstage and cold-cocked the legally blind Myers. The guy escaped the bartender's tackle and hightailed it out. Next morning, cops informed Myers they'd arrested his assailant, who was already scheduled to begin a four-year stretch at Huntsville for armed robbery.

"If the cops hadn't found him, I was gonna have him killed myself," says Myers, who maintains that his old Chicago underworld connections are still pistol-hot.

In April 1986, Anson Funderburgh drove to Jackson, Mississippi, in a borrowed van and moved Sam Myers and all of his worldly belongings to Dallas. "I'm glad he's with Anson," says Hash Brown, "because Sam was workin' a mattress factory in Jackson at the time. It's pretty hard for a white blues band to get anywhere. The realism is not there. With Sam, they've got it."

"I love the old man," says Funderburgh, who performed two of Sam's songs before ever meeting him. "On a good night, there is no better singer I'd rather listen to."

"Personally, I've never really liked the harmonica," Sam says, an odd admission from a player who is easily one of America's top ten in the blues. "I only blow with the Rockets to fill out the sound." With a Hohner endorsement, Myers says he plays harp as if it were trumpet. His belt holds seven Marine Band harps, arranged alphabetically by key. Though he plays less now, he's having a new four-hundred-dollar belt custom made to hold fourteen, including his Chromonica Super 64.

It's said Myers's greatest notoriety is in Norway, a country he's toured often since first arriving in the '50s, as a member of the Windy City Six. From Oslo to Trondheim, he's recognized in airports, even followed by Nordic girls. One fan dubbed him "the king of Norway" with a special beer mug. In America, however, distinguished musicians suffer constant indignities. At last year's King Biscuit Blues Festival, in Helena, Arkansas, headliner Buddy Guy arrived in his Silver Shadow bus. Guy's entourage ordered James Cotton's bus out of the load-in area. And then, before his entrance onstage, Buddy's handlers demanded that other acts vacate the backstage area—including Anson and the Rockets, featuring Sam Myers, and festival honoree Robert Lockwood Jr., stepson-protégé of Robert Johnson.

"With that attitude, Buddy Guy will be pulled back down in a few years by those who put him there. He can't handle it," says Sam, who refused to budge. He offers a bit of slightly askew philosophy: "The music business—and life—is like a luggage-rack carousel at the airport. If you miss your bag the first time, it'll come round the next time."

But seniority is punished in the music business. It would be a cultural loss if Sam Myers doesn't get the chance to record a solo album, while his musical powers are still strong. "That would be the greatest thing I'd like to do," he admits. On acoustic guitar, he'd fly his old friend, Robert Lockwood Jr. in from Cleveland. From Chicago, he'd summon Chess drummer Odie Payne out of retirement and gather his favorite old horn players. "I still have unreleased material I'd like to see on wax, tape, or CD, with my name on it."

And what would this landmark album be called?

"*Sam Myers' Contribution to Music*," he says.

—1996

Note: *Sam finally recorded his solo album,* Coming from the Old School, *in 2004. He was buried back in Mississippi with a loaded harmonica belt strapped across his chest in July 2006.*

Born to Wah: Andrew Baxter Jr. fronts a blues jam in Dallas.

(©1999 James B. Wells)

CHAPTER 14

Little Boy Blues

ndrew Baxter Jr. is a little guitar picker whose control, timing, and taste make him an impressive blues musician. The fact the he just turned eleven is what turns people's heads. The fifth grader, not quite five feet tall, has been regularly showcasing at blues festivals and weekly jams. In order to accommodate nightly requests for autographs, Andrew's father and roadie, Andrew Sr., ordered a hundred eight-by-tens. They sell for five dollars, the proceeds funneling into Andrew Jr's. music fund. Only five are left at the moment. The music fund defrays maintenance costs for five stage guitars, two blues amps, strings, repairs, and customized picks bearing the Andrew Baxter Jr. name.

"We got all the time in the world," says Andrew Baxter Sr., in no particular rush to see his boy turn pro. But considering Andrew's once-a-month Friday paid gig with the Hash Brown Band at the Blue Mule in Dallas's West End, and his first booking as bandleader at the Hole in the Wall . . . he already is a pro.

Music-gear industry sharks are circling, and would like his endorsement early. A Nashville guitar company is building him an instrument from scratch. D'Aquisto Strings, in New York, sent a dozen sets and a letter saying they'd love to have Andrew "join our team of endorsers." The kid has yet to write his first song. But the American public's obsession with baseball-card celebrity strikes nightly when the Baxters visit clubs.

"*There's that kid*," people whisper. "Is he gonna play?" Drunks plunge napkins or matchbooks before him, requesting an autograph with today's date, so they can prove they knew him when.

"Sometimes they spit when they talk," complains Andrew, of such late-night demands on a school night.

The Baxter home appears happy and healthy, in the middle-class suburb of Carrollton, Texas. Neither Andrew's dad, a distribution manager for a computer warehouse; his mom, Angela, a travel agent; or fourteen-year-old brother Morgan are musicians. All of them avoid using the term *child prodigy*. Can there even be such a thing as a child prodigy of the blues?

Dallas-based blues artist Lucky Peterson, whom Andrew recently played with at the Blue Cat, was a "prodigy," appearing on *Ed Sullivan* when he was five years old. Little Stevie Wonder was, of course. Is Andrew one? Hash Brown, who once worked for Andrew Sr. a decade ago, thinks so: "He plays as well as guys in their twenties, with tons of room to grow. He's a hard worker. I've given him a couple of lessons. Then he goes home and woodsheds."

Andrew clears his plate at the family dinner table, just like in *Leave It to Beaver.* He plays solitaire, shuffling cards. He's a picker, not a talker, and looks to his father as spokesman. Andrew Sr. fetches their 1998 Charley's Guitar Shop calendar, which serves as a personal diary for music events. At the Tandy Center in Fort Worth, Andrew "took the cake," his father says, during a "Young Gun Shoot-Out" between adolescent guitarists. As other boys fell silent after their solos, Andrew was the only kid who could also play rhythm. Other highlights read like an education in the blues. At the East Texas Pinetop Blues Festival he sat in with Tutu Jones. "Armand Hussein [blues impresario and ex–pro wrestling champ] invited us out," says Dad, "and drove Andrew around on a golf cart. We met Bobby Blue Bland, then met the guys from [South Dallas blues institution] R. L. Griffin's, who invited us to their club."

Andrew met Lou Ann Barton at the Texas Independence Day Festival at Sons of Hermann Hall. Antone's house guitarist Derek O'Brien gave him his number. Lou Ann requested he learn "It's Raining" before coming to Austin to sit in. He met Buddy Miles last year at the Robert Ealey Blues Festival in Fort Worth, and sits in with Ealey every three months. The Baxters attended the First Annual Blind Lemon Jefferson Festival in Wortham, Texas, where Andrew sat in with family friends Jim Suhler and Monkey Beat, then played a local juke joint that night. "They turned it up to eight and just blew that little shack down," says Dad.

"He's so young, it's a novelty," marvels Jim Suhler. "His hands are so tiny, people think, 'Isn't that cute.' But he can really play, and he seems to be in it for the long haul. He never gets rattled, never a bead of sweat, always real poised."

Sounds almost like the JonBenét Ramsey of blues. But observing Andrew at home and onstage proves his precocious love of the blues generates from within. Andrew sets his own pace; his parents merely accommodate. This writer first saw Andrew play when he was ushered onstage at Poor David's with Anson and the Rockets. Weeks later, he sat in with Little Charlie and the Nightcats. How did a little boy manage to land onstage with Little Charlie, a California-based act on Alligator Records, who'd never seen him?

"I played Little Charlie's guitar during break," explains Andrew.

"They were talking shop, and Charlie Baty saw those little fingers working, could tell Andrew was good," says his dad.

The Baxters attended the last four Greater Southwest Guitar Shows. Event producer Mark Pollock booked Andrew as a feature attraction for next year. The *Southwest Blues* newspaper invited him to sit at their booth and play. Andrew brought his little tweed amp, and blues senior Joe Jonas accompanied him on harmonica.

"This guy comes over, and goes, 'Hey, your kid is good, he's got good timing. C'mere, you need to talk to me.'" Jimmy Triggs, a

Nashville luthier, approached the Baxters to custom build a guitar. "I go, 'How much is this gonna cost us?' He goes, 'No I *wanna build* you one.'" Andrew's only specification was for a fat neck, not a skinny one. He also wants a Tele, a good slide guitar, and a red Brian Setzer 6120 model Gretsch, with the dice volume knobs (the size of which would dwarf him). He keeps a poster of it in his music room.

Andrew Sr. is quick to assert his son's normality; he likes Nintendo and basketball. A trip to Andrew's bedroom shows Beanie Babies, Legos, Ninja Turtles, Donald Duck dolls, and a picture of his girl-friend. Favorite TV shows are *Family Matters, Step by Step,* and *Hangin' With Mr. Cooper.* The blues stuff stays in the blues room. But he clicks on his radio by the bed, set at 98.7 KLUV. On comes Jackie Wilson's "Lonely Teardrops," and Andrew reclines on his bed like a kid from an earlier decade. His clothes closet indicates a budding showbiz career. Pointy cowboy boots adorned with music notes. He wants tips for all his boots.

This is where he dresses to the nines in blues regalia before hit-ting the clubs. His style is modeled on Jimmy Vaughan's retro R&B threads—the wardrobe of Mississippi sharecroppers who moved to Chicago in the 1940s, went electric, and dressed up Delta blues. A mil-lion miles from today's fifth graders, who get tattoos and piercings and experiment with drugs. But they make fun of his hair—which Andrew models equally on "Jimmy Vaughan and Ricky Ricardo." He slicks gel in his hair every day (favorite brand: Dippity-Do). Andrew's life of blues seems more about his natural feel for guitar—rather than suffering the thoughts of a Percy Mayfield or Howlin' Wolf.

But the kid is not just into style—he's got substance. He leads me to his music room to jam. This place is serious business. The walls are covered with Texas blues festival posters, most of which Andrew has attended. The first guitar he used for live performance is a three-quar-ters-scale, child's-size Fender Duosonic. His first tube amp was a tweed Fender Blues Jr. Then his folks purchased a full-size Silvertone hollow body for a hundred bucks. Then a blond Vibrolux amp, now fueled by his number-one axe, a man-size '60s reissue Strat. The local Van Zandt company dropped in Vintage Plus pickups.

I grab the Strat, Andrew takes his Guild X-170 hollow body. I start off the rhythm on Freddy King's "Side Tracked," letting Andrew play lead. He doesn't hit a wrong note or lose a moment's rhythm, even when I do. Doesn't add any flash or rock licks to his blues; he *keeps it country*—unlike anyone remotely his age. He plays a moment behind his head, but does this only as a concession to showmanship. When this kid plays blues, it just sounds bluesier than my own playing. He practices against records.

"One night at Muddy Waters, Shawn Pittman got me up there and said I could use anything [effects pedals]. Okay. We're doin' like a funk song in D, and I just pressed the wah-wah pedal and heard it snap on." According to reports, he was born to wah. His dad thereafter got him a Vox wah-wah for his eleventh birthday.

"Do some 'Soul Sister,'" says Dad, and Andrew obliges.

"I don't wanna take a whole buncha time with the lead, because that would be rude," explains Andrew, on playing tastefully behind vocalists. He begins his solos softly, when cued by a singer, then builds from their vocals.

Andrew is unsure of what the obsolete word *record* means, when I ask what his favorites are. "Tell him your favorite *CDs*," says his dad. And then he lists Johnny Moeller's *Return of the Funky Worm*, along with anything by Mike Morgan & the Crawl. Morgan, whom his parents knew before Andrew was born, happens to be Andrew Baxter Jr.'s role model.

"Poor kid," says Morgan, when told of this. "But he's a great little kid. I wish I woulda been born with talent and a work ethic like that. If he keeps goin' . . ."

Andrew Sr. worked at the original Stubbs Barbeque in Lubbock in the 1970s, the region's premiere blues club. The Baxters have a photo of three-year-old Andrew onstage with a guitar at the short-lived Dallas franchise of Stubbs Barbecue ("I had 40 percent of nothin' of that," says Andrew Sr.) on Greenville Ave. He's onstage with Jim Suhler, Mike Morgan, Lee McBee, and Doyle Bramhall Sr. Andrew holds a real guitar but was playing air guitar. "Picking up the rhythms and the grooves," his dad says. His maternal grandfather taught Andrew the riff from "Secret Agent Man," the first lick for millions of kids.

Father-son LPs on the top shelf in the music room include the
Palladins (with whom Andrew recently posed for pictures backstage
at Sons of Hermann), the Thunderbirds, SRV, Freddy King, George
Thorogood, Anson Funderburgh, Marcia Ball, Angela Strehli, Roomful
of Blues. "All the blacks are down there," points out Andrew Jr. And
sure enough, segregated on the bottom shelf is the deep stuff, on vinyl:
Willie Dixon, Little Walter, Howlin' Wolf, T-Bone Walker, Albert King,
Junior Wells' *Hoodoo Man Blues*, Iceman Albert Collins. He practices
against these records, and next wants to learn "Okie Dokie Stomp"
from a Gatemouth Brown LP.

"Play some 'Snatch It Back and Hold It,'" says Andrew's dad,
not unlike a gym coach. "How 'bout some 'My babe don't stand no
cheatin.'" Andrew obliges with each of these blues motifs. He's played
two Polser Elementary School talent shows, and one "pancake breakfast." He performed "Johnny B. Goode" and "Kansas City" with the
school principal, Mr. Wagner, on rhythm guitar, and another fifth
grader on drums. The parents loved it. But not one friend or peer in
Andrew's fifth grade at the Lewisville school shares his interest in blues.
They prefer Marilyn Manson.

"[Manson] sucks" laughs Andrew. "I think he's stupid."

"Some people at school say I show off, playing guitar," Andrew
shrugs, but this doesn't give him any pause. He can think of only one
girl who likes his playing. Andrew will be joining the school orchestra
next year, tackling upright bass.

Angela Baxter, his mom, tells of a time exactly ten years ago when
her son was three weeks old. They were in Little Rock visiting her family. The Stevie Ray Vaughan bus was in town, and since the Baxters knew
Tommy Shannon, they were invited in. SRV himself held little Andrew
and gave him a kiss. She thinks this may have been an omen.

Andrew's first album is not even a dream, considering he's yet to
write a whole song. "When his brother was in the hospital for three
days, we all cried. I told Andrew to go in his room, try to write something," says his dad. But Andrew wasn't ready. In the meanwhile, father
and son hit two or three clubs a night, when on the prowl. The clubs
never charge them a cover. "We don't go out for beers. He goes to

hear music, that's the sole purpose. All the guitarists in town give him a chance. They know he's not gonna hog the stage or his head's not gonna pop," says his dad.

"I was his caretaker first, now I'm his roadie," continues Dad, who never played guitar. "I'll make sure his amp is on, he's tuned up. But it's between him and the folks onstage. A lot of people at the jams request Andrew. If he likes who's playin', if he's comfortable, he'll say yeah, and if he doesn't, he'll tell ya, 'I don't wanna play with 'em.'"

"There's this bass player who looks like a bulldog," says Andrew Jr. "He smells. . . . But it doesn't bother me, except when they spit in my face," he says, of drunks. "They ask, 'Are you gonna be the next Jimmie Ray Vaughan?'"

"There ain't no rush," insists his dad.

—1998

Note: *Several months after this article appeared, Andrew Baxter Sr. unexpectedly died of cancer.*

Exhibit B: Official publicity shot of Rick Sikes (middle) & the Rhythm Rebels, which was used against them in court to convict them of bank robbery.

(Fred Knobbs. Courtesy of Rick Sikes)

CHAPTER 15

Rick Sikes and the Rhythm Rebels

A scraggly teenage boy ambles up to the sixty-five-year-old proprietor of Coleman's roadside antique shop.

"Mister, are you Rick Sikes?"

"Yeah."

"Can I talk to you a minute?"

"All right," comes Sikes.

"How do you rob a bank?"

Reputations die hard, and Rick Sikes's legend is an untold footnote in Texas music history. It's been fifteen years since the once-fearsome country band leader–cum–bank robber was released from Leavenworth Penitentiary in Kansas. He's raised two stepdaughters now in college and owns a sign shop in addition to the antiques store. He and his wife of fifteen years, Jan, live in a charming compound, behind dusty, unpaved streets. He is one of Coleman's most revered citizens. But his past has taken on a life of its own.

"Boy, I danced a million miles to y'all's music," says one starry-eyed local old-timer, reminiscing at the shop. Rick Sikes and the Rhythm Rebels scored a handful of regional hits that made the little girls squeal—the rockabilly ballad "Give Me a Little" in 1965, and "Den of Sin" a year later ("I'm not cryin' because my baby left me/ I'm cryin' cause she's comin' home to stay"). Sikes had his own half-hour live-music program on KPAR, then Abilene's CBS affiliate. His theme song was "Standing Room Only When I Die." The band was the first to ever attract an audience of cowpokes, rednecks, and hippies—before Willie, Waylon, and the boys.

But then, in 1971, three-fifths of the band were convicted of robbing two banks. A bank teller recognized Rick's hands on TV—"My fingers are too big on the tips," says Rick—as the same hands that held a gun to her back. Rick Sikes and the Rhythm Rebels' longest engagement became the federal penitentiary at Leavenworth. From behind bars, Sikes resigned himself to watching the outlaw country movement take off without him. "I didn't blame those guys. But it still pisses me off," he says. "We were the real outlaws in country music. We had numbers to prove it."

When Sikes got busted, he called Jan, instructing her not to do the planting in the garden. The FBI told Sikes they would get his time reduced if he only told them where he'd buried the loot. "You think I left my kids and old lady down there without any groceries? There ain't no fuckin' buried money!" Sikes told them. Sure enough, the FBI came and dug up the whole yard, finding nothing. The next day, Rick called home, saying, "Okay, honey, go ahead and do your planting."

Rick and Jan stroll into RiJan Music, a shotgun-railroad building on the homestead. Resembling a Nashville booking agency forty years ago, this is the music world Rick left behind for prison. A space-age bachelor-pad bar is stocked with Jim Beam, quaint ashtrays, and beer coasters. A hundred framed publicity photos exhibit a former generation of country musicians whose careers crossed paths with Rick's. There's Sikes with Bob Wills, onstage with Red Foley, and there's Grand Ole Opry and television star Little Jimmy Dickens. A *Cashbox* magazine clipping shows Rick presenting Dewey Groom, the proprietor of Dallas's Longhorn Ballroom, with a pair of longhorns. Rick points to a plaque in memory of Curtis Leach, the Okie who wrote "Golden Guitar."

"Curtis's girlfriend sliced him in the groin and he bled to death. He would have become the next Hank Williams," Rick believes. There are photos of other Coleman luminaries, like his songwriting collaborator Dean Beard (one of the original Champs, of "Tequila" fame). There's songwriter Bobby Bare, honky-tonk queen Wanda Jackson, and Johnny Horton ("The Battle of New Orleans"). An old photo of Willie Nelson playing bass with "one of his ex–old ladies." Time here is frozen in the early '60s, when Rick Sikes and the Rhythm Rebels headlined the Mayan Dude Ranch in Bandara, when draught beer was ten cents a mug, and you could watch the girl in the gilded cage, Diamond Lil, and her Famous Can-Can Girls.

"There was a song I did they loved in Round Rock," recalls Rick, who had a deep, resonant country croon. "'Blue Eyes Crying in the Rain,' an old Fred Rose song that nobody sang since Roy Acuff. When I went to prison, Willie had burned out in Nashville, so he come back to Austin and started playin' at Big G's out in Round Rock. I never talked to Willie about it. But I'm sure all those people kept requesting that song."

The Rhythm Rebels' 1968 publicity photo was used as evidence against them at their trial. It depicted the band mocking their secret avocation, posing as bandits on train tracks with guns and knives. They even told the wary photographer they intended to rob a train. Then a little switch engine came by and the two guys on board threw up their hands in jest. But the quivering photographer, a World War II correspondent named Fred Knobbs, sensed the musicians weren't joking.

"I can't say I wasn't guilty," Sikes admits of his two robbery convictions. "That'd be a lie. But I can swear that I never in my life held up a bank with a *gun*." He says he merely "*cased out* banks for associates to rob. Let's just leave it at that."

The Rhythm Rebels boarded their instruments of music and crime in a teardrop-shaped utility trailer. After they did their banking business, they went back to retrieve the trailer and ride off to the next gig. In San Antonio, Austin, and Houston, Sikes's band was drawing the same size crowds as George Jones and Charley Pride. They would play "The Pusher Man," "Stardust," and "San Antonio Rose," all in the same set.

"We were mixing the music before anyone. We were pulling the college kids out of Georgetown and the cowboys out of Austin, over at Big G's in Round Rock. We were sorta cowboy hippies. We'd play a matinee at Fort Hood wearing Nehru shirts for a rock gig, then haul ass to Austin or San Angelo, put on our Western shirts and cowboy hats and Levi's, and play shit-kicker music at night."

Jan Sikes was a go-go dancer in Abilene when she and Rick met. "I was the first country musician to ever hire go-go girls," he claims. It was 1970, the year before he was incarcerated, and she kept in touch throughout the fourteen years he was behind bars. By the late sixties, Rick had been through some bad marriages and bad record deals; his career was going to hell. "I was thirty-five, drinking too much, eatin' a few pills—amphetamines was plentiful. The days of free love and nickel beer. I was disgusted with the music business. Didn't even want to play anymore, didn't give a damn anymore. I wanted off the merry-go-round but couldn't see where to get off."

Rick Sikes says he can hardly believe how stupid he was back then. "I was a big ol' boy, drank and raised hell, playin' in honky-tonks, screwin' all these broads. I'm supposed to be the bandleader, keeping us working, so they could feed their families. I felt obligated to keep things going. So I had a boyhood friend who was an outlaw. We was playing these little old towns. I'd go into the bank to get some change. I'd see how many tellers there were, how many doors in and out. I'd go back to the motel and sketch out the place and the escape route, how many farm-to-market roads to get back on the interstate. This was valuable to people in that business. Let's put it that way. I'd get a few bucks out of it."

"Everybody was afraid of him," says Jan, who left a strict, religious home in Shreveport to become a go-go dancer.

"I was probably one of the most arrogant bastards in the world," Rick adds. "There were a lot of decent people had it in for us, you know what I mean?"

One man who had it in for Sikes was Emory Walton, Eastland County district attorney. "A little sawed-off bald-headed guy" recalls Rick. The D.A. came before an Eastland County holding cell that Sikes shared with a seventeen-year-old boy who'd been crying all day. The kid faced five years for drug possession. Walton began to taunt the kid, Rick recalls, threatening, "I'm'a getcha five more years when I prove you intended to sell it."

Sikes went ballistic. "Hey, you sonofabitch, you wanna fuck with somebody, why don't you fuck with me!?" he exploded.

"I'll fuck with you, all right, boy," came Walton, from outside the bars. "You want me to come in there?" He reached into his vest pocket, says Sikes, and patted a derringer.

"Come in here," Sikes told the man about to prosecute him, "and I'll stick that derringer up yo' ass sideways."

Walton nailed Sikes with fifty years from the state of Texas. He convinced a jury that Sikes donned a disguise and pulled a gun while robbing the First State Bank of Rising Star. Sikes says his Abilene-based attorney was drunk during most of the trial. Key evidence hinged upon the testimony of a frail woman, Mrs. Effie Harris, who had just been widowed and recovered from a heart attack when she happened into the First Bank of Rising Star. She was whirled around by a man who then held a gun to her back, seeing him for an instant. Walton presented that infamous photo of the band posing as outlaws on the tracks—from which she identified Sikes. In a separate trial for another bank robbery, the Feds sentenced him to twenty-five years. (Shortly after, Eastland County D.A. Emory Walton shot himself in the head.)

Off federal parole, Sikes remains on state parole until the sentence is up in 2021. "I doubt I'm gonna make it," he says, referring to his life span.

Since Sikes got out early, in 1985, he has become a sterling model for prisoner rehabilitation. Leavenworth was considered the second-toughest maximum-security prison in America. It's for career criminals and killers—not first-timers or country musicians. In his book *The Hot House: Life Inside Leavenworth Prison*, Pete Earley quotes former Leavenworth prison warden Jerry O'Brien as saying, "The only real thing that rehabilitates a convict in Leavenworth is old age. When they get so old they can't run out of a bank, they retire."

"But I got it all out of my system," says Sikes. "People don't know what bottoming out is until you really don't have nothin', not even the freedom of what you eat, what you wear. There's no way that I would do *anything* to go back in there."

Rick got his GED in prison, studied graphic arts, wrote hundreds of songs, now stored away in unopened boxes. (In one 1980 clipping on Rick's music wall, Boxcar Willie credits a song he was planning to record called "The Hobo King" as written by inmate No. 87047-132—that's Rick—at Leavenworth.) He invented devices like the prototype "bead-o-matic" which simplifies Indian bead making. He remodeled guitars; he strums a brilliant-toned chord on a Dobro-like instrument. The resonators are made out of little aluminum tins that once held pecan pies from Leavenworth's commissary. He named another instrument, a silver battle-axe with a Martin neck and a banjo body, the "gitjo." "You had to have permits to keep each one in the cell," he says. Other convicts kept their distance from Sikes, and no one dared mess with his guitars.

Sikes was so industrious in his solo endeavors that he was taken to the prison psychiatrist for being "antisocial." The shrink, whose Viennese accent has become one of Rick's stock character routines, wore his wristwatch on his ankle for fear a convict would steal it from his wrist. "He'd be walking down the hallway, some guard would ask the time, and he'd stop to pull up his pants leg up."

"'Mr. Sikes,' he said, 'I unnerstandt you don't associate wit anyone; you haf no friends.' I said, 'Do you realize that over 90 percent of the people in here are felons. Killers, thugs, drug pushers. What kinda people you want me to hang out with, man? We're not allowed to patronize the officers.' He told me to go."

Not in the Rhythm Rebels band, but part of their gang, Big Sandy was convicted along with Rick and the boys. "Sandy was huge, four hundred pounds, 6'7"," says Rick. "He had a real bad thing against black people. Sandy believed Leavenworth was the best prison in the federal system. But he got sent to Atlanta. First thing, he pops some black guy in the mouth. They take him in front of the IDC. 'What do you mean assaulting this inmate?' He said, 'No goddamn nigger gets up in my face.' Of course, some of the associate wardens were black. They said, 'We'll tell you what, big boy, the next trouble you cause, we're putting your ass on the bus to Leavenworth.' Sandy said, 'Why don't you put me on the next sonofabitch to Leavenworth now.' They said, 'We damn sure will!'

"So Sandy got up here, where he wanted to be. First thing, they sent him to the Viennese prison psychiatrist. 'Mr. Sanders, I see you haf trouble down in Atlanta.'

"'What, for knockin' the shit outta some nigger?'

"'Ah, Mr. Sanders, you be racist, too?'

"'I ain't no racist. I just don't like niggers.'

"'Ah, Mr. Sanders, we gonta haf to do somezing. We gonta put you on Thorazine.'

"'I don't want no goddamn Thorazine.'" (Prisoners on Thorazine were immediately recognized by their gait when they swayed down the hall—the *Thorazine shuffle*.)

"'But, Mr. Sanders, you take Thorazine, it make you feel better. I take Thorazine, it make *me* feel better.'

"So Sandy said, 'Then why don't you take mine, you goofy sonofabitch, and you'll feel twice as good.'"

B. B. King played Kansas City, which is thirty miles from Leavenworth, and he performed at the prison free. "Last time B. B. came, I carried his guitar in, and he said, 'Boys, we like to play for y'all, but it's just got to be too much of a hassle.' The guards would shake down B. B.'s band, tearing up the amps looking for contraband drugs. B. B.'s band was black, so the guards figured they were smuggling dope in."

The warden was mightily impressed with a song Sikes wrote called "From the Bottle to the Needle." Rick didn't sing his way out of prison, like Leadbelly, but he did convince the warden to let him build a recording studio at Leavenworth. It was the first one ever in a federal pen, he says, and it became a Nashville pipeline that enabled prison songwriters to submit demos. Before the studio, convict musicians had to send in their demos on sheet music. An incarcerated trumpet player, who was paid off in cigarettes from the commissary, had been writing everybody's charts.

Rick painted music notes across the recording studio walls, to make it appear less institutional. Given an old broken 2-track recorder for starters, he built a homemade console using old radio parts. He glued egg crates on the walls for sound baffling. Then Steam Train Maury, the real "King of the Hobos," befriended Rick during a Leavenworth visit. Tight with Peavey Instruments in Mississippi, Maury arranged for it to donate a truckload of amps, a PA, mics, and a Peavey soundboard.

"Rick's greatest talent is taking pieces of nothing and making something out of them," says Jan Sikes, leading a tour of the main house. All the cabinets, furniture, and Native American–style crafts were built by her husband. He constructed a bunkhouse for their kids, now refitted with a hot tub. A 130-year-old trunk from Jan's grandmother has been refurbished to look like a museum piece. "He still repairs most things with a nail clippers and toothbrush—the only things allowed in his cell," she adds. The master bedroom's king-size bed is decked out in red satin sheets. The landscaped grounds, which stretch out to the Davis Feed Mill nearby, could be mistaken for some sort of West Texas resort. A rebuilt nineteenth-century woodstove outside can smoke eight briskets at a time.

Five years ago, a cardiologist gave Rick a death sentence. The doctor warned him to eat nothing but rice, beans, and pasta, and he *might* last six months. "But I'll die when I get goddamned good and ready," says Rick, digging into a fresh steak delivered from his next-door neighbor's restaurant, Caroline's Coldwater Cattle Company. (Folks drive all the way in from Abilene to eat at Caroline's.) Jan spent "thousands of hours" learning about low-fat diets to reverse heart disease, he says. "She straightened me out more than anybody in the world. She's to blame for keeping me alive, man."

The rest of Rick's former band, the Rhythm Rebels, haven't fared as well. Rick's brother, Bobby, who played keyboards, died of kidney failure a few years back. Tommy "Red Hoss" Jenkins, the tall skinny bass player, was cell partners with Rick at Leavenworth. After eleven years, Jenkins disappeared forever. "One morning guards came in and took him," Rick recalls. "He had a bad eye, and they said they were taking him over to

Kansas City to take the bad eye out and put in a glass one. I never seen him since." His prison number and whereabouts are nowhere to be found to this day. Gary Marquis, the lead guitarist, died of a heart attack in the late '80s. Though Sikes once helped out Preacher Williams, the drummer, when he went AWOL from the army—"I had some friends in Nashville," Rick says; "I sent him down there to hide the poor little bastard out"—Preacher returned the favor by turning state's evidence, claiming Rick forced him to steal and rob banks. Rick doesn't know his whereabouts either, and "he never done a day in jail."

Sikes has Native American ancestry in his blood, and developed a close friendship with the late, great American Indian poet Roxy Gordon when Roxy returned home from Dallas to the Coleman area during his last years. Both were Civil War buffs, members of the Nashville chapter of Sons of the Confederate Veterans. A large framed daguerreotype of Roxy's great-great-grandfather, a Confederate chaplain who died in a Northern prison camp, hangs in the Rick's living room. Roxy had been encouraging Rick to get back onstage. So for the first time in thirty years, Rick Sikes performed, at Roxy's memorial in May 2000, at Sons of Hermann Hall in Dallas. He liked it, the audience liked him, and he aims to do some more.

Finally, one wonders whether Sikes keeps a bank account today. "My best supporter since I've been home has been the First National Bank of Coleman," he says. "They loaned me money for the antique shop, the sign works shop. They back me all the way."

—2000

Acknowledgments

Special thanks to Peggy Bennett, Robert Wilonsky, Al Aronowitz, and Mike Edison. Thanks also to Polly Watson and Jessica Burr for editorial support.

The following extra sources provided or confirmed bits of information used in "Kiss My Big Black *Tokhis*!": "Ain't Nothin' but a 'Hound Dog'," by George A. Moonoogian, from *Whiskey, Women, and . . .* Number 14 (June 1984); *Baby, That Was Rock 'n' Roll: The Legendary Leiber & Stoller,* by Robert Palmer, with an introduction by John Lahr (Harvest/HBJ, 1978); *Every Goy's Guide to Common Jewish Expressions,* by Arthur Naiman (Ballantine Books, 1983); *50 Coastin' Classics,* Rhino R2 71090, liner notes by Randy Poe; "Lullaby of Tin Pan Alley," by Ben Yagoda, AmericanHeritage.com (October/November 1983); *Music Publishing,* by Randy Poe (Writer's Digest Books, 1990); "Rhythm-and-Jews," by Mark Lisheron, *CommonQuest: The Magazine of Black/Jewish Relations* (Summer 1997); *Rhythm and the Blues: A Life in American Music,* by Jerry Wexler and David Ritz (Knopf, 1993); *Yiddish Radio Project: Stories from the Golden Age of Yiddish Radio,* as heard on NPR's *All Things Considered*; and the YIVO Institute in New York.

Index

INDEX

INDEX

Lyrics Acknowledgments

The author gratefully acknowledges the following for permission to reprint lyrics from the songs indicated:

Audre Mae Music: "Feel So Good" (p. 142), by Mose Allison, Audre Mae Music (BMI). All rights reserved. Used by permission. "How Does It Feel to Be Good Lookin" (p. 148), by Mose Allison, Audre Mae Music (BMI). All rights reserved. Used by permission. "MJA Jr." (p. 137), by Mose Allison, Audre Mae Music (BMI). All rights reserved. Used by permission. "My Backyard" (p. 145), by Mose Allison, Audre Mae Music (BMI). All rights reserved. Used by permission. "Who's In, Who's Out" (p. 141), by Mose Allison, Audre Mae Music (BMI). All rights reserved. Used by permission.

Bullseye Management: "Dallas" (p. 176), by Johnny Winter, Winter Blues Music Publishing (BMI). All rights reserved. Used by permission.

Hal Leonard Corporation: "Bear Cat" (p. 21), words and music by Rufus Thomas, copyright © 1970 Almo Music Corp. Copyright renewed. All rights reserved. Used by permission. "Hound Dog" (p. 7), words and music by Jerry Leiber and Mike Stoller, copyright © 1956 Elvis Presley Music, Inc., and Lion Publishing Co., Inc. Copyright renewed, assigned to Gladys Music and Universal Music Corp. All rights administered by Cherry Lane Music Publishing Company, Inc. All rights reserved. International copyright secured. "Mr. Hound Dog's in Town" (p. 21), words and music by Roy Brown, copyright © 1953 by Trio Music Company and Fort Knox Music, Inc. Copyright renewed. All rights reserved. Used by permission. International copyright secured. "On Broadway" (p. 13), words and music by Barry Mann, Cynthia Weil, Mike Stoller and Jerry Leiber, copyright © 1962, 1963 (renewed 1990, 1991) Screen Gems-EMI Music Inc. All rights reserved. Used by permission. International